WEIGHT **WATCHERS**®

Simply
the
Best

Simply the Best

250 Prizewinning

Family Recipes

MACMILLAN • USA

MACMILLAN
A Simon & Schuster Macmillan Company
1633 Broadway
New York, NY 10019

A Word about Weight Watchers™

Since 1963, Weight Watchers has grown from a handful of people to millions of enrollees annually. Today, Weight Watchers is recognized as the leading name in safe and sensible weight control. Weight Watchers members form a diverse group, from youths to senior citizens, attending meetings virtually around the globe.

Weight-loss and weight-management results vary by individual, but we recommend that you attend Weight Watchers meetings, follow the Weight Watchers food plan and participate in regular physical activity. For the Weight Watchers meeting nearest you, call 1-800-651-6000.

Weight Watchers Publishing Group
Editorial Director: Nancy Gagliardi
Senior Editor: Martha Schueneman
Food and Nutrition Editor: Regina Ragone, M.S., R.D.
Editorial Assistant: Christine Senft, M.S.

Thanks to the people who contributed to this book:
Editorial Consultant: Eileen Runyan
Nutrition Consultants: Lynne S. Hill, M.S., R.D., L.D., and William A. Hill, M.S., R.D., L.D.
Photographer: Steven Mark Needham
Food Stylist: Mariann Sauvion
And to all the members, staff members and magazine readers who entered their recipes.
Interior Design by Nick Anderson
Photograph on cover by Dennis Gottlieb

Library of Congress Cataloging-in-Publication Data
Weight Watchers simply the best 250 prizewinning family recipes.
   p. cm
   Includes index.
   ISBN 0-02-861940-4
   1. Reducing diets--Recipes. I. Weight Watchers International.
RM222.2.W326 1997
641.5'635--dc21   97-4287
                                                  CIP

Manufactured in the United States of America

Contents

Recipe Symbols

Make Ahead

Microwavable

One Pot

Rush Hour

Spicy

Vegetarian

Introduction

Although you might try a recipe from a magazine that looks tasty or get ideas for a new way to prepare a dish from a cookbook, you probably have your favorites—the reliable standbys that you turn to again and again: The easy skillet meals that you can toss together on the nights you get home late, the pot-luck dishes that are the first to disappear at a summer picnic or the special occasion entrée that was handed down from a dear family member. In fact, research shows that most cooks rely on a mere ten recipes they use repeatedly. The recipes they feel are, to put it plainly, simply the best.

If you've been on the Weight Watchers program, you know the strength that comes from group support—swapping success stories, receiving encouragement in times of setbacks and sharing recipes. *Weight Watchers Simply the Best*, our third collection of members' favorite recipes, is a testament to the power of sharing. Nearly 2,000 members, staff and magazine readers sent in their favorite recipes, which we reviewed, tested, tasted, tested again and pared down to the 250 best recipes. We then took on the task of choosing the eight very best, grand-prizewinning recipes (we chose two entries, a Weight Watchers member and a staff member, from each of the four categories: Main Meals; Light Meals; Appetizers, Soups, Side Dishes and Salads; and Desserts, Snacks, Baked Goods and Beverages. Although we think that each and every one of these recipes is worth adding to your "reliable standby" collection, here are the eight grand-prizewinners: Celia K. Schwartz's Manhattan Fish Chowder; Kathy Rheinhart's Confetti Couscous; Jennifer Straus's Spinach-Veggie Pizza; Barbara Gardner's Twice-Baked Garlic Potatoes; Julie Clawson's Bella Braised Chicken; Tonya Sarina's Beef in a Leaf; De'Ann Tollefsrud's Chocolate-Amaretto Cheesecake; and Annette Snoek's Cranberry-Blueberry Muffins.

One of the most intriguing aspects of the contest was discovering the story behind each recipe. The contest entry form included space for a brief essay: The entrants told us about themselves, their dizzyingly busy lives, their weight loss journeys, and the recipe they were submitting. Although some creative cooks duplicated favorite restaurant dishes or concocted a delectable treat with whatever was on hand, many members echoed these words from member Kim Cullison: "The original recipe comes from my grandmother and was one of those 'comfort' foods, loaded with fat, cholesterol and calories. With the knowledge I gained from my Weight Watchers meetings, I trimmed down the recipe and fit it into my food plan. The best part is, no one can tell the difference from the original recipe."

Your recipes confirm what we've suspected: You're pressed for time and have no interest in cooking "diet" food for yourself and "real" food for your family. You want to cook healthfully, but aren't willing to compromise flavor. We are delighted to share with you the 250 recipes that we think are *Simply the Best*.

CHAPTER

I

Appetizers, Snacks and Beverages

$\mathscr{S}$even Layer Dip

MAKES 8 SERVINGS

Brenda Oliver
Nepean, Ontario, Canada

Brenda has given us a delicious low-fat alternative to the popular, but high-calorie Mexican bean dip. Make it spicier by sprinkling the top with a minced jalapeño pepper and serve it with baked corn chips.

One 16-ounce can pinto beans, rinsed and drained

Several drops hot red pepper sauce, or to taste

1 tomato, chopped

$1/2$ green bell pepper, seeded and chopped

1 cup salsa

1 cup nonfat sour cream

$3/4$ cup shredded nonfat cheddar cheese

4 scallions, thinly sliced

10 pitted small black olives, sliced

(See photo.)

1. In a blender or food processor, puree the beans, pepper sauce and 2 tablespoons water. Transfer to a 12" serving platter; spread in a thin layer on the platter.

2. Leaving a 1" border, top the bean mixture evenly with the tomato, bell pepper and salsa. Leaving a 1" border, top the tomato layer evenly with the sour cream and cheese. Sprinkle with the scallions and olives.

PER SERVING: 89 Calories, 1 g Total Fat, 0 g Saturated Fat, 1 mg Cholesterol, 365 mg Sodium, 12 g Total Carbohydrate, 2 g Dietary Fiber, 8 g Protein, 150 mg Calcium.

SERVING PROVIDES: 1 Fruit/Vegetable, 2 Protein/Milks.

POINTS PER SERVING: 1.

Cucumber-Yogurt Dip

MAKES 2 SERVINGS

Karen Marshall
Scarborough, Ontario, Canada

Karen works as a center coordinator for Weight Watchers in Toronto. She loves creating recipes with a Middle Eastern flavor like this refreshing dip. Serve it with vegetable crudités and toasted pita bread wedges. The recipe can easily be doubled.

1 cucumber, peeled, seeded and finely chopped

³/4 cup yogurt cheese★

1 tablespoon fresh lemon juice

1 teaspoon extra virgin olive oil

1 garlic clove, minced

¹/4 teaspoon salt

¹/4 teaspoon freshly ground black pepper

Parsley sprigs

In a medium bowl, combine the cucumber, yogurt cheese, lemon juice, oil, garlic, salt and pepper. Refrigerate, covered, until the flavors are blended, at least 1 hour. Serve garnished with the parsley.

PER SERVING: 91 Calories, 2 g Total Fat, 0 g Saturated Fat, 0 mg Cholesterol, 333 mg Sodium, 9 g Total Carbohydrate, 0 g Dietary Fiber, 7 g Protein, 224 mg Calcium.

SERVING PROVIDES: 1 Fruit/Vegetable, 1 Protein/Milk, 1 Fat.

POINTS PER SERVING: 2.

★*To prepare yogurt cheese, spoon 1¹/2 cups plain nonfat yogurt into a coffee filter or a cheesecloth-lined strainer; place it over a bowl. Refrigerate, covered, at least 5 hours or overnight. Discard the liquid in the bowl. Makes ³/4 cup yogurt cheese.*

$\mathcal{G}$uilt-Free Guacamole

MAKES 6 SERVINGS

Linda A. Grant
Stockton, California

*"It was the afternoon of Day 7 of a b-a-a-a-d week," said Linda. "I had used
all my Bonus Calories and I was HUNGRY. All the raw veggies were slated for the
night's dinner and I didn't want to rob Peter to pay Paul. Then I remembered an old favorite
of Jean Nidetch [the founder of Weight Watchers]: Green Bean Pea Soup. I raced to the
cupboard—alas, no green beans! The only green anything was a can of asparagus. I pureed
the contents and then did a double take: The stuff looked exactly liked mashed avocado!"
Following this discovery, Linda came up with this remarkably delicious guacamole
that's even better with fresh asparagus. Serve it as a dip with
baked corn chips or raw vegetable sticks.*

24 asparagus spears,
 trimmed and halved

1/2 cup salsa

1 tablespoon cilantro leaves

2 garlic cloves

4 scallions, thinly sliced

1. In a large nonstick skillet, combine the asparagus and 1/2 cup water; bring to a boil. Reduce the heat and simmer, covered, until the asparagus is tender-crisp, about 5 minutes; drain and run under cold water to cool.

2. In a blender or food processor, puree the asparagus, salsa, cilantro and garlic. Add the scallions; pulse several times until chunky-smooth. Transfer to a serving bowl. Refrigerate, covered, until chilled, at least 1 hour.

PER SERVING: 22 Calories, 0 g Total Fat, 0 g Saturated Fat, 0 mg Cholesterol, 96 mg Sodium, 4 g Total Carbohydrate, 1 g Dietary Fiber, 2 g Protein, 18 mg Calcium.

SERVING PROVIDES: 1 Fruit/Vegetable.

POINTS PER SERVING: 0.

Hummus

MAKES 8 SERVINGS

Jacquelin T. Duffek
Eastham, Massachusetts

Jacquelin, a Weight Watchers lifetime member, has lost (and kept off) 90 pounds over the past four years. Recipes such as this garlicky hummus have helped her stay on her food plan while enjoying delicious foods. Try serving it with an assortment of raw vegetables, for added crunch and color.

2 teaspoons olive oil

2 onions, chopped

3 garlic cloves, minced

One 19-ounce can chickpeas, rinsed and drained

3 tablespoons fresh lemon juice

2 tablespoons tahini (sesame paste)

$1/4$ teaspoon salt

$1/4$ teaspoon freshly ground black pepper

1. In a medium nonstick skillet, heat the oil. Add the onions and garlic; cook, stirring as needed, until the onions are softened, about 5 minutes.

2. In a blender or food processor, puree the chickpeas, lemon juice, tahini, salt and pepper with the onion mixture. Refrigerate, covered, until chilled, at least 1 hour.

PER SERVING: 89 Calories, 4 g Total Fat, 0 g Saturated Fat, 0 mg Cholesterol, 147 mg Sodium, 10 g Total Carbohydrate, 3 g Dietary Fiber, 3 g Protein, 37 mg Calcium.

SERVING PROVIDES: 1 Protein/Milk.

POINTS PER SERVING: 2.

$\mathcal{L}$ow-Fat Spinach Dip

MAKES 4 SERVINGS

Karen Schultz
Williamsburg, Michigan

*Karen loves dips and often brings this one along to parties to help her
stay on the program. Try it with fat-free crackers.*

½ cup nonfat sour cream

½ cup part-skim ricotta
  cheese

2 teaspoons fresh lemon
  juice

1 garlic clove

½ teaspoon salt

¼ teaspoon freshly ground
  black pepper

Half 10-ounce package
  frozen chopped spinach,
  thawed and squeezed dry

¼ cup water chestnuts,
  chopped

4 scallions, thinly sliced

1. In a blender or food processor, puree the sour cream,
cheese, lemon juice, garlic, salt and pepper. Transfer to a
medium bowl.

2. Stir in the spinach, water chestnuts and scallions.
Refrigerate, covered, until the flavors are blended, at least
1 hour.

PER SERVING: 83 Calories, 3 g Total Fat, 2 g Saturated Fat,
10 mg Cholesterol, 360 mg Sodium, 8 g Total Carbohydrate,
1 g Dietary Fiber, 7 g Protein, 171 mg Calcium.

SERVING PROVIDES: 1 Fruit/Vegetable.

POINTS PER SERVING: 2.

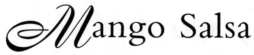ango Salsa

MAKES 4 SERVINGS

Hildie Block
Arlington, Virginia

Fresh as a tropical breeze, Hildie's Mango Salsa works well in so many ways.
Serve it as an accompaniment to grilled fish, or use it as a dip for
low-fat tortilla chips. Just be sure to make enough!

2 small mangoes, peeled and cut into 1/2" pieces

4 scallions, thinly sliced

1/4 green bell pepper, seeded and diced

2 tablespoons minced cilantro

1 tablespoon fresh lime juice

1/8 teaspoon crushed red pepper flakes

In a medium nonreactive bowl, combine the mangoes, scallions, bell pepper, cilantro, lime juice and pepper flakes. Transfer to a serving bowl and refrigerate, covered, until the flavors are blended, at least 1 hour.

PER SERVING: 56 Calories, 0 g Total Fat, 0 g Saturated Fat, 0 mg Cholesterol, 3 mg Sodium, 15 g Total Carbohydrate, 1 g Dietary Fiber, 1 g Protein, 14 mg Calcium.

SERVING PROVIDES: 1 Fruit/Vegetable.

POINTS PER SERVING: 1.

Pico de Gallo

MAKES 6 SERVINGS

Wanda Moore
Madison Heights, Virginia

*Wanda and her friend Mary have a favorite grilled chicken salad they order
at a local restaurant. They always ask for extra Pico de Gallo on the side. Since
this particular salsa is not available in a jar, Wanda came up with her own fresh version.
Literally meaning "rooster's beak," this is a hot, sharp salsa. Serve it as a dip
with baked corn chips, as a topping for baked potatoes
or on the side with grilled chicken salad.*

3 tomatoes, chopped

1 green bell pepper, seeded
and diced

1/4 red onion, chopped

1 tablespoon minced
cilantro

2 teaspoons fresh lime juice

1 jalapeño pepper, seeded
and chopped (wear
gloves to prevent
irritation)

1/4 teaspoon salt

In a medium nonreactive bowl, combine the tomatoes,
bell pepper, onion, cilantro, lime juice, jalapeño and salt.
Refrigerate, covered, until ready to serve, at least 1 hour.

PER SERVING: 23 Calories, 0 g Total Fat, 0 g Saturated Fat,
0 mg Cholesterol, 98 mg Sodium, 5 g Total Carbohydrate,
1 g Dietary Fiber, 1 g Protein, 8 mg Calcium.

SERVING PROVIDES: 1 Fruit/Vegetable.

POINTS PER SERVING: 1.

Shrimp Salsa

MAKES 6 SERVINGS

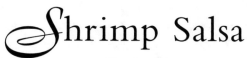

Peggy Villarreal
Mesa, Arizona

This zippy Mexican chip-and-dip appetizer comes special delivery from letter carrier Peggy Villarreal. It satisfies her urge to munch and fills the need for something spicy.

1/2 pound peeled cooked shrimp, coarsely chopped

1 1/2 cups salsa

4 scallions, thinly sliced

1/4 cup minced cilantro

1 tablespoon fresh lime juice

1 garlic clove, minced

1/2 teaspoon dried oregano

1/4 teaspoon freshly ground black pepper

One 7-ounce bag baked tortilla chips

In a medium bowl, combine the shrimp, salsa, scallions, cilantro, lime juice, garlic, oregano and pepper. Refrigerate, covered, until the flavors are blended, about 1 hour. Serve with the tortilla chips.

PER SERVING: 171 Calories, 2 g Total Fat, 0 g Saturated Fat, 74 mg Cholesterol, 366 mg Sodium, 26 g Total Carbohydrate, 2 g Dietary Fiber, 11 g Protein, 102 mg Calcium.

SERVING PROVIDES: 1 Bread, 1 Fruit/Vegetable, 1 Protein/Milk, 80 Bonus Calories.

POINTS PER SERVING: 4.

*E*ggplant Spread

MAKES 6 SERVINGS

Janet Aloia
Washington, Pennsylvania

*When Janet wants to prepare something out of the ordinary for parties,
she whips up this exotic eggplant spread, redolent of Middle Eastern flavors.
Served with pita bread, it makes for great foreign intrigue.*

1 large (1½-pound)
  eggplant

14 sun-dried tomato halves
  (not oil-packed)

10 garlic cloves, peeled

2 tablespoons fresh lemon
  juice

1 teaspoon dried oregano

1 teaspoon olive oil

¼ teaspoon ground cumin

¼ teaspoon crushed red
  pepper flakes

I. Preheat the oven to 450° F.

2. Halve the eggplant lengthwise; cut 2 deep slits in each
of the cut sides. Insert the tomatoes and garlic into the
slits. Place the eggplant in a 12 × 8" baking pan; bake, covered, until the eggplant is tender, about 45 minutes. Cool
until comfortable to handle, about 15 minutes.

3. Scoop out the eggplant pulp, tomatoes and garlic; place
in a blender or food processor. Add the lemon juice,
oregano, oil, cumin and pepper flakes; puree. Transfer to a
serving bowl and serve at room temperature.

PER SERVING: 58 Calories, 1 g Total Fat, 0 g Saturated Fat,
0 mg Cholesterol, 11 mg Sodium, 12 g Total Carbohydrate,
3 g Dietary Fiber, 3 g Protein, 47 mg Calcium.

SERVING PROVIDES: 1 Fruit/Vegetable.

POINTS PER SERVING: 1.

Sushi Salad Appetizer

MAKES 8 SERVINGS

Peggy Allen
Pasadena, California

You might have to pay a visit to an Asian market or a gourmet grocery to pick up some of the ingredients for Peggy's Japanese-inspired appetizer, but this delicious recipe is worth a special trip. If fresh crabmeat is beyond your budget, use canned crab.

3 tablespoons rice-wine vinegar

1 tablespoon wasabi powder★

2 teaspoons Asian sesame oil

1 teaspoon grated peeled gingerroot

8 ounces cooked crabmeat, picked over and flaked

1 cup cold cooked sushi rice†

1 tomato, chopped

1/2 carrot, shredded

1/2 cucumber, peeled and chopped

32 Boston lettuce leaves

1 nori (dried seaweed) sheet, cut into strips (optional)

1. In a small bowl, combine the vinegar, wasabi powder, oil and ginger.

2. In a large bowl, combine the crab, rice, tomato, carrot and cucumber. Add the vinegar mixture and toss to coat. Serve the lettuce, topped with the crabmeat mixture and garnished with the nori (if using).

PER SERVING: 84 Calories, 2 g Total Fat, 0 g Saturated Fat, 28 mg Cholesterol, 85 mg Sodium, 10 g Total Carbohydrate, 1 g Dietary Fiber, 7 g Protein, 46 mg Calcium.

SERVING PROVIDES: 1 Fruit/Vegetable, 1 Protein/Milk.

POINTS PER SERVING: 2.

★*Wasabi, the Japanese version of horseradish, has a sharp, pungent, fiery flavor. It is available in Asian markets and some supermarkets.*

†*Sushi rice, once cooled, has a glossy sheen and separates easily. It is available in Asian markets and some supermarkets.*

Tortilla Swirls

MAKES 12 SERVINGS

Barbara L. Pryor
Cuyahoga Falls, Ohio

Barbara developed the recipe for these festive Tortilla Swirls because she needed to get through the holidays without gaining weight. Guess what? Total success!

3/4 cup nonfat cream cheese

1/2 cup nonfat sour cream

1 cup shredded nonfat sharp cheddar cheese

1/2 green bell pepper, seeded and finely chopped

8 scallions, thinly sliced

2 teaspoons fresh lime juice

Nine 6" fat-free flour tortillas

1/4 cup salsa

(See photo.)

1. In a small bowl, with an electric mixer at medium speed, beat the cream cheese and sour cream until smooth. With the mixer at low speed, blend in the cheddar cheese, pepper, scallions and lime juice.

2. Place the tortillas on a work surface. Spread about 1/4 cup of the cheese mixture on each tortilla; roll up and place, seam-side down, on a plate. Cover the rolls with plastic wrap and refrigerate until chilled, at least 1 hour.

3. With a serrated knife, cut each tortilla roll into 6 equal slices; arrange, cut-side up, on a serving platter. Top each swirl with 1/4 teaspoon salsa.

PER SERVING: 99 Calories, 0 g Total Fat, 0 g Saturated Fat, 2 mg Cholesterol, 354 mg Sodium, 16 g Total Carbohydrate, 1 g Dietary Fiber, 8 g Protein, 140 mg Calcium.

SERVING PROVIDES: 1 Bread.

POINTS PER SERVING: 2.

*H*ot Asiago Spread

MAKES 8 SERVINGS

Tonya Sarina
Aurora, Colorado

"This is my yummy version of a rich and fattening spread I enjoyed at a local microbrewery,"
Tonya writes, adding that come the holidays, she puts it out with sliced apples and toasted
English muffins. As an alternative, serve it with a colorful assortment of crudités.

1 cup nonfat cottage cheese

¹/₄ cup + 2 tablespoons nonfat cream cheese

1¹/₂ teaspoons Dijon mustard

¹/₄ cup grated Asiago or Parmesan cheese

2 scallions, sliced

1 jalapeño pepper, seeded, deveined and minced (wear gloves to prevent irritation)

1. In a blender or food processor, puree the cottage and cream cheeses; add the mustard. Add the Asiago cheese, scallions and jalapeño; pulse to combine.

2. Transfer the mixture to a 2-cup microwavable dish; microwave on High until heated through, 3 minutes. Serve at once.

PER SERVING: 49 Calories, 1 g Total Fat, 1 g Saturated Fat, 6 mg Cholesterol, 214 mg Sodium, 3 g Total Carbohydrate, 0 g Dietary Fiber, 6 g Protein, 77 mg Calcium.

SERVING PROVIDES: 1 Protein/Milk.

POINTS PER SERVING: 1.

$\mathscr{A}$sian Meatballs

MAKES 8 SERVINGS

Rebecca Raiewski
Petaluma, California

Rebecca enjoys being able to stay at home full time with her three sons. This recipe was first produced as an appetizer for a family get-together, and they all loved it. Sometimes Rebecca serves it as a quick dinner over rice.

10 ounces ground skinless turkey breast

1/2 green bell pepper, seeded and minced

4 scallions, thinly sliced

1/3 cup fine dried bread crumbs

2 tablespoons minced water chestnuts

1 egg white

1 tablespoon reduced-sodium soy sauce

1/4 cup sweet and sour sauce

1/2 cup unsweetened applesauce

(See photo.)

1. Preheat the oven to 375° F. Spray a nonstick jelly-roll pan with nonstick cooking spray.

2. In a medium bowl, lightly combine the turkey, pepper, scallions, bread crumbs, water chestnuts, egg white and soy sauce. Shape into 32 equal meatballs, about 1" each; place on the pan. Bake until cooked through and browned, about 15 minutes.

3. Meanwhile, in a 2-quart microwavable dish, combine the sweet and sour sauce and applesauce; microwave on High until hot and bubbling, 2 minutes. Stir in the meatballs and serve with toothpicks.

PER SERVING: 82 Calories, 1 g Total Fat, 0 g Saturated Fat, 22 mg Cholesterol, 163 mg Sodium, 9 g Total Carbohydrate, 1 g Dietary Fiber, 12 g Protein, 19 mg Calcium.

SERVING PROVIDES: 1 Protein/Milk.

POINTS PER SERVING: 2.

ot Shrimp Dip

MAKES 8 SERVINGS

Patty Paulsen
Monterey, California

When Patty found that a friend's recipe for hot shrimp dip was loaded with calories and contained many hard-to-find ingredients, she went to the drawing board and came up with this supereasy, ultratasty low-fat dip. We think it works every bit as well chilled.

²/₃ cup part-skim ricotta cheese

¹/₄ cup nonfat cream cheese

¹/₂ pound cooked peeled shrimp, diced

1 tomato, chopped

1 onion, chopped

¹/₄ cup chopped canned green chiles, drained

2 garlic cloves, minced

¹/₄ teaspoon salt

One 8-ounce loaf whole-wheat Italian bread, cut into 24 slices and toasted

In a large nonstick skillet over low heat, melt the ricotta and cream cheeses. Add the shrimp, tomato, onion, chiles, garlic and salt; cook, stirring as needed, until heated through, 4–5 minutes. Transfer to a serving bowl and serve at once with the toast.

PER SERVING: 143 Calories, 3 g Total Fat, 1 g Saturated Fat, 62 mg Cholesterol, 368 mg Sodium, 17 g Total Carbohydrate, 2 g Dietary Fiber, 12 g Protein, 113 mg Calcium.

SERVING PROVIDES: 1 Bread, 1 Protein/Milk.

POINTS PER SERVING: 3.

Roasted Vegetable Dip

MAKES 4 SERVINGS

Jane Barg
Princeton, New Jersey

*"I'm always looking for things to serve with crudités," writes Jane,
who is justifiably proud of her Roasted Vegetable Dip, which packs more than
a little "kick." Roasting brings out the vegetables' natural sweetness, so you may want to add
an additional pinch or two of cayenne pepper. Besides crudités, toasted pita wedges
or baked tortilla chips also go well with this.*

1 medium zucchini, sliced

1 medium yellow squash, sliced

1 red bell pepper, seeded and sliced

1 red onion, thinly sliced

2 garlic cloves, peeled

¼ teaspoon salt

¼ teaspoon cayenne pepper, or to taste

1. Preheat the oven to 400° F.

2. Place the zucchini, squash, bell pepper, onion and garlic on a jelly-roll pan. Spray evenly with nonstick cooking spray; sprinkle evenly with the salt and cayenne. Bake, turning once, until the vegetables are tender and lightly browned, about 15 minutes on each side.

3. Transfer the vegetables to a blender or food processor; puree. Transfer to a serving bowl and serve warm, or refrigerate, covered, until chilled, at least 2 hours.

PER SERVING: 33 Calories, 1 g Total Fat, 0 g Saturated Fat, 0 mg Cholesterol, 140 mg Sodium, 7 g Total Carbohydrate, 1 g Dietary Fiber, 1 g Protein, 26 mg Calcium.

SERVING PROVIDES: 1 Fruit/Vegetable.

POINTS PER SERVING: 1.

Mushroom-Salsa Wrapper

MAKES 2 SERVINGS

Merri Fromm
St. Paul, Minnesota

*As a busy graphic designer, Merri has no time for fussy recipes and no patience
for dull flavors. Hence, this lively vegetable-and-salsa-filled tortilla. Merri's motto?
"Creative food choices are what keep me going and happy."*

1 cup sliced mushrooms

1/2 green bell pepper,
  seeded and chopped

1/4 cup salsa

1 tablespoon minced
  cilantro

Two 6" fat-free flour
  tortillas, warmed

1. Spray a small nonstick skillet with nonstick cooking
spray; heat. Add the mushrooms and pepper; cook, stirring as needed, until the vegetables are softened, about 5
minutes.

2. Add the salsa and cilantro; cook, stirring constantly,
until heated through, about 1 minute. Divide the mixture between the 2 tortillas and roll up.

PER SERVING: 109 Calories, 1 g Total Fat, 0 g Saturated Fat,
0 mg Cholesterol, 389 mg Sodium, 23 g Total Carbohydrate,
2 g Dietary Fiber, 3 g Protein, 4 mg Calcium.

SERVING PROVIDES: 1 Bread, 1 Fruit/Vegetable.

POINTS PER SERVING: 2.

Banana Pudding Pops

MAKES 8 SERVINGS

Debra Marzka
Luna Pier, Michigan

*Debra likes to vary her pudding pops by using chocolate pudding
and fresh whole strawberries, or pineapple chunks with a sprinkling of coconut.
It is a great no-mess dessert that adults and kids will love.*

1 envelope (four ½-cup servings) reduced-calorie instant vanilla pudding mix

2 cups skim milk

2 bananas, peeled and cut into 4 chunks each

1. Prepare the pudding with the milk, following package directions.

2. Push 1 wooden ice-cream stick into each banana chunk; place each in one 5-ounce plastic drinking cup. Pour the pudding into the cups, filling each two-thirds full. Freeze until firm, at least 4 hours.

PER SERVING: 59 Calories, 0 g Total Fat, 0 g Saturated Fat, 1 mg Cholesterol, 192 mg Sodium, 12 g Total Carbohydrate, 0 g Dietary Fiber, 2 g Protein, 77 mg Calcium.

SERVING PROVIDES: 1 Fruit/Vegetable.

POINTS PER SERVING: 1.

Berry Brown Rice

MAKES 4 SERVINGS

Theresa Schlarb
Sacramento, California

*More than just rice pudding, this creamy snack marries the whole-grain goodness
of brown rice with the tart sweetness of cranberries.*

2 cups cooked brown rice

2 cups skim milk

1/2 cup dried cranberries

2 tablespoons firmly packed
light brown sugar

1 teaspoon lemon zest

1/8 teaspoon cinnamon
(optional)

In a medium nonstick saucepan, bring the rice, milk and cranberries to a boil. Reduce the heat and simmer, uncovered, until the cranberries are softened, about 5 minutes. Remove from the heat and stir in the sugar, lemon zest and cinnamon (if using). Cool 30 minutes. Serve warm, or refrigerate, covered, until chilled, at least 2 hours.

PER SERVING: 222 Calories, 1 g Total Fat, 0 g Saturated Fat, 2 mg Cholesterol, 71 mg Sodium, 46 g Total Carbohydrate, 3 g Dietary Fiber, 7 g Protein, 167 mg Calcium.

SERVING PROVIDES: 1 Bread, 1 Fruit/Vegetable.

POINTS PER SERVING: 4.

Granola-Yogurt Snack

MAKES 2 SERVINGS

Erika J. Shatz
Lemon Grove, California

As a vegetarian, Erika finds the Weight Watchers program an easy fit. Although she makes her own yogurt from scratch every week, store-bought yogurt works just as well. Serve this for a tasty breakfast or an after-school snack.

1 cup plain nonfat yogurt

1 small apple, cored and diced (or 1/2 banana, peeled and sliced)

1/2 cup low-fat granola

1/4 cup dried cranberries

2 tablespoons pumpkin seeds

In a medium bowl, combine the yogurt, apple, granola, cranberries and pumpkin seeds. Serve at once.

PER SERVING: 235 Calories, 2 g Total Fat, 0 g Saturated Fat, 2 mg Cholesterol, 138 mg Sodium, 46 g Total Carbohydrate, 3 g Dietary Fiber, 9 g Protein, 239 mg Calcium.

SERVING PROVIDES: 1 Bread, 2 Fruit/Vegetables, 1 Protein/Milk, 1 Fat.

POINTS PER SERVING: 4.

Marshmallow-Fruit Squares

MAKES 12 SERVINGS

Karen Marshall
Scarborough, Ontario, Canada

Karen, who lost 98 pounds, is now a center coordinator in Toronto. While these fruity, crunchy marshmallow squares look and taste sinful, they're reasonably virtuous.

4 teaspoons reduced-calorie margarine

20 marshmallows

2 cups cornflakes

24 dried apricot halves, chopped

$^1/_2$ cup unsalted sunflower seeds

$^1/_4$ cup sliced unblanched almonds

4 pitted dates, chopped

2 tablespoons sesame seeds

$^1/_4$ teaspoon vanilla extract

1. Spray a 10 × 6" baking pan with nonstick cooking spray.

2. In a large nonstick saucepan over low heat, melt the margarine. Add the marshmallows and cook, stirring constantly, until the marshmallows are melted, about 5 minutes.

3. Remove from the heat; stir in the cornflakes, apricots, sunflower seeds, almonds, dates, sesame seeds and vanilla.

4. With moistened hands, press the mixture evenly into the baking pan. Refrigerate, covered, until firm, at least 30 minutes.

PER SERVING: 145 Calories, 6 g Total Fat, 1 g Saturated Fat, 0 mg Cholesterol, 69 mg Sodium, 22 g Total Carbohydrate, 1 g Dietary Fiber, 3 g Protein, 34 mg Calcium.

SERVING PROVIDES: 1 Fruit/Vegetable, 1 Fat, 40 Bonus Calories.

POINTS PER SERVING: 3.

Cranberry–Ice Cream Soda

MAKES 1 SERVING

Monica Kramer
Tulsa, Oklahoma

*Monica's grandmother traditionally served this drink at Christmas,
but now Monica enjoys her own low-calorie version all year.*

1 cup chilled low-calorie
 cranberry juice cocktail
¹/₄ cup chilled club soda
¹/₂ cup nonfat ice cream
Mint sprigs

In a chilled 16-ounce glass, combine the cranberry juice and soda. Add the ice cream; garnish with the mint and serve at once with a tall spoon.

PER SERVING: 145 Calories, 0 g Total Fat, 0 g Saturated Fat, 0 mg Cholesterol, 70 mg Sodium, 34 g Total Carbohydrate, 0 g Dietary Fiber, 2 g Protein, 124 mg Calcium.

SERVING PROVIDES: 2 Fruit/Vegetables, 90 Bonus Calories.

POINTS PER SERVING: 3.

Fruit and Spice Iced Tea

MAKES 8 SERVINGS

Lois Luttrell
Newcastle, California

Although Lois has for years mixed teas and fruit juices for summertime drinks, a redecorating crewman told her, "You should bottle this and sell it," when he tasted this fruity, refreshing drink.

3 English breakfast teabags

3 orange and spice teabags

3 cups boiling water

Sugar substitute to equal
   2 tablespoons sugar

2 cups grapefruit juice

Ice cubes

Mint sprigs

(See photo.)

1. Place the teabags in a large teapot. Add the boiling water; let stand, covered, 10 minutes. Remove the teabags and stir in the sugar substitute until it dissolves; let cool.

2. Pour the grapefruit juice and 3 cups cold water into a large pitcher; stir in the cooled tea. Pour over ice and serve, garnished with the mint.

PER SERVING: 27 Calories, 0 g Total Fat, 0 g Saturated Fat, 0 mg Cholesterol, 6 mg Sodium, 6 g Total Carbohydrate, 0 g Dietary Fiber, 1 g Protein, 4 mg Calcium.

SERVING PROVIDES: 1 Fruit/Vegetable.

POINTS PER SERVING: 1.

Strawberry-Orange Yogurt Shake

MAKES 4 SERVINGS

Erika Baril
Atkinson, New Hampshire

"I make this recipe because I love fruity yogurt shakes for breakfast," Erika writes.
Most recipes, she found, needed artificial sweetener or honey. Erika makes
hers with orange juice and finds it to be as sweet as she needs.
Serve it as she does, in tall fountain glasses with straws.

2 cups strawberries (reserve 2 berries and slice)

1 cup skim milk

1 cup plain nonfat yogurt

½ cup orange juice

8 ice cubes

In a blender, puree the strawberries, milk, yogurt and orange juice. Add the ice and blend until the ice is coarsely chopped. Serve in chilled glasses, garnished with the reserved strawberry slices.

PER SERVING: 90 Calories, 1 g Total Fat, 0 g Saturated Fat, 2 mg Cholesterol, 76 mg Sodium, 16 g Total Carbohydrate, 2 g Dietary Fiber, 6 g Protein, 202 mg Calcium.

SERVING PROVIDES: 1 Fruit/Vegetable.

POINTS PER SERVING: 1.

Cinnamon Cappuccino

MAKES 1 SERVING

Randi D. Hamilton
Van Buren, Arkansas

As a lover of all cappuccino and espresso drinks, and as an avid inventor of recipes that fit the Weight Watchers program, Randi developed this very satisfying Cinnamon Cappuccino.

³/₄ cup skim milk

1 teaspoon vanilla extract

¹/₄ teaspoon cinnamon

¹/₂ cup hot, very strong coffee

¹/₄ teaspoon sifted unsweetened cocoa powder

1 cinnamon stick

In a medium nonstick saucepan, bring the milk, vanilla and cinnamon just to a boil. Remove from the heat and whisk until frothy, about 1 minute. In a large mug, combine the coffee and the milk mixture. Sprinkle with the cocoa and garnish with the cinnamon stick; serve.

PER SERVING: 86 Calories, 0 g Total Fat, 0 g Saturated Fat, 4 mg Cholesterol, 98 mg Sodium, 12 g Total Carbohydrate, 0 g Dietary Fiber, 6 g Protein, 243 mg Calcium.

SERVING PROVIDES: 1 Protein/Milk.

POINTS PER SERVING: 2.

Hot Eggnog

MAKES 8 SERVINGS

Annette Broussard
New Orleans, Louisiana

Annette came up with this recipe after her Weight Watchers group expressed
a desire for a slimmed-down version of the classic holiday eggnog. "My family loved it!" she
wrote. "We rang in the New Year toasting with 'Nettie's Nog' topped with a dollop of
frozen light whipped topping and a sprinkling of nutmeg."

One 12-ounce can evaporated skimmed milk

1 1/3 cups fat-free egg substitute

3 tablespoons sugar

3 cups skim milk

2 tablespoons vanilla extract

1/2 teaspoon cinnamon

1/4 teaspoon grated nutmeg

Freshly grated nutmeg (optional)

1. In a large nonstick saucepan over low heat, combine the evaporated milk, egg substitute and sugar; cook, stirring constantly, until bubbles just begin to form around the edges and the mixture thickens, 12–15 minutes.

2. Add the skim milk, vanilla, cinnamon and nutmeg; increase the heat to medium and cook, whisking constantly, until just heated through, about 5 minutes. Serve at once, sprinkled with the freshly grated nutmeg (if using).

PER SERVING: 120 Calories, 0 g Total Fat, 0 g Saturated Fat, 4 mg Cholesterol, 169 mg Sodium, 16 g Total Carbohydrate, 0 g Dietary Fiber, 11 g Protein, 267 mg Calcium.

SERVING PROVIDES: 1 Protein/Milk.

POINTS PER SERVING: 2.

CHAPTER
2

Soups

Cream of Broccoli-Cheese Soup

MAKES 4 SERVINGS

Fern Anita Chapman
Sioux Lookout, Ontario, Canada

As a professional singer who is also the busy mother of a toddler, Fern needs food on the run that's both satisfying and nutritious. This savory soup, which she likes to serve with a dollop of nonfat yogurt and a sprinkling of sliced scallions, can be frozen in portions and simply microwaved as needed.

1 onion, chopped

4 cups chopped broccoli

3 small all-purpose pota-
toes, peeled and cubed

4 cups skim milk

3 packets low-sodium
instant chicken broth and
seasoning mix

1 carrot, shredded

³/₄ cup shredded reduced-
fat sharp cheddar cheese

¹/₄ teaspoon dried sage

¹/₄ teaspoon freshly ground
black pepper

1. Spray a large nonstick saucepan or Dutch oven with nonstick cooking spray; heat. Add the onion and cook, stirring constantly, until softened, about 5 minutes. Add the broccoli, potatoes and 2 cups water; bring to a boil. Reduce the heat and simmer, covered, until the vegetables are tender, about 20 minutes.

2. With a slotted spoon, transfer the vegetables to a blender or food processor. Puree, then return them to the liquid. Add the milk, broth mix and carrot; bring to a boil. Reduce the heat and simmer, stirring as needed, until the carrot is softened, about 5 minutes.

3. Remove the pan from the heat; cool about 1 minute. Add the cheese, sage and pepper; stir until the cheese is melted.

PER SERVING: 278 Calories, 5 g Total Fat, 3 g Saturated Fat, 20 mg Cholesterol, 335 mg Sodium, 40 g Total Carbohydrate, 5 g Dietary Fiber, 20 g Protein, 550 mg Calcium.

SERVING PROVIDES: 1 Bread, 1 Fruit/Vegetable, 2 Protein/Milks.

POINTS PER SERVING: 5.

Corn and Bean Chowder

MAKES 4 SERVINGS

Marlene Bayers
St. John's, Newfoundland, Canada

*Marlene, a Weight Watchers member and leader for 10 years, serves this
hearty corn chowder—an updated childhood favorite—with warm dinner rolls and
a side salad for a no-fuss dinner. Like most soups, the leftovers refrigerate
or freeze well and the flavors are even better the next day.*

2 cups low-sodium chicken or vegetable broth

2 carrots, diced

2 celery stalks, diced

1 small all-purpose potato, diced

1 onion, chopped

1¹/₂ cups fresh or thawed frozen corn kernels

1 cup drained rinsed canned cannellini beans

1 cup skim milk

¹/₄ teaspoon freshly ground black pepper

1. In a large nonstick saucepan or Dutch oven, combine the broth, carrots, celery, potato and onion; bring to a boil. Reduce the heat and simmer, covered, until the vegetables are tender, about 15 minutes.

2. Stir in the corn, beans, milk and pepper; increase the heat and bring to a boil. Reduce the heat and simmer, uncovered, stirring as needed, until the corn is tender, about 3 minutes.

PER SERVING: 194 Calories, 2 g Total Fat, 1 g Saturated Fat, 3 mg Cholesterol, 214 mg Sodium, 36 g Total Carbohydrate, 7 g Dietary Fiber, 11 g Protein, 128 mg Calcium.

SERVING PROVIDES: 1 Bread, 1 Fruit/Vegetable, 1 Protein/Milk.

POINTS PER SERVING: 3.

Saffron Carrot Soup

MAKES 6 SERVINGS

Karin Theophile
Washington, D.C.

*When Karin sent her husband to the supermarket to buy some carrots,
little did she imagine that he would return with a 10-pound bag! Accordingly, she
set about to find ways to use up this fortuitous bounty. One recipe she came up with
was this saffron-spiked soup, every bit as delicious as it is low-fat and low-calorie.*

2 cups low-sodium veg-
   etable broth

3 carrots, cut into
   2" chunks

4 onions, chopped

3 small all-purpose pota-
   toes, peeled and cut into
   2" chunks

1 cup parsley leaves

1 teaspoon olive oil

2 carrots, sliced

1 cup sliced mushrooms

1/2 teaspoon freshly ground
   black pepper

1/8 teaspoon saffron threads,
   crumbled

1/2 cup plain nonfat yogurt

Minced parsley

1. In a large nonstick saucepan or Dutch oven, bring the broth, carrot chunks, onions, potatoes, parsley leaves and 7 cups water to a boil. Reduce the heat and simmer, covered, until the vegetables are tender, about 1 hour.

2. Meanwhile, in a large nonstick skillet, heat the oil. Add the sliced carrots and mushrooms; cook, covered, stirring as needed, until the carrots are tender, about 10 minutes, adding 1 tablespoon water at a time, if necessary. Stir in the pepper and saffron.

3. With a slotted spoon, transfer the vegetables from the saucepan to a blender or food processor. Puree, then return them to the broth. Whisk in the yogurt and stir in the sautéed vegetables; cook, stirring as needed, until heated through, 2–3 minutes. Serve, garnished with the minced parsley.

PER SERVING: 143 Calories, 1 g Total Fat, 0 g Saturated Fat, 0 mg Cholesterol, 78 mg Sodium, 30 g Total Carbohydrate, 5 g Dietary Fiber, 5 g Protein, 90 mg Calcium.

SERVING PROVIDES: 1 Bread, 1 Fruit/Vegetable.

POINTS PER SERVING: 2.

*F*rench Onion Soup

MAKES 2 SERVINGS

Lorraine Yaremchuk
Edmonton, Alberta, Canada

As the mother of two toddlers, Lorraine has no time to bother with difficult and time-consuming fare. This soul-warming soup is adapted from a classic recipe given to her many years ago by a friend. Sometimes, the simplest things are the best.

1 teaspoon unsalted stick margarine

1 onion, chopped

1½ cups low-sodium beef broth

2 ounces French bread, cut into two slices and toasted

⅓ cup shredded part-skim mozzarella cheese

(See photo.)

1. Preheat the broiler. In a medium saucepan, melt the margarine. Add the onion and cook, stirring as needed, until softened, about 5 minutes. Add the broth; bring to a boil. Reduce the heat and simmer, uncovered, until the onion is very tender, about 3 minutes.

2. Place one slice of the toast in each of two flameproof soup bowls; pour the soup over the toast. Sprinkle each with the cheese and broil until the cheese is melted and lightly browned, about 1 minute. Serve at once.

PER SERVING: 180 Calories, 6 g Total Fat, 3 g Saturated Fat, 12 mg Cholesterol, 326 mg Sodium, 19 g Total Carbohydrate, 1 g Dietary Fiber, 12 g Protein, 168 mg Calcium.

SERVING PROVIDES: 1 Bread, 1 Protein/Milk, 1 Fat.

POINTS PER SERVING: 4.

$\mathcal{G}$oulash Soup

MAKES 4 SERVINGS

Karen Senn
Mississauga, Ontario, Canada

*"Traveling through Germany and Austria, I enjoyed goulash soup
nearly every day," Karen writes. When she returned home, she knew she
had to come up with a recipe that she could make easily and was both
satisfying and low-calorie. Happily for all of us, she did!*

1 tablespoon vegetable oil

2 onions, chopped

2 garlic cloves, minced

4 cups low-sodium beef broth

1 pound lean boneless beef round, cut into 1" pieces

1 tablespoon paprika

1 teaspoon caraway seeds

1/4 teaspoon freshly ground black pepper

3 small all-purpose potatoes, peeled and cubed

2 carrots, diced

1 tomato, chopped

1 teaspoon dried marjoram

1. In a large nonstick saucepan or Dutch oven, heat the oil. Add the onions and garlic; cook, stirring as needed, until the onions are softened, about 5 minutes.

2. Add the broth, beef, paprika, caraway seeds and pepper; bring to a boil. Reduce the heat and simmer, covered, stirring as needed, until the beef is almost tender, about 45 minutes.

3. Increase the heat and stir in the potatoes and carrots; return to a boil. Reduce the heat and simmer, covered, stirring as needed, until the vegetables are tender and the beef is cooked through, about 20 minutes.

4. Add the tomato and marjoram; cook until the tomato is heated through, about 3 minutes.

PER SERVING: 338 Calories, 10 g Total Fat, 2 g Saturated Fat, 66 mg Cholesterol, 164 mg Sodium, 30 g Total Carbohydrate, 4 g Dietary Fiber, 34 g Protein, 48 mg Calcium.

SERVING PROVIDES: 1 Bread, 1 Fruit/Vegetable, 3 Protein/Milks, 1 Fat.

POINTS PER SERVING: 7.

Leek and Potato Soup

MAKES 4 SERVINGS

Elaine Bray
Niagara Falls, Ontario, Canada

*Elaine is a Weight Watchers lifetime member and an elementary-school
teacher who takes homemade vegetable soup to work for lunch most days.
It helps her maintain her goal weight while providing her with a
satisfying, filling lunch. This is one of her favorites.*

2 teaspoons unsalted stick
    margarine

4-5 leeks, cleaned and
    sliced (about 7 cups)

3 shallots, chopped

4 cups low-sodium veg-
    etable broth

2 small all-purpose pota-
    toes, peeled and diced

2 cups skim milk

1/4 cup dry white wine

1/2 teaspoon freshly ground
    black pepper

Dash curry powder
    (optional)

1. In a large nonstick saucepan or Dutch oven, melt the margarine. Add the leeks and shallots; cook, stirring as needed, until softened, 6–8 minutes.

2. Add the broth and potatoes; bring to a boil. Reduce the heat and simmer, covered, until the potatoes are tender, about 20 minutes.

3. Stir in the milk, wine, pepper and curry powder (if using); cook, stirring as needed, just until the mixture comes to a boil.

PER SERVING: 270 Calories, 4 g Total Fat, 1 g Saturated Fat, 6 mg Cholesterol, 211 mg Sodium, 47 g Total Carbohydrate, 3 g Dietary Fiber, 12 g Protein, 284 mg Calcium.

SERVING PROVIDES: 1 Bread, 1 Fruit/Vegetable, 1 Fat.

POINTS PER SERVING: 5.

*L*ettuce Soup

MAKES 4 SERVINGS

Nancy Drechsler
Hendersonville, North Carolina

*Nancy was introduced to Weight Watchers by her daughter, who sends her copies
of recipes from Weight Watchers Magazine. She concocted this simple recipe
to help her lose a few pounds after the holidays. Lettuce may seem like an
unusual ingredient for soup, but it is delicious with or without the cheese.
It's not too different from the Italian classic escarole soup.*

2 teaspoons unsalted stick margarine

2 celery stalks, chopped

4 scallions, thinly sliced

6 cups shredded green leaf lettuce

4 cups low-sodium vegetable broth

1/4 cup minced parsley

1/4 teaspoon freshly ground black pepper

2 tablespoons grated Parmesan cheese

1. In a large nonstick saucepan or Dutch oven, melt the margarine. Add the celery and scallions; cook, stirring as needed, until softened, about 5 minutes.

2. Stir in the lettuce, broth, parsley, pepper and 1 cup water; bring to a boil. Reduce the heat and simmer, stirring as needed, until the lettuce is wilted, about 5 minutes. Serve, sprinkled with the cheese.

PER SERVING: 83 Calories, 3 g Total Fat, 1 g Saturated Fat, 2 mg Cholesterol, 141 mg Sodium, 11 g Total Carbohydrate, 1 g Dietary Fiber, 3 g Protein, 107 mg Calcium.

SERVING PROVIDES: 2 Fruit/Vegetables, 1 Fat.

POINTS PER SERVING: 2.

*L*entil-Spinach Soup

MAKES 4 SERVINGS

Karen Kutno
Trumbull, Connecticut

*Karen, a working mother who loves to exercise, developed this recipe during a blizzard—
a lot more healthful, she writes, than "baking cookies and eating them."*

4 teaspoons olive oil

3 onions, chopped

3 celery stalks, diced

4 garlic cloves, minced

1 cup lentils, picked over, rinsed and drained

One 8-ounce can tomato sauce (no salt added)

1 cup low-sodium vegetable broth

4 teaspoons dried oregano

One 10-ounce package frozen chopped spinach, thawed

1. In a large nonstick saucepan, heat the oil. Add the onions, celery and garlic; cook, stirring as needed, until softened, about 5 minutes.

2. Add the lentils, tomato sauce, broth, oregano and 3 cups water; bring to a boil. Reduce the heat and simmer, covered, stirring as needed, until the lentils are tender, about 45 minutes.

3. Stir in the spinach and cook, stirring as needed, until the spinach is heated through, about 5 minutes.

PER SERVING: 263 Calories, 6 g Total Fat, 1 g Saturated Fat, 0 mg Cholesterol, 120 mg Sodium, 40 g Total Carbohydrate, 9 g Dietary Fiber, 17 g Protein, 155 mg Calcium.

SERVING PROVIDES: 2 Fruit/Vegetables, 2 Protein/Milks, 1 Fat.

POINTS PER SERVING: 4.

Minestrone

MAKES 6 SERVINGS

Marie A. Geocos
Dumont, New Jersey

Marie's family thinks this hearty vegetable soup is just buono *as an appetizer
or a meal in itself. Double the recipe if you are serving a crowd.*

1 tablespoon olive oil

2 onions, chopped

2 garlic cloves, minced

One 28-ounce can crushed
   tomatoes (no salt added)

3 cups low-sodium veg-
   etable broth

2 carrots, sliced

4 celery stalks, sliced

3/4 cup ditalini pasta

One 19-ounce can
   cannellini beans, rinsed
   and drained

One 10-ounce package
   frozen chopped spinach,
   thawed

2 teaspoons dried oregano

1/2 teaspoon freshly ground
   black pepper

2 tablespoons grated
   Parmesan cheese

1. In a large nonstick saucepan or Dutch oven, heat the oil. Add the onions and garlic; cook, stirring as needed, until softened, about 5 minutes.

2. Add the tomatoes, broth, carrots, celery, pasta and 3 cups water; bring to a boil, stirring as needed to prevent the pasta from sticking to the bottom of the pan. Reduce the heat and simmer, covered, stirring as needed, until the pasta is tender, about 15 minutes.

3. Add the beans, spinach, oregano and pepper; return to a boil, stirring as needed. Serve, sprinkled with the cheese.

PER SERVING: 268 Calories, 6 g Total Fat, 2 g Saturated Fat, 3 mg Cholesterol, 209 mg Sodium, 44 g Total Carbohydrate, 7 g Dietary Fiber, 15 g Protein, 203 mg Calcium.

SERVING PROVIDES: 1 Bread, 2 Fruit/Vegetables, 1 Protein/Milk, 1 Fat.

POINTS PER SERVING: 4.

*M*ushroom-Barley Soup

MAKES 6 SERVINGS

Mary Ann Palestino
Brooklyn, New York

"A hot bowl of soup," Mary Ann writes, "makes you feel warm and cozy."
Savor a comforting bowl of this one on a blustery winter day. Beef broth adds lots of
flavor, but if you prefer a vegetarian soup, use vegetable broth instead.

3/4 cup pearl barley

1 tablespoon olive oil

4 onions, chopped

2 celery stalks, chopped

1 1/2 pounds mushrooms, sliced

4 cups low-sodium beef broth

3 carrots, sliced

2 tablespoons tomato paste (no salt added)

1/2 teaspoon salt

Freshly ground black pepper, to taste

Minced parsley

(See photo.)

1. In a large saucepan, stir the barley and 4 cups water; bring to a boil. Reduce the heat and simmer, partially covered, until the barley is partially cooked, about 30 minutes.

2. Meanwhile, in a Dutch oven, heat the oil. Add the onions and celery; cook, stirring as needed, until softened, 6–8 minutes. Add the mushrooms and cook, stirring as needed, until the mushrooms begin to soften and release their liquid, about 5 minutes.

3. Add the broth, carrots, tomato paste and barley with its liquid; bring to a boil. Reduce the heat and simmer, partially covered, stirring as needed, until the barley and carrots are tender, about 30 minutes. Stir in the salt and pepper; serve, garnished with the parsley.

PER SERVING: 182 Calories, 3 g Total Fat, 0 g Saturated Fat, 0 mg Cholesterol, 264 mg Sodium, 32 g Total Carbohydrate, 7 g Dietary Fiber, 9 g Protein, 42 mg Calcium.

SERVING PROVIDES: 1 Bread, 3 Fruit/Vegetables, 1 Fat.

POINTS PER SERVING: 2.

Herbed Split Pea Soup

MAKES 8 SERVINGS

Karla Larsen
Billings, Montana

*Karla likes to serve this substantial soup with a tablespoon of nonfat yogurt on top
and a warm slice of homemade whole-wheat bread on the side.*

1 pound green split peas,
   picked over, rinsed and
   drained

4 cups low-sodium veg-
   etable broth

2-3 leeks, cleaned and
   sliced (about 3 cups)

2 carrots, diced

1/2 teaspoon dried
   marjoram

1/4 teaspoon freshly ground
   black pepper

1/4 teaspoon grated nutmeg

Half 10-ounce package
   frozen chopped spinach,
   thawed

1 tablespoon lemon juice

1. In a large nonstick saucepan or Dutch oven, bring the peas, broth, leeks, carrots, marjoram, pepper, nutmeg and 4 cups water to a boil. Reduce the heat and simmer, covered, until the peas are tender, about 40 minutes.

2. With a slotted spoon, transfer the vegetables to a blender or food processor. Puree, then return to the saucepan. Stir in the spinach and lemon juice. Cook until heated through, about 5 minutes.

PER SERVING: 250 Calories, 1 g Total Fat, 0 g Saturated Fat, 0 mg Cholesterol, 74 mg Sodium, 47 g Total Carbohydrate, 5 g Dietary Fiber, 16 g Protein, 82 mg Calcium.

SERVING PROVIDES: 1 Fruit/Vegetable, 2 Protein/Milks.

POINTS PER SERVING: 4.

Tomato-Tofu Bisque

MAKES 4 SERVINGS

Cindy Waldt
St. Paul, Minnesota

Says Cindy: "People who swear they'd never eat tofu love this soup!" Why?
Because the tofu gives the soup its rich and sinfully creamy texture.

1 tablespoon unsalted stick margarine

1 onion, chopped

1 tablespoon all-purpose flour

Two 14¹/₂-ounce cans diced tomatoes (no salt added)

2 cups low-sodium vegetable broth

1 teaspoon dried oregano

¹/₄ teaspoon freshly ground black pepper

³/₄ pound reduced-fat soft tofu (reserve ¹/₂ cup of the liquid)

¹/₂ cup minced parsley

2 tablespoons minced dill

1 tablespoon honey

1. In a large nonstick saucepan or Dutch oven, melt the margarine. Add the onion and cook, stirring as needed, until softened, about 5 minutes. Add the flour and cook, stirring constantly, until the flour is lightly browned, about 1 minute.

2. Add the tomatoes, broth, oregano and pepper; bring to a boil. Reduce the heat and simmer, covered, until heated through, about 10 minutes.

3. Meanwhile, in a blender or food processor, puree the tofu and the reserved liquid. Add the tofu, parsley, dill and honey to the tomato mixture; cook, stirring as needed, until just heated through, about 3 minutes.

PER SERVING: 165 Calories, 6 g Total Fat, 1 g Saturated Fat, 0 mg Cholesterol, 72 mg Sodium, 23 g Total Carbohydrate, 2 g Dietary Fiber, 7 g Protein, 107 mg Calcium.

SERVING PROVIDES: 1 Fruit/Vegetable, 1 Protein/Milk, 1 Fat, 40 Bonus Calories.

POINTS PER SERVING: 3.

Tortellini Soup

MAKES 6 SERVINGS

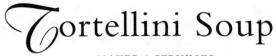

Lisa Godin
Welland, Ontario, Canada

Lisa is married, works full time and needs quick recipes that her husband enjoys.
This hearty soup is one of their favorites on a cold winter's night.

1 tablespoon unsalted stick margarine

2 cups sliced mushrooms

1 garlic clove, minced

2 cups low-sodium vegetable broth

One 14½-ounce can Italian-style stewed tomatoes (no salt added)

3 cups frozen cheese tortellini

One 10-ounce package frozen chopped spinach, thawed and squeezed dry

Freshly ground black pepper, to taste

1. In a large nonstick saucepan or Dutch oven, melt the margarine. Add the mushrooms and garlic; cook, stirring as needed, until softened, 2–3 minutes.

2. Add the broth, tomatoes and 3 cups water; bring to a boil. Add the tortellini; return to a boil. Reduce the heat and simmer, stirring as needed, until the tortellini are cooked, about 10 minutes. Stir in the spinach and return to a boil. Serve, sprinkled with the pepper.

PER SERVING: 237 Calories, 6 g Total Fat, 2 g Saturated Fat, 23 mg Cholesterol, 265 mg Sodium, 37 g Total Carbohydrate, 4 g Dietary Fiber, 10 g Protein, 144 mg Calcium.

SERVING PROVIDES: 1 Bread, 1 Fruit/Vegetable, 1 Fat.

POINTS PER SERVING: 4.

"Faux" Pho (Vietnamese Soup)

MAKES 2 SERVINGS

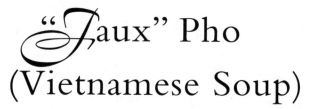

Hildie Block
Arlington, Virginia

*Perhaps it's not prepared exactly as it would be in Saigon, but this fresh,
flavorful, hearty soup is guaranteed to wake up your taste buds and dress up your dinner table.
Best of all, you can have it on the table in about 20 minutes—including prep time.*

3 cups low-sodium chicken broth

3 ounces capellini (angel-hair pasta)

¹/₂ cup chopped watercress

¹/₂ cup sliced radishes

¹/₂ pound reduced-fat firm tofu, cubed

¹/₂ cup bean sprouts

1 tablespoon rice vinegar

2 teaspoons tamari sauce

1 teaspoon Asian sesame oil

1 tablespoon sesame seeds, toasted★

(See photo.)

1. In a medium nonstick saucepan, bring the broth, capellini, watercress and radishes to a boil. Reduce the heat and simmer, covered, until the capellini is tender, about 3 minutes.

2. Increase the heat and stir in the tofu, bean sprouts, vinegar, tamari and oil; cook, stirring as needed, until heated though, about 3 minutes. Serve, sprinkled with the sesame seeds.

PER SERVING: 314 Calories, 9 g Total Fat, 2 g Saturated Fat, 6 mg Cholesterol, 603 mg Sodium, 40 g Total Carbohydrate, 2 g Dietary Fiber, 19 g Protein, 135 mg Calcium.

SERVING PROVIDES: 2 Breads, 1 Fruit/Vegetable, 2 Protein/Milks, 1 Fat.

POINTS PER SERVING: 7.

★*To toast the sesame seeds, place a small nonstick skillet over medium heat. Add the sesame seeds and cook, stirring constantly, until lightly browned, 1–2 minutes.*

Manhattan Fish Chowder

MAKES 6 SERVINGS

Celia K. Schwartz
Cathedral City, California

Celia, a Weight Watchers leader, swears by this vibrant fish soup. "I can make the soup stock in advance and add the fish before I serve it," she writes. Our tasters praised its rich broth and excellent flavor and commented that it "wasn't too fishy." With a salad and some French bread, it makes an ideal light meal.

1 tablespoon olive oil

2 celery stalks, diced

2 onions, chopped

2 garlic cloves, minced

Two 28-ounce cans whole tomatoes (no salt added), coarsely chopped

1/2 cup dry white wine

1 teaspoon dried basil

1 teaspoon dried oregano

1/2 teaspoon dried thyme leaves

1/2 teaspoon freshly ground black pepper

1/4 teaspoon salt

2 pounds sole or flounder fillets, cut into 1" pieces

1/2 cup minced parsley

1. In a large nonstick saucepan or Dutch oven, heat the oil. Add the celery, onions and garlic; cook, stirring as needed, until softened, about 5 minutes.

2. Add the tomatoes, wine, basil, oregano, thyme, pepper and salt; bring to a boil. Reduce the heat and simmer, covered, until the flavors are blended, about 25 minutes.

3. Add the fish and parsley; increase the heat and bring to a boil, stirring gently. Reduce the heat and simmer, uncovered, stirring as needed, until the fish is opaque, about 5 minutes.

PER SERVING: 240 Calories, 5 g Total Fat, 1 g Saturated Fat, 73 mg Cholesterol, 260 mg Sodium, 15 g Total Carbohydrate, 3 g Dietary Fiber, 32 g Protein, 122 mg Calcium.

SERVING PROVIDES: 2 Fruit/Vegetables, 2 Protein/Milks, 1 Fat.

POINTS PER SERVING: 5.

Manhattan Clam Chowder

MAKES 8 SERVINGS

Emily F. Fritts
North Haven, Connecticut

Emily likes to make this chill-chasing soup during the cold winter months.
As a Weight Watchers receptionist, she often tells members about how a cup of her soup
helps "allay the 'hungries'" while she's preparing dinner for her family.

2 tablespoons canola oil

3 onions, chopped

One 28-ounce can crushed tomatoes (no salt added)

4 carrots, diced

2 small all-purpose potatoes, peeled and diced

2 celery stalks, chopped

1 teaspoon dried thyme leaves

1/2 teaspoon salt

1/4 teaspoon freshly ground black pepper

1 bay leaf

Three 6 1/2-ounce cans minced clams, drained (reserve 1 1/2 cups of the liquid)

1/4 cup minced parsley

6 drops hot red pepper sauce, or to taste

1. In a large nonstick saucepan or Dutch oven, heat the oil. Add the onions and cook, stirring as needed, until softened, about 5 minutes.

2. Add the tomatoes, carrots, potatoes, celery, thyme, salt, black pepper, bay leaf and 2 cups water; bring to a boil. Reduce the heat and simmer, covered, stirring as needed, until the vegetables are tender, about 20 minutes.

3. Discard the bay leaf. Stir in the clams, the reserved liquid, the parsley and pepper sauce; cook until heated through, about 3 minutes.

PER SERVING: 166 Calories, 5 g Total Fat, 0 g Saturated Fat, 24 mg Cholesterol, 220 mg Sodium, 20 g Total Carbohydrate, 4 g Dietary Fiber, 12 g Protein, 96 mg Calcium.

SERVING PROVIDES: 1 Fruit/Vegetable, 1 Fat.

POINTS PER SERVING: 3.

Skinny New England Clam Chowder

MAKES 2 SERVINGS

Hildie Block
Arlington, Virginia

When Hildie got a craving for some clam chowder, she searched through cookbooks for one that was easy to make and not loaded with cream or butter. Unable to find one, she came up with her own.

2 teaspoons unsalted stick margarine

1 onion, chopped

$^1/_2$ green bell pepper, seeded and chopped

1 small all-purpose potato, peeled and diced

$^1/_4$ teaspoon salt

$^1/_4$ teaspoon freshly ground black pepper

One 6$^1/_2$-ounce can chopped clams, drained (reserve $^1/_2$ cup of the liquid)

1 cup evaporated skimmed milk

1. In a medium nonstick saucepan, melt the margarine. Add the onion and bell pepper; cook, stirring as needed, until softened, about 5 minutes.

2. Add the potato, salt, black pepper and 1 cup water; bring to a boil. Reduce the heat and simmer, covered, stirring, as needed, until the potato is tender, about 15 minutes.

3. Add the clams, the reserved liquid and the milk; cook, stirring as needed, until the soup is just heated through, about 3 minutes.

PER SERVING: 279 Calories, 5 g Total Fat, 1 g Saturated Fat, 37 mg Cholesterol, 476 mg Sodium, 34 g Total Carbohydrate, 2 g Dietary Fiber, 24 g Protein, 439 mg Calcium.

SERVING PROVIDES: 1 Bread, 1 Fruit/Vegetable, 1 Protein/Milk, 1 Fat.

POINTS PER SERVING: 6.

Harvest Chicken Chowder

MAKES 4 SERVINGS

Barbara A. Bentley
Nampa, Idaho

*Barbara, a Weight Watchers leader for several years now, serves this robust
chicken chowder to her two children, who think it positively yummy.*

2 teaspoons olive oil

4 onions, chopped

3 garlic cloves, minced

1 pound skinless boneless
chicken breasts, cubed

2 cups low-sodium chicken
broth

2 celery stalks, sliced

1 carrot, sliced

One 15-ounce can pump-
kin puree

One 12-ounce can evapo-
rated skimmed milk

¼ cup minced parsley

1 tablespoon minced fresh
sage, or ½ teaspoon
dried

1 teaspoon dried thyme
leaves

Freshly ground black pep-
per (optional)

1. In a large nonstick saucepan or Dutch oven, heat the
oil. Add the onions and garlic; cook, stirring as needed,
until softened, about 5 minutes.

2. Add the chicken, broth, celery and carrot; bring to a
boil. Reduce the heat and simmer, stirring as needed,
until the chicken is cooked through and the vegetables
are tender, about 10 minutes.

3. Add the pumpkin, milk, parsley, sage and thyme;
return to a boil, stirring as needed. Serve, sprinkled with
the pepper (if using).

PER SERVING: 317 Calories, 6 g Total Fat, 1 g Saturated Fat,
65 mg Cholesterol, 269 mg Sodium, 33 g Total Carbohydrate,
5 g Dietary Fiber, 36 g Protein, 376 mg Calcium.

SERVING PROVIDES: 2 Fruit/Vegetables, 4 Protein/Milks, 1 Fat.

POINTS PER SERVING: 6.

Hearty Chicken-Vegetable Soup

MAKES 8 SERVINGS

Suzan Bell
Union, Kentucky

*This robust and colorful chicken soup comes from Suzan, a Weight Watchers leader
who proudly states that "living the program has made me a good cook." The proof
is in this recipe, which will warm both your tummy and your heart.*

One 14¹/₂-ounce can diced
  tomatoes (no salt added)

3 packets low-sodium
  instant chicken broth and
  seasoning mix

2 carrots, sliced

2 onions, coarsely chopped

2 celery stalks, sliced

1 medium zucchini, diced

³/₄ cup elbow macaroni

2 garlic cloves, minced

¹/₂ pound skinless boneless
  chicken breast, cut into
  1" pieces

¹/₄ cup minced parsley

¹/₂ teaspoon salt

¹/₄ teaspoon freshly ground
  black pepper

1. In a large nonstick saucepan or Dutch oven, bring the tomatoes, broth mix and 6 cups water to a boil. Add the carrots, onions, celery, zucchini, macaroni and garlic; return to a boil, stirring as needed. Reduce the heat and simmer, covered, stirring as needed, until the vegetables and macaroni are tender, about 30 minutes.

2. Increase the heat and stir in the chicken, parsley, salt and pepper; return to a boil. Reduce the heat and simmer, covered, until the chicken is cooked through, about 10 minutes.

PER SERVING: 109 Calories, 1 g Total Fat, 0 g Saturated Fat, 16 mg Cholesterol, 182 mg Sodium, 16 g Total Carbohydrate, 2 g Dietary Fiber, 9 g Protein, 40 mg Calcium.

SERVING PROVIDES: 1 Bread, 1 Fruit/Vegetable, 1 Protein/Milk.

POINTS PER SERVING: 2.

*G*azpacho
MAKES 4 SERVINGS

Jill Disser
Bloomingdale, New Jersey

*A recipe that's been in Jill's family for years, this festive chilled soup
works best in summer, when sweet, ripe tomatoes are packed with flavor and
can be picked off the vine or purchased at the farm stand. Make sure you chill the soup
in a glass or plastic bowl—the acid in the tomatoes and vinegar will "react"
with a metal bowl and the soup will have an "off" taste.*

1 green bell pepper, halved and seeded

1 cucumber, peeled and halved

3 cups reduced-sodium tomato juice

1 onion, halved

2 garlic cloves

1/8 teaspoon hot red pepper sauce, or to taste

1/4 cup red-wine vinegar

2 tomatoes, chopped

4 scallions, thinly sliced

1/2 cup packaged seasoned croutons

1. Coarsely chop half of the bell pepper and half of the cucumber. In a blender or food processor, combine 2 cups of the tomato juice, the onion, chopped bell pepper, chopped cucumber, garlic and pepper sauce; pulse until the vegetables are finely chopped.

2. Pour the mixture into a large nonreactive bowl; stir in the remaining 1 cup of the tomato juice and the vinegar. Refrigerate, covered, until chilled, at least 2 hours.

3. Meanwhile, finely dice the remaining bell pepper and cucumber halves. Serve the chilled soup topped with the diced bell pepper, cucumber, tomatoes, scallions and croutons.

PER SERVING: 95 Calories, 1 g Total Fat, 0 g Saturated Fat, 0 mg Cholesterol, 95 mg Sodium, 20 g Total Carbohydrate, 2 g Dietary Fiber, 3 g Protein, 43 mg Calcium.

SERVING PROVIDES: 2 Fruit/Vegetables.

POINTS PER SERVING: 2.

CHAPTER

3

Brunch and Lunch Dishes

Blueberry-Cashew Pancakes

MAKES 4 SERVINGS

Sandra Case
Palmdale, California

*Twice a year, Sandra and her husband travel to Phoenix to attend stock-car races.
There, they frequent a restaurant that serves delicious blueberry cashew pancakes. Now that
Sandra has figured out a way to make these pancakes according to Weight Watchers
guidelines, she and her family enjoy them year-round.*

PANCAKES:

2/3 cup all-purpose flour

1/2 cup whole-wheat flour

1 tablespoon sugar

1 teaspoon double-acting
baking powder

1/4 teaspoon salt

1 1/4 cups low-fat (1%)
buttermilk

1/3 cup fat-free egg
substitute

1 cup fresh or frozen
blueberries

1/2 cup unsalted dry-roasted
cashews, halved

TOPPING:

1/4 teaspoon cornstarch

1 cup fresh or frozen
blueberries

2 teaspoons sugar

1/2 teaspoon fresh lemon
juice

(See photo.)

1. To prepare the pancakes, in a medium bowl, combine the flours, the sugar, baking powder and salt. Add the buttermilk and egg substitute; stir until just blended. Stir in the blueberries and cashews.

2. Spray a large nonstick skillet or griddle with nonstick cooking spray; heat. Spoon the batter, 1/4 cup at a time, into the skillet, making 4 pancakes. Cook about 2 minutes on each side. Remove the pancakes and keep warm. Repeat with the remaining batter, making 16 pancakes.

3. Meanwhile, to prepare the topping, in a small saucepan, blend the cornstarch with 2 1/2 tablespoons water. Stir in the blueberries, sugar and lemon juice; cook until the mixture boils and thickens, about 3 minutes.

4. Arrange 4 pancakes on each of 4 warm plates. Top each portion with 2 tablespoons of the warm sauce.

PER SERVING: 342 Calories, 10 g Total Fat, 2 g Saturated Fat, 5 mg Cholesterol, 408 mg Sodium, 53 g Total Carbohydrate, 5 g Dietary Fiber, 12 g Protein, 205 mg Calcium.

SERVING PROVIDES: 2 Breads, 1 Fruit/Vegetable, 1 Protein/Milk, 1 Fat.

POINTS PER SERVING: 7.

*O*range French Toast

MAKES 2 SERVINGS

Samantha Peterson
New Ringgold, Pennsylvania

When fresh blueberries are in season, sprinkle a few on top of the yogurt for added taste appeal—but very few calories.

1/2 cup skim milk

1/3 cup fat-free egg substitute

1 tablespoon orange zest

1 teaspoon vanilla extract

Dash cinnamon

4 slices reduced-calorie whole-wheat bread

1/2 cup vanilla nonfat yogurt

1 large navel orange, cut into 8 slices

1. In a shallow bowl, combine the milk, egg substitute, orange zest, vanilla and cinnamon. Dip the bread slices into the egg mixture, coating both sides; all the liquid should be absorbed.

2. Spray a large nonstick skillet with nonstick cooking spray; heat. Add the bread, 2 slices at a time, and cook until browned on one side, about 3 minutes; turn over and cook 2 minutes longer. Cut each French toast slice diagonally in half. Place 4 halves on each of 2 plates; top with the yogurt and garnish with the orange slices.

PER SERVING: 250 Calories, 2 g Total Fat, 0 g Saturated Fat, 3 mg Cholesterol, 374 mg Sodium, 48 g Total Carbohydrate, 8 g Dietary Fiber, 14 g Protein, 261 mg Calcium.

SERVING PROVIDES: 1 Bread, 1 Fruit/Vegetable, 1 Protein/Milk.

POINTS PER SERVING: 4.

Broccoli-Mushroom Quiche

MAKES 6 SERVINGS

Marie A. Geocos
Dumont, New Jersey

*"I owe my success to tasty, healthful meals that I can serve to my family
as well as to company," says Marie, who lost 24 pounds. Part of the credit for her success
goes to recipes such as this crustless quiche—perfect as a festive luncheon entrée.*

1 tablespoon unsalted stick margarine

4 cups broccoli florets

2 onions, chopped

1 cup sliced mushrooms

1 cup all-purpose flour

2 teaspoons double-acting baking powder

1 cup fat-free egg substitute

1 cup skim milk

2 cups shredded nonfat mozzarella cheese

1. Preheat the oven to 350° F. Spray a 9" pie plate with nonstick cooking spray.

2. In a large nonstick skillet, melt the margarine. Add the broccoli, onions and mushrooms; cook, stirring constantly, until softened, about 5 minutes.

3. In a large bowl, combine the flour and baking powder. Add the egg substitute and milk; mix with a wooden spoon until smooth. Stir in the cheese and the broccoli mixture. Transfer to the pie plate. Bake until the top is golden and a knife inserted in the center comes out clean, about 35 minutes.

PER SERVING: 229 Calories, 3 g Total Fat, 0 g Saturated Fat, 5 mg Cholesterol, 663 mg Sodium, 29 g Total Carbohydrate, 4 g Dietary Fiber, 22 g Protein, 472 mg Calcium.

SERVING PROVIDES: 1 Bread, 1 Fruit/Vegetable, 1 Protein/Milk, 1 Fat.

POINTS PER SERVING: 4.

Rice and Zucchini Quiche

MAKES 6 SERVINGS

Rebecca Raiewski
Petaluma, California

*This quiche has been a favorite of Rebecca's for brunches and potluck suppers
for a long time. It originally had a higher fat content, but over the years
Rebecca has learned to cook in a healthier fashion.*

1½ cups cooked brown rice

1½ medium zucchini, shredded and drained

2 tablespoons canned chopped green chiles

1 cup shredded reduced-fat sharp cheddar cheese

1 cup skim milk

2 eggs

3 egg whites

¼ teaspoon freshly ground black pepper

1. Preheat the oven to 375° F. Spray a 9" pie plate with nonstick cooking spray.

2. With moistened hands, press the rice evenly onto the bottom and up the sides of the pie plate. Top evenly with the zucchini and chiles.

3. In a medium bowl, combine ½ cup of the cheese, the milk, eggs, egg whites and pepper. Pour over the zucchini mixture; sprinkle evenly with the remaining ½ cup of the cheese. Bake until the top is golden and a knife inserted in the center comes out clean, about 45 minutes. Let stand 5 minutes before serving.

PER SERVING: 175 Calories, 5 g Total Fat, 3 g Saturated Fat, 85 mg Cholesterol, 236 mg Sodium, 18 g Total Carbohydrate, 0 g Dietary Fiber, 13 g Protein, 239 mg Calcium.

SERVING PROVIDES: 1 Bread, 2 Protein/Milks.

POINTS PER SERVING: 4.

Quick and Easy Frittata

MAKES 4 SERVINGS

Karen J. Jackson
Little Rock, Arkansas

*The secret to making a frittata (an open-face Italian omelet) is to use
low heat so that the egg cooks through without burning the bottom.
Serve this with a biscuit or toast for a satisfying meal.*

1 onion, chopped

1/2 green bell pepper,
seeded and chopped

1 tomato, diced

1/2 teaspoon dried oregano

2 cups fat-free egg
substitute

1/3 cup shredded reduced-
fat Monterey Jack cheese

Freshly ground black
pepper, to taste

I. Spray a medium nonstick skillet with nonstick cooking spray; heat. Add the onion and bell pepper; cook, stirring as needed, until softened, about 5 minutes. Add the tomato and oregano; cook, stirring as needed, until the tomato is softened, about 2 minutes.

2. Meanwhile, spray a large nonstick skillet with nonstick cooking spray; place over medium–low heat. Add the egg substitute and cook until set, about 8 minutes, lifting the edges frequently with a spatula to let the uncooked egg substitute flow underneath.

3. Sprinkle the frittata evenly with the tomato mixture and the cheese; cook, covered, until the cheese is melted, about 3 minutes. Serve, sprinkled with the black pepper.

PER SERVING: 112 Calories, 2 g Total Fat, 1 g Saturated Fat, 7 mg Cholesterol, 279 mg Sodium, 7 g Total Carbohydrate, 1 g Dietary Fiber, 16 g Protein, 134 mg Calcium.

SERVING PROVIDES: 1 Fruit/Vegetable, 2 Protein/Milks.

POINTS PER SERVING: 2.

iesta Eggs

MAKES 2 SERVINGS

Kim Nickelson
Trenton, New Jersey

Kim makes this eye-opening breakfast dish on weekends, when the pace is more leisurely and she has time to sit down and savor something special.

2 eggs, lightly beaten

1 plum tomato, chopped

Two 6" fat-free flour tortillas

1/4 cup salsa

3 tablespoons shredded nonfat Monterey Jack cheese

1. Spray a small nonstick skillet with nonstick cooking spray; heat. Add the eggs and tomato; cook, stirring constantly, until the eggs are scrambled, about 2 minutes.

2. Spoon the egg mixture evenly over the tortillas; top evenly with the salsa and cheese. Microwave the tortillas one at a time on Medium-High until heated through and the cheese is melted, about 1 minute.

PER SERVING: 192 Calories, 6 g Total Fat, 2 g Saturated Fat, 213 mg Cholesterol, 556 mg Sodium, 22 g Total Carbohydrate, 1 g Dietary Fiber, 12 g Protein, 26 mg Calcium.

SERVING PROVIDES: 1 Bread, 1 Fruit/Vegetable, 1 Protein/Milk.

POINTS PER SERVING: 4.

*M*exican Egg Brunch

MAKES 6 SERVINGS

Tara Meier
Greenwood, Indiana

*As an accomplished hostess, Tara has it all down to a system: Prepare and
refrigerate everything the night before, and then cook when you're ready. The payoff?
You get to relax and enjoy your company.*

2 cups fat-free egg
substitute

One 14¹/₂-ounce can
stewed tomatoes (no salt
added)

1 onion, finely chopped

¹/₂ green bell pepper,
seeded and diced

¹/₂ cup boiled ham strips

Three 6" fat-free flour tortillas, cut into 2 × ¹/₂"
strips

³/₄ cup shredded reduced-
fat Monterey Jack cheese

1. Preheat the oven to 350° F. Spray a 10 × 6" baking
dish with nonstick cooking spray; set aside.

2. In a medium bowl, combine the egg substitute,
tomatoes, onion and pepper. Stir in the ham and tortilla
strips until the tortillas are just moistened.

3. Pour into the dish; sprinkle with the cheese and bake
until a knife inserted in the center comes out clean,
about 40 minutes.

PER SERVING: 163 Calories, 3 g Total Fat, 2 g Saturated Fat,
16 mg Cholesterol, 520 mg Sodium, 16 g Total Carbohydrate,
2 g Dietary Fiber, 17 g Protein, 179 mg Calcium.

SERVING PROVIDES: 1 Bread, 1 Fruit/Vegetable, 2 Protein/Milks.

POINTS PER SERVING: 3.

Cheese and Tomato Strata

MAKES 6 SERVINGS

Mariemma Thompson
Wall, New Jersey

*Mariemma likes to serve this delicious casserole with a salad on the side,
and for dessert, a fat-free pudding. And they call this dieting?*

12 slices reduced-calorie whole-wheat bread

2 cups shredded nonfat sharp cheddar cheese

2 tomatoes, sliced

1 teaspoon vegetable oil

2 onions, chopped

2 cups skim milk

1 cup fat-free egg substitute

1 tablespoon Dijon mustard

1/4 teaspoon freshly ground black pepper

3 slices crisp-cooked bacon, crumbled

1. Spray a 13 × 9" baking dish with nonstick cooking spray. Arrange 6 slices of bread in the baking dish. Sprinkle evenly with one-third of the cheese and one-half of the tomatoes. Repeat layers. Top with the remaining one-third of the cheese.

2. In a small nonstick skillet, heat the oil. Add the onions and cook, stirring as needed, until softened, about 5 minutes.

3. In a medium bowl, combine the onions, milk, egg substitute, mustard and pepper; pour over the bread mixture. Refrigerate, covered, at least 1 hour or overnight.

4. Preheat the oven to 350° F. Bake the strata until puffed and golden, about 1 hour. Sprinkle with the bacon; serve.

PER SERVING: 250 Calories, 4 g Total Fat, 1 g Saturated Fat, 8 mg Cholesterol, 740 mg Sodium, 32 g Total Carbohydrate, 6 g Dietary Fiber, 26 g Protein, 493 mg Calcium.

SERVING PROVIDES: 1 Bread, 1 Fruit/Vegetable, 2 Protein/Milks.

POINTS PER SERVING: 4.

$\mathcal{E}$asy Brunch Bake

MAKES 4 SERVINGS

Sarah J. McCutcheon
Hopewell, Virginia

Sarah likes to prepare this casserole the night before, so that she can simply pop it in the oven the next morning. It's a favorite of the whole family, especially at holiday time.

1 cup fat-free egg substitute

1 cup skim milk

4 ounces Italian bread, cubed

³/₄ cup sliced cooked turkey sausage

³/₄ cup shredded reduced-fat sharp cheddar cheese

¹/₄ teaspoon freshly ground black pepper

3 canned whole pimientos, drained and julienned

1. Preheat the oven to 350° F. Spray an 8" square baking pan with nonstick cooking spray.

2. In a medium bowl, combine the egg substitute and milk. Add the bread, sausage, half of the cheese and the pepper; stir until all of the bread is moistened.

3. Pour the mixture into the pan; sprinkle evenly with the remaining cheese. Bake until the top is golden and a knife inserted in the center comes out clean, about 40 minutes. Serve, garnished with the pimientos.

PER SERVING: 263 Calories, 9 g Total Fat, 5 g Saturated Fat, 40 mg Cholesterol, 712 mg Sodium, 20 g Total Carbohydrate, 1 g Dietary Fiber, 24 g Protein, 313 mg Calcium.

SERVING PROVIDES: 1 Bread, 3 Protein/Milks.

POINTS PER SERVING: 5.

$\mathscr{A}$pple Pancake Soufflé

MAKES 8 SERVINGS

Diane Honer
Ivoryton, Connecticut

*As a festive breakfast or luncheon entrée, a light supper dish or even as a dessert,
this fluffy golden soufflé more than satisfies. Diane's family and guests
look forward to having it as often as possible.*

1 cup + 2 tablespoons all-purpose flour

3 tablespoons sugar

^{1}/$_2$ teaspoon salt

^{1}/$_2$ teaspoon cinnamon

2 cups fat-free egg substitute

2 cups skim milk

1 teaspoon vanilla extract

2 tablespoons unsalted stick margarine

6 apples, peeled and thinly sliced

3 tablespoons firmly packed light brown sugar

1. Preheat the oven to 425° F.

2. In a large bowl, combine the flour, sugar, salt and cinnamon; make a well in the center. Add the egg substitute, milk and vanilla; whisk until thoroughly combined.

3. Place the margarine in a 13 × 9" baking dish; place in the oven until the margarine is melted and sizzling, about 3 minutes. Add the apples and mix gently to coat. Bake until the apples are heated through, about 5 minutes. Pour the egg mixture over the apples; sprinkle with the brown sugar. Bake until the soufflé is puffed and golden and a knife inserted in the center comes out clean, about 35 minutes. Serve at once.

PER SERVING: 222 Calories, 3 g Total Fat, 1 g Saturated Fat, 1 mg Cholesterol, 271 mg Sodium, 38 g Total Carbohydrate, 2 g Dietary Fiber, 10 g Protein, 109 mg Calcium.

SERVING PROVIDES: 1 Bread, 1 Fruit/Vegetable, 1 Protein/Milk, 1 Fat, 40 Bonus Calories.

POINTS PER SERVING: 4.

Hearty Grilled Eggplant Sandwich

MAKES 2 SERVINGS

Adrienne M. Byrne
Brewster, New York

*As a Weight Watchers weigher and receptionist, Adrienne enjoys meeting new people
and trading pointers on eating well. One of her best tips is this delicious hot sandwich—
so nice to sit down to for a hearty weekend lunch.*

½ eggplant (½ to ¾ pound), cut into four ½" rounds

1 onion, sliced

One 4-ounce jar sliced pimientos, drained

¼ teaspoon freshly ground black pepper

Two small rolls, split and warmed

1 tablespoon reduced-calorie balsamic vinaigrette salad dressing

1. Spray a large nonstick skillet with nonstick cooking spray; heat. Add the eggplant and cook, turning occasionally, until lightly browned and softened, 5–6 minutes. Transfer to a plate; keep warm.

2. Spray the same skillet with more nonstick cooking spray; add the onion and cook, stirring as needed, until tender-crisp, 1–2 minutes. Add the pimientos and black pepper; cook, stirring as needed, until the onion is softened, 1–2 minutes.

3. To assemble the sandwiches, place a roll half on each of 2 plates. Layer with the eggplant slices and the onion mixture, then drizzle with the vinaigrette. Top with the remaining roll halves.

PER SERVING: 251 Calories, 6 g Total Fat, 1 g Saturated Fat, 1 mg Cholesterol, 385 mg Sodium, 44 g Total Carbohydrate, 4 g Dietary Fiber, 7 g Protein, 127 mg Calcium.

SERVING PROVIDES: 2 Breads, 1 Fruit/Vegetable.

POINTS PER SERVING: 5.

Open-Face Reuben Sandwich

MAKES 1 SERVING

Nicky Slobodnjak
Elk Grove, California

*Nicky swears by this streamlined version—which, she says,
is nothing like "diet food"—of the traditional Reuben sandwich.*

2 slices reduced-calorie rye
  bread, toasted
1 teaspoon Dijon mustard
1 thin slice deli ham,
  halved
3 tablespoons shredded
  Gruyère cheese
2 tablespoons drained
  rinsed sauerkraut

1. Preheat the broiler.

2. Spread the toast with the mustard; top each slice evenly with the ham and cheese. Place on a broiler rack and broil 5" from the heat, until the cheese is melted, about 1 minute.

3. Meanwhile, place the sauerkraut in a small microwavable dish; microwave, covered, on High until heated through, about 30 seconds. Top each sandwich with the sauerkraut.

PER SERVING: 234 Calories, 10 g Total Fat, 5 g Saturated Fat, 38 mg Cholesterol, 894 mg Sodium, 20 g Total Carbohydrate, 0 g Dietary Fiber, 17 g Protein, 257 mg Calcium.

SERVING PROVIDES: 1 Bread, 2 Protein/Milks.

POINTS PER SERVING: 6.

Grilled Portobello Sandwich

MAKES 4 SERVINGS

Beth L. Hendrix
Hendersonville, Tennessee

*Although Beth watches cooking shows on television and reads
all the latest cookbooks, this "meaty" portobello sandwich is a Hendrix original.
Beth and her husband love to cook and eat, and recipes like this allow them to
indulge their gourmet tastes and still remain on the program.*

4 teaspoons extra virgin olive oil

1 tablespoon fresh lemon juice

1 teaspoon dried basil

1/2 teaspoon dried oregano

1/4 teaspoon freshly ground black pepper

8 ounces portobello mushrooms, sliced

1 onion, sliced

4 slices reduced-fat Swiss cheese

2 large sourdough rolls, halved

1. Spray the broiler or grill rack with nonstick cooking spray; set aside. Preheat the broiler, or prepare the grill.

2. In a large bowl, combine the oil, lemon juice, basil, oregano and pepper; add the mushrooms and toss to coat. Set aside 10 minutes to marinate.

3. Meanwhile, spray a large nonstick skillet with nonstick cooking spray; heat. Add the onion and cook, stirring as needed, until softened, about 5 minutes; set aside.

4. Broil the mushrooms 5" from the heat until browned, about 4 minutes on each side; transfer to a medium bowl.

5. Place 1 slice of cheese on each of the 4 roll halves and broil 2 minutes until the cheese is melted. Top each with the mushrooms and onions.

PER SERVING: 282 Calories, 10 g Total Fat, 3 g Saturated Fat, 11 mg Cholesterol, 387 mg Sodium, 35 g Total Carbohydrate, 3 g Dietary Fiber, 13 g Protein, 286 mg Calcium.

SERVING PROVIDES: 2 Breads, 1 Fruit/Vegetable, 1 Protein/Milk, 1 Fat.

POINTS PER SERVING: 6.

$\mathcal{R}$oast Beef Pita Supreme

MAKES 2 SERVINGS

Lisa Noble
Red Deer, Alberta, Canada

If you need a new taste in sandwiches, try this unique roast beef salad in a pita for a welcomed change. The oranges add color and sweetness, while the pecans impart crunch. Couldn't you just picture this on the menu at some trendy California-style café?

¼ pound sliced lean roast beef, cut into strips

2 cups torn romaine lettuce

1 small orange, peeled and cut into chunks

2 tablespoons balsamic vinegar

1 tablespoon pecans, coarsely chopped

¼ teaspoon dried basil

2 small oat-bran pita breads, halved

In a medium bowl, combine the beef, lettuce, orange, vinegar, pecans and basil. Divide the beef mixture among the 4 pita halves.

PER SERVING: 243 Calories, 7 g Total Fat, 2 g Saturated Fat, 46 mg Cholesterol, 193 mg Sodium, 25 g Total Carbohydrate, 5 g Dietary Fiber, 21 g Protein, 59 mg Calcium.

SERVING PROVIDES: 1 Bread, 2 Fruit/Vegetables, 2 Protein/Milks, 1 Fat.

POINTS PER SERVING: 4.

Roasted Veggie Sandwiches

MAKES 4 SERVINGS

Tonett Wojtasik
Etobicoke, Ontario, Canada

Tonett, who has lost 64 pounds in one year, finds that her entire family enjoys the Weight Watchers meals she prepares. These colorful vegetarian sandwiches have become favorites of the entire household.

1 small (³/₄ pound) egg-
   plant, cut into ¹/₄" slices

2 red bell peppers, halved
   and seeded

2 portobello mushrooms,
   sliced

1 medium zucchini, cut
   into ¹/₄" slices

¹/₂ teaspoon freshly ground
   black pepper

¹/₄ teaspoon salt

4 small crusty Italian rolls

2 tablespoons fat-free
   vinaigrette salad dressing

¹/₂ red onion, coarsely
   chopped

(See photo.)

1. Arrange the oven racks to divide the oven into thirds; preheat the oven to 500° F. Spray two 15 × 10" jelly-roll or large roasting pans with nonstick cooking spray.

2. Arrange the eggplant, bell peppers, mushrooms and zucchini on the pans; spray lightly with nonstick cooking spray and sprinkle with the black pepper and salt. Bake until lightly charred, 6–7 minutes on each side.

3. Transfer the bell peppers to a paper bag; fold the bag closed and let the peppers steam 10 minutes. Peel the peppers. Layer 4 roll halves evenly with the peppers, eggplant, mushrooms and zucchini; then sprinkle with the dressing and onion. Top with the remaining 4 roll halves.

PER SERVING: 216 Calories, 3 g Total Fat, 1 g Saturated Fat, 0 mg Cholesterol, 570 mg Sodium, 41 g Total Carbohydrate, 5 g Dietary Fiber, 8 g Protein, 93 mg Calcium.

SERVING PROVIDES: 2 Breads, 2 Fruit/Vegetables.

POINTS PER SERVING: 4.

*T*arragon Turkey Salad Sandwich

MAKES 2 SERVINGS

Maria A. Cerino
Colchester, Connecticut

Maria, a busy mom with two young sons, came up with this satisfying turkey-salad sandwich whose secret ingredient (well, maybe it's not so secret anymore) is the tarragon.

1 cup finely chopped cooked turkey breast

1 carrot, shredded

1 celery stalk, finely chopped

2 scallions, thinly sliced

2 teaspoons reduced-calorie mayonnaise

2 teaspoons minced fresh tarragon, or 1/2 teaspoon dried

1/8 teaspoon freshly ground black pepper

2 small oat-bran pita breads, halved

In a medium bowl, combine the turkey, carrot, celery, scallions, mayonnaise, tarragon and pepper. Spoon about 1/3 cup of the turkey mixture into each pita half.

PER SERVING: 193 Calories, 3 g Total Fat, 1 g Saturated Fat, 49 mg Cholesterol, 239 mg Sodium, 22 g Total Carbohydrate, 4 g Dietary Fiber, 21 g Protein, 41 mg Calcium.

SERVING PROVIDES: 1 Bread, 1 Fruit/Vegetable, 2 Protein/Milks, 1 Fat.

POINTS PER SERVING: 3.

Tuna Melts

MAKES 2 SERVINGS

Sharon Clark
St. Charles, Ontario, Canada

Sharon, who lost 40 pounds in six months, loves to experiment in the kitchen.
Through trial and error, she came up with this oh-so-satisfying hot sandwich, which she
often serves with a tossed salad or some cucumber and carrot sticks.

One 6-ounce can water-packed tuna, drained and flaked

1 celery stalk, finely chopped

4 scallions, thinly sliced

2 teaspoons reduced-calorie mayonnaise

1/8 teaspoon freshly ground black pepper

4 slices reduced-calorie whole-wheat bread, toasted

3 tablespoons shredded reduced-fat Swiss cheese

1. Preheat the broiler.

2. In a medium bowl, combine the tuna, celery, scallions, mayonnaise and pepper. Divide the mixture among the 4 slices of toast; sprinkle with the cheese. Broil 5" from the heat, until the cheese is melted, 1–2 minutes.

PER SERVING: 270 Calories, 5 g Total Fat, 1 g Saturated Fat, 37 mg Cholesterol, 648 mg Sodium, 27 g Total Carbohydrate, 7 g Dietary Fiber, 31 g Protein, 146 mg Calcium.

SERVING PROVIDES: 1 Bread, 1 Protein/Milk, 1 Fat.

POINTS PER SERVING: 4.

*M*onterey Turkey Melt

MAKES 4 SERVINGS

Stephanie W. Tice
Charlottesville, Virginia

"The sooner I can get dinner on the table after work, the less likely I am to pick at food while I am cooking," writes Stephanie. Hence, this simple and savory dinner-on-a-bun, which calls for minimum effort but yields maximum satisfaction.

1 tablespoon unsalted stick margarine

2 cups chopped mushrooms

2 onions, chopped

2 cups cooked skinless turkey breast strips

4 small potato rolls, split and toasted

3/4 cup shredded reduced-fat Monterey Jack cheese

1. Preheat the broiler.

2. In a large nonstick skillet, melt the margarine. Add the mushrooms and onions; cook, stirring as needed, until softened, about 5 minutes. Add the turkey and cook until heated through, about 1 minute.

3. Arrange the toasted rolls on a nonstick baking sheet; divide the turkey mixture among the rolls and sprinkle with the cheese. Broil until the cheese is melted, 1–2 minutes.

PER SERVING: 338 Calories, 9 g Total Fat, 4 g Saturated Fat, 63 mg Cholesterol, 502 mg Sodium, 33 g Total Carbohydrate, 2 g Dietary Fiber, 30 g Protein, 266 mg Calcium.

SERVING PROVIDES: 2 Breads, 1 Fruit/Vegetable, 3 Protein/Milks, 1 Fat.

POINTS PER SERVING: 7.

Chicken Waldorf Salad

MAKES 4 SERVINGS

Jonna Marie Gabriele
Stamford, Connecticut

*Owners of a construction company, Jonna and her husband work hard
but still find time to cook good food. Here is one of their favorite recipes.
Serve it with bread sticks or Melba toast.*

2 Red Delicious apples, cored and diced

1 tablespoon fresh lime juice

2 cups diced cooked skinless chicken breast

2 cups small seedless grapes, halved

1/4 cup walnuts, coarsely chopped

1/4 cup nonfat sour cream

2 teaspoons reduced-calorie mayonnaise

2 teaspoons Dijon mustard

1/4 teaspoon salt

1/4 teaspoon freshly ground black pepper

12 loose-leaf lettuce leaves

In a large bowl, combine the apples and lime juice; toss to coat. Add the chicken, grapes, walnuts, sour cream, mayonnaise, mustard, salt and pepper; toss to combine. Place the lettuce leaves on plates; top with the salad mixture.

PER SERVING: 286 Calories, 10 g Total Fat, 2 g Saturated Fat, 62 mg Cholesterol, 286 mg Sodium, 26 g Total Carbohydrate, 3 g Dietary Fiber, 23 g Protein, 58 mg Calcium.

SERVING PROVIDES: 1 Fruit/Vegetable, 2 Protein/Milks, 1 Fat.

POINTS PER SERVING: 6.

ℱestive Pasta Salad

MAKES 4 SERVINGS

Erika Baril
Atkinson, New Hampshire

"This recipe has been a big hit at barbecues and on camping trips because it doesn't taste low-fat, and it's loaded with strong flavors and bright colors," writes Erika. We promise we won't tell your friends about this recipe's health secret; just bring it to your next family outing and watch it disappear.

2²/₃ cups tricolor fusilli

8 sun-dried tomato halves (not oil-packed)

¹/₂ cup boiling water

2 tablespoons balsamic vinegar

2 teaspoons extra virgin olive oil

2 garlic cloves, minced

1 teaspoon dried basil

¹/₄ teaspoon coarsely ground black pepper

1 medium zucchini, diced

1 red bell pepper, seeded and diced

4 scallions, sliced

¹/₃ cup diced reduced-fat sharp cheddar cheese

1. Cook the pasta according to package directions. Drain and rinse under cold running water.

2. In a small bowl, combine the tomatoes and boiling water; let soak 5 minutes. Drain, squeezing out any excess water, and chop.

3. In a large bowl, combine the vinegar, oil, garlic, basil and black pepper. Add the pasta, tomatoes, zucchini, bell pepper, scallions and cheese; toss to coat. Refrigerate, covered, until chilled, at least 1 hour.

PER SERVING: 287 Calories, 5 g Total Fat, 2 g Saturated Fat, 7 mg Cholesterol, 105 mg Sodium, 49 g Total Carbohydrate, 4 g Dietary Fiber, 12 g Protein, 126 mg Calcium.

SERVING PROVIDES: 2 Breads, 2 Fruit/Vegetables, 1 Fat.

POINTS PER SERVING: 5.

$\mathcal{T}$una Salad Platter

MAKES 2 SERVINGS

Anne Kern
Spring Valley, New York

Anne's colorful tuna salad is so much better than the conventional version that we're
willing to bet it will soon become a classic in your household.
Try serving it with whole-wheat breadsticks.

1 cup broccoli slaw or
   finely chopped broccoli

1 tomato, chopped

One 6-ounce can water-
   packed tuna, drained and
   flaked

2 teaspoons reduced-calorie
   mayonnaise

2 teaspoons cider vinegar

1/8 teaspoon freshly ground
   black pepper

2 cups torn mixed salad
   greens

1/2 cucumber, peeled and
   cut into spears

In a medium bowl, combine the broccoli, tomato, tuna, mayonnaise, vinegar and pepper. Place 1 cup of the salad greens on each of 2 plates. Top with the tuna mixture and serve, garnished with the cucumber.

PER SERVING: 160 Calories, 2 g Total Fat, 0 g Saturated Fat, 33 mg Cholesterol, 320 mg Sodium, 9 g Total Carbohydrate, 3 g Dietary Fiber, 26 g Protein, 67 mg Calcium.

SERVING PROVIDES: 2 Fruit/Vegetables, 1 Protein/Milk, 1 Fat.

POINTS PER SERVING: 3.

Confetti Couscous

MAKES 8 SERVINGS

Kathy Rheinhart
Virginia Beach, Virginia

When Kathy takes her family camping, she's always sure to pack this portable couscous salad. Our tasters loved its refreshing flavors and bright colors. It works especially well when paired with sesame breadsticks. Try it for lunch or as a dinnertime side dish.

2 cups vegetable broth

One 10-ounce box couscous

2 teaspoons extra virgin olive oil

1 red onion, chopped

3 garlic cloves, minced

1 medium zucchini, diced

1 medium yellow squash, diced

1 red bell pepper, seeded and diced

One 19-ounce can chickpeas, rinsed and drained

3 tablespoons fresh lemon juice

1/2 teaspoon coarsely ground black pepper, or to taste

24 loose-leaf lettuce leaves

2 tablespoons minced parsley

1. In a medium saucepan, bring the broth to a boil; stir in the couscous. Remove from the heat; cover and set aside until all of the liquid is absorbed, about 10 minutes.

2. Meanwhile, in a large nonstick skillet, heat the oil. Add the onion and garlic; cook, stirring as needed, until softened, about 5 minutes. Add the zucchini, yellow squash and bell pepper; cook, stirring as needed, until the vegetables are tender-crisp, about 5 minutes.

3. Transfer the couscous to a large serving bowl; fluff with a fork. Add the vegetables, chickpeas, lemon juice and black pepper; toss with a fork. Refrigerate, covered, until chilled, at least 2 hours. Line each of 8 salad plates with 3 lettuce leaves; top with the couscous mixture and serve, sprinkled with the parsley.

PER SERVING: 216 Calories, 3 g Total Fat, 0 g Saturated Fat, 0 mg Cholesterol, 304 mg Sodium, 40 g Total Carbohydrate, 4 g Dietary Fiber, 8 g Protein, 43 mg Calcium.

SERVING PROVIDES: 1 Bread, 1 Fruit/Vegetable, 1 Protein/Milk.

POINTS PER SERVING: 4.

Garden Pasta Toss

MAKES 4 SERVINGS

Bonnie A. Richards
Dalton, Pennsylvania

"I have a very big garden that my family lives off all year," Bonnie writes. What a treat to pick from one's own backyard most of the ingredients for this colorful low-fat pasta!

1 teaspoon olive oil

2 medium zucchini, sliced

2 cups broccoli florets

3 garlic cloves, minced

2 tomatoes, coarsely chopped

1 tablespoon minced fresh basil, or 1 teaspoon dried

1 tablespoon minced fresh oregano, or 1 teaspoon dried

1 1/2 teaspoons minced fresh rosemary, or 1/2 teaspoon dried rosemary leaves, crumbled

6 ounces capellini (angel-hair pasta)

1/4 cup grated Parmesan cheese

Freshly ground black pepper, to taste

(See photo.)

1. In a large nonstick skillet, heat the oil. Add the zucchini, broccoli and garlic; cook, stirring as needed, until tender-crisp, about 5 minutes.

2. Add the tomatoes, basil, oregano and rosemary; cook, stirring as needed, until the tomatoes are softened, about 5 minutes.

3. Meanwhile, cook the pasta according to package directions. Drain, reserving 1/4 cup of the pasta water, and place the pasta in a serving bowl. Add the vegetable mixture, cheese and the reserved pasta water; toss to combine. Serve, sprinkled with the pepper.

PER SERVING: 244 Calories, 4 g Total Fat, 1 g Saturated Fat, 4 mg Cholesterol, 122 mg Sodium, 43 g Total Carbohydrate, 5 g Dietary Fiber, 12 g Protein, 140 mg Calcium.

SERVING PROVIDES: 2 Breads, 2 Fruit/Vegetables.

POINTS PER SERVING: 4.

Spaghetti with Spinach and Cheese

MAKES 2 SERVINGS

Donna Sawicki
Mentor, Ohio

Donna's busy daily schedule doesn't stop her from creating exciting new pasta recipes. This one, a family favorite, really shines in the summer, when fresh basil and tomatoes are abundant in gardens and at farm stands.

2 shallots, chopped

2 garlic cloves, minced

1 bunch spinach, cleaned and torn (about 4 cups)

2 tomatoes, chopped

¼ cup minced basil

¾ cup shredded part–skim mozzarella cheese

¼ teaspoon coarsely ground black pepper

2 cups hot cooked spaghetti

2 tablespoons grated Parmesan cheese

1. Spray a large nonstick skillet with nonstick cooking spray; heat. Add the shallots and garlic; cook, stirring as needed, until softened, about 5 minutes.

2. Add the spinach, tomatoes and basil; toss lightly. Reduce the heat and simmer, covered, until the spinach is wilted, 4–5 minutes. Remove from the heat. Add the mozzarella cheese and pepper; toss to combine. Place 1 cup of the spaghetti on each of 2 plates. Top with the spinach mixture and serve, sprinkled with the Parmesan cheese.

PER SERVING: 401 Calories, 11 g Total Fat, 6 g Saturated Fat, 29 mg Cholesterol, 366 mg Sodium, 56 g Total Carbohydrate, 6 g Dietary Fiber, 23 g Protein, 491 mg Calcium.

SERVING PROVIDES: 2 Breads, 3 Fruit/Vegetables, 2 Protein/Milks.

POINTS PER SERVING: 8.

$\mathcal{L}$ow Cal-zone

MAKES 2 SERVINGS

Arlene Pafumi
Franklin Square, New York

These calzones also cook well in the microwave. Simply place the filled and rolled tortillas, two at a time, seam-side down, on a microwavable plate; cover with plastic wrap and microwave on Medium-High 1 minute 20 seconds. Either way you'll love them.

1 cup part-skim ricotta cheese

1/3 cup shredded nonfat mozzarella cheese

1 plum tomato, diced

1/4 cup chopped lean ham

1/8 teaspoon freshly ground black pepper

Four 6" fat-free flour tortillas

1. Preheat the oven to 400° F.

2. In a medium bowl, combine the cheeses, tomato, ham and pepper. Divide the mixture evenly among the tortillas; roll up and wrap in foil. Place the foil packets on a baking sheet. Bake until heated through, about 10 minutes. Open the packets carefully, as steam will escape.

PER SERVING: 387 Calories, 11 g Total Fat, 6 g Saturated Fat, 49 mg Cholesterol, 1,000 mg Sodium, 43 g Total Carbohydrate, 2 g Dietary Fiber, 28 g Protein, 470 mg Calcium.

SERVING PROVIDES: 2 Breads, 2 Protein/Milks.

POINTS PER SERVING: 8.

Ham, Cheese and Veggie Scramble

MAKES 2 SERVINGS

Stephanie Storms
Coon Rapids, Minnesota

Stephanie finds this hearty lunchtime dish a surefire way of making sure to get in those daily vegetables. Serve with toasted oat-bran English muffins for a healthful, filling meal.

1 carrot, finely chopped

1 medium zucchini, diced

4 scallions, sliced

$1/4$ cup chopped mushrooms

2 eggs, lightly beaten

$1/4$ cup julienned lean ham

$1/8$ teaspoon freshly ground black pepper

$1/3$ cup shredded nonfat sharp cheddar cheese

1. Spray a large nonstick skillet with nonstick cooking spray; heat. Add the carrot, zucchini, scallions and mushrooms; cook, stirring constantly, until the vegetables are softened, 5–6 minutes.

2. Add the eggs, ham and pepper; cook, stirring constantly, until the eggs are cooked, 2–3 minutes. Add the cheese and cook, stirring constantly, until the cheese is melted, about 30 seconds.

PER SERVING: 169 Calories, 7 g Total Fat, 2 g Saturated Fat, 222 mg Cholesterol, 395 mg Sodium, 11 g Total Carbohydrate, 3 g Dietary Fiber, 18 g Protein, 228 mg Calcium.

SERVING PROVIDES: 1 Fruit/Vegetable, 2 Protein/Milks.

POINTS PER SERVING: 3.

Polenta with Broccoli Rabe

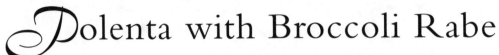

MAKES 4 SERVINGS

Maria Colabella
Point Pleasant, New Jersey

*"Polenta is a dish my mother always made," writes Maria, who took a
traditional family recipe and put a new, healthful spin on it.*

One 6-ounce box polenta

$^1/_4$ cup grated Parmesan
cheese

$^1/_4$ teaspoon freshly ground
black pepper

2 teaspoons olive oil

3 garlic cloves, minced

1 bunch broccoli rabe,
cleaned and coarsely
chopped (about 8 cups)

$^1/_4$ teaspoon crushed red
pepper flakes

Four 1-ounce slices part-
skim mozzarella cheese

1. Spray an 8" square baking pan with nonstick cooking
spray.

2. Prepare the polents according to package directions.
Remove from the heat and stir in the Parmesan cheese
and black pepper. Pour the polenta into the pan and cool
10 minutes. Refrigerate, covered, until firm, at least 2
hours.

3. Preheat the oven to 400° F. In a large saucepan, heat
the oil. Add the garlic and cook, stirring constantly, until
lightly browned, about 1 minute. Stir in the broccoli
rabe and pepper flakes. Reduce the heat and simmer,
covered, stirring as needed, until the broccoli rabe is tender, 10–12 minutes.

4. Cut the polenta into 4 squares and place on a baking
sheet. Divide the broccoli rabe among the polenta
squares; top each with a slice of mozzarella cheese. Bake
until heated through and the cheese is melted, 8–10
minutes.

PER SERVING: 284 Calories, 10 g Total Fat, 4 g Saturated Fat,
20 mg Cholesterol, 295 mg Sodium, 35 g Total Carbohydrate,
6 g Dietary Fiber, 16 g Protein, 356 mg Calcium.

SERVING PROVIDES: 2 Breads, 2 Fruit/Vegetables, 2 Protein/Milks,
1 Fat.

POINTS PER SERVING: 5.

Spinach-Veggie Pizza

MAKES 4 SERVINGS

Jennifer Straus
Sterling Heights, Michigan

*Jennifer, a graphic designer and the mother of two, has lost more than
40 pounds with Weight Watchers. She came up with this winning low-fat
pizza recipe as a dinnertime solution for a family that likes to eat well but has
no time for fuss. Our tasters raved about the great flavor and about how pretty they are.
A bonus: These pizzas freeze well and there's no need to thaw them before baking,
but you may have to add 2–3 minutes to the baking time.*

Half 10-ounce package
   frozen chopped spinach,
   thawed and squeezed dry

1 cup nonfat ricotta cheese

2 garlic cloves, minced

1 teaspoon dried basil

1/2 teaspoon dried oregano

2 teaspoons olive oil

1 medium zucchini, sliced

1 red bell pepper, seeded
   and cut into 1" strips

1 onion, thinly sliced

4 large whole-wheat pita
   breads

1/2 cup tomato sauce
   (no salt added)

1 cup shredded part-skim
   mozzarella cheese

1. Preheat the oven to 400° F.

2. In a medium bowl, combine the spinach, ricotta cheese, garlic, basil and oregano.

3. In a large nonstick skillet, heat the oil. Add the zucchini, pepper and onion; cook, stirring as needed, until tender-crisp, about 4 minutes.

4. Arrange the pita breads on a nonstick baking sheet. Spread 1/2 cup of the spinach mixture over each pita bread; top each with the tomato sauce and the sautéed vegetables. Sprinkle the mozzarella cheese evenly over each. Bake until heated through and the cheese is melted, about 15 minutes.

PER SERVING: 335 Calories, 9 g Total Fat, 3 g Saturated Fat, 16 mg Cholesterol, 539 mg Sodium, 43 g Total Carbohydrate, 6 g Dietary Fiber, 23 g Protein, 557 mg Calcium.

SERVING PROVIDES: 2 Breads, 1 Fruit/Vegetable, 2 Protein/Milks, 1 Fat.

POINTS PER SERVING: 6.

Quick Tortillas and Peppers

MAKES 2 SERVINGS

Ann Marie Kynoch
Fairfield, Connecticut

Whenever Ann Marie wants something quick, she throws together this piquant Mexican-inspired dish. To make it more substantial, she sometimes adds chicken.

1 green bell pepper, seeded and sliced

1 onion, sliced

1/2 cup salsa

1/3 cup shredded reduced-fat sharp cheddar cheese

Two 6" fat-free flour tortillas

1. Spray a large nonstick skillet with nonstick cooking spray; heat. Add the pepper and onion; cook, stirring as needed, until softened, about 5 minutes. Stir in the salsa and cook until heated through, about 1 minute.

2. Divide the cheese evenly between the tortillas. Microwave the tortillas, one at a time, on Medium-High 30 seconds, until the cheese is melted. Top each with the pepper mixture.

PER SERVING: 185 Calories, 4 g Total Fat, 2 g Saturated Fat, 13 mg Cholesterol, 675 mg Sodium, 28 g Total Carbohydrate, 2 g Dietary Fiber, 9 g Protein, 178 mg Calcium.

SERVING PROVIDES: 1 Bread, 1 Fruit/Vegetable, 1 Protein/Milk.

POINTS PER SERVING: 4.

$\mathcal{V}$egetable Pancakes

MAKES 4 SERVINGS

Suzanne Ullyot
Winnipeg, Manitoba, Canada

Suzanne got the idea for this recipe from a cousin who spent time in Korea.
It's great for lunch, but we think it goes well with almost any entrée—
Eastern or Western—especially with a dollop of applesauce.

1 cup + 2 tablespoons all-purpose flour

1 teaspoon double-acting baking powder

1/2 teaspoon salt

2 eggs

1 large baking potato, scrubbed and grated

2 carrots, grated

1 onion, grated

1. In a large bowl, combine the flour, baking powder and salt. Add the eggs and 1 cup water; stir until just blended (do not overmix). Stir in the potato, carrots and onion.

2. Spray a large nonstick skillet or griddle with nonstick cooking spray; heat. Pour the batter by 1/4-cup measures into the skillet. Cook just until bubbles begin to appear at the edges of the pancakes, 3–4 minutes; turn over and cook 2–3 minutes longer. Repeat with the remaining batter, making 12 pancakes.

PER SERVING: 254 Calories, 4 g Total Fat, 1 g Saturated Fat, 106 mg Cholesterol, 451 mg Sodium, 46 g Total Carbohydrate, 4 g Dietary Fiber, 9 g Protein, 114 mg Calcium.

SERVING PROVIDES: 2 Breads, 1 Fruit/Vegetable.

POINTS PER SERVING: 5.

Spinach and Clam Linguine

MAKES 4 SERVINGS

Nancy Mutchler
Wethersfield, Connecticut

Dinner guests at Nancy's house don't have a clue that this savory pasta dish is low in fat and calories. What they do know is that they love the way it tastes!

2 teaspoons extra virgin olive oil

6 garlic cloves, minced

Two 6-ounce cans minced clams, drained (reserve the liquid)

8 cups cleaned spinach leaves

1/4 teaspoon freshly ground black pepper

6 ounces linguine

2 tablespoons grated Parmesan cheese

1. In a large nonstick skillet, heat the oil. Add the garlic and cook, stirring constantly, until lightly browned, about 1 minute.

2. Add the clam liquid, spinach and pepper; toss lightly. Bring to a boil; reduce the heat and simmer, covered, stirring as needed, until the spinach is wilted, 3–4 minutes. Add the clams and cook, stirring as needed, until heated through, about 2 minutes.

3. Meanwhile, cook the linguine according to package directions. Drain and place in a large serving bowl. Immediately add the clam mixture and toss to combine. Serve, sprinkled with the cheese.

PER SERVING: 287 Calories, 5 g Total Fat, 1 g Saturated Fat, 32 mg Cholesterol, 188 mg Sodium, 40 g Total Carbohydrate, 4 g Dietary Fiber, 21 g Protein, 208 mg Calcium.

SERVING PROVIDES: 2 Breads, 2 Fruit/Vegetables, 1 Protein/Milk, 1 Fat.

POINTS PER SERVING: 5.

CHAPTER

4

Sides and Salads

Oven-Roasted Potatoes

MAKES 4 SERVINGS

Jane McCormick
North Canton, Ohio

Now retired, Jane devotes her energies to homemaking. She knows Weight Watchers is the key to losing weight and eating well. This easily prepared side dish proves her point deliciously.

4 small red potatoes, scrubbed and quartered

1 onion, chopped

2 teaspoons unsalted stick margarine

1/2 teaspoon salt

1/4 teaspoon freshly ground black pepper

Rosemary sprig (optional)

1. Preheat the oven to 350° F. Spray a 2-quart casserole with nonstick cooking spray.

2. Place the potatoes and onion in the casserole. Dot with the margarine and sprinkle with the salt and pepper; top with the rosemary (if using). Bake, covered, until the potatoes are tender, about 50 minutes.

PER SERVING: 142 Calories, 2 g Total Fat, 0 g Saturated Fat, 0 mg Cholesterol, 285 mg Sodium, 27 g Total Carbohydrate, 3 g Dietary Fiber, 3 g Protein, 7 mg Calcium.

SERVING PROVIDES: 1 Bread, 1 Fat.

POINTS PER SERVING: 2.

Scalloped Potatoes

MAKES 4 SERVINGS

Karen Marshall
Scarborough, Ontario, Canada

Save time and labor by using your food processor to slice the potatoes and onions.
Assemble the dish, sit back and enjoy the tempting aromas as these scrumptious potatoes bake.

2 large baking potatoes, thinly sliced

2 onions, thinly sliced

1/4 cup minced parsley

3 tablespoons all-purpose flour

1/4 teaspoon salt

1/4 teaspoon freshly ground black pepper

2 cups hot skim milk

1/3 cup shredded reduced-fat cheddar cheese

1. Preheat the oven to 350° F. Spray a 10 × 6" baking pan with nonstick cooking spray.

2. Arrange one-third of the potatoes and onions in the bottom of the pan. Sprinkle evenly with half of the parsley and flour. Repeat the layering once more, ending with the potatoes and onion. Sprinkle evenly with the salt and pepper.

3. Pour the milk over all and sprinkle with the cheese. Bake until the potatoes are tender and the top is browned, about 1 hour and 10 minutes.

PER SERVING: 215 Calories, 2 g Total Fat, 1 g Saturated Fat, 9 mg Cholesterol, 284 mg Sodium, 38 g Total Carbohydrate, 4 g Dietary Fiber, 11 g Protein, 267 mg Calcium.

SERVING PROVIDES: 1 Bread, 1 Protein/Milk.

POINTS PER SERVING: 4.

*T*asty Home-Fried Potatoes

MAKES 2 SERVINGS

Jean Murray
Ottawa, Ontario, Canada

*These home-fried potatoes—originally developed to beat a craving for french fries—
are so good that Jean often quadruples the recipe to feed her whole family.*

1 teaspoon olive oil

2 small all-purpose pota-
toes, cooked and cubed

1 garlic clove, minced

1 teaspoon grated
Parmesan cheese

Freshly ground black pep-
per, to taste

In a large nonstick skillet, heat the oil. Add the potatoes and garlic; cook, stirring constantly, until the potatoes are lightly browned, about 5 minutes. Remove from the heat and sprinkle with the cheese and pepper.

PER SERVING: 123 Calories, 3 g Total Fat, 0 g Saturated Fat, 1 mg Cholesterol, 21 mg Sodium, 23 g Total Carbohydrate, 2 g Dietary Fiber, 2 g Protein, 23 mg Calcium.

SERVING PROVIDES: 1 Bread, 1 Fat.

POINTS PER SERVING: 2.

*T*wice-Baked Garlic Potatoes

MAKES 8 SERVINGS

Barbara Gardner
Hesperia, California

Once is not enough, so we bake these winning stuffed potatoes a second time to make them fragrant with garlic and meltingly lush. Barbara first served this dish at a Christmas dinner and, not surprisingly, everyone left with the recipe. After selecting this a hands-down winner, our tasters left with a copy of the recipe, too.

4 large baking potatoes, scrubbed

1 garlic bulb

1/2 cup low-sodium chicken broth

1/2 cup nonfat sour cream

1/2 teaspoon freshly ground black pepper

1/4 cup grated Parmesan cheese

Paprika

(See photo.)

1. Preheat the oven to 425° F.

2. Pierce the potatoes several times with a fork; place on a baking sheet. Wrap the garlic in foil and place alongside the potatoes. Bake until the potatoes are tender and the garlic is browned and softened, 50–60 minutes. Let the potatoes and garlic cool until comfortable to handle, about 15 minutes.

3. Halve the potatoes lengthwise; scoop the pulp into a large bowl, leaving the skins intact. Cut the garlic bulb in half; squeeze out the pulp and add to the potato. Add the broth, sour cream and pepper; stir and mash with a fork to the desired texture. Spoon the stuffing back into the potato skins; sprinkle with the cheese and paprika.

4. Return the potatoes to the baking sheet and bake until heated through and lightly browned, about 15 minutes.

PER SERVING: 153 Calories, 1 g Total Fat, 1 g Saturated Fat, 2 mg Cholesterol, 73 mg Sodium, 31 g Total Carbohydrate, 3 g Dietary Fiber, 5 g Protein, 73 mg Calcium.

SERVING PROVIDES: 1 Bread.

POINTS PER SERVING: 3.

Baked Yams with Pineapple

MAKES 4 SERVINGS

Darla Pulliam
Los Angeles, California

*Darla, a young African-American woman who is as proud of her cultural heritage
as she is of her family's culinary traditions, puts a low-fat spin on many ethnic favorites.
What's more, she gets rave reviews at the frequent family gatherings she attends. Try her baked
yams, and you'll see why Darla—who is also an artist—views cooking as an art form.*

2 large yams or sweet potatoes, peeled and cut into
1" slices

1/2 navel orange, cut into
4 slices

One 8-ounce can unsweet-
ened pineapple tidbits
(reserve juice)

1/2 teaspoon cinnamon

1/4 teaspoon grated nutmeg

2 teaspoons reduced-calorie
margarine

1. Preheat the oven to 375° F.

2. In a 2-quart casserole, combine the yams, orange, pineapple and its juice, cinnamon and nutmeg; dot with the margarine. Bake, covered, until the yams are tender, about 45 minutes.

PER SERVING: 191 Calories, 1 g Total Fat, 0 g Saturated Fat, 0 mg Cholesterol, 34 mg Sodium, 44 g Total Carbohydrate, 6 g Dietary Fiber, 2 g Protein, 43 mg Calcium.

SERVING PROVIDES: 1 Bread, 1 Fruit/Vegetable.

POINTS PER SERVING: 3.

Brown Rice and Lentil Pilaf

MAKES 4 SERVINGS

Hildie Block
Arlington, Virginia

Hildie developed this delicious pilaf for her vegetarian roommate.
It serves 4 as a side dish, 2 as an entrée.

1 teaspoon olive oil

2 celery stalks, chopped

1 onion, chopped

2 garlic cloves, minced

1 cup brown rice

1/4 cup lentils, picked over, rinsed and drained

2 tablespoons raisins

1 1/2 teaspoons curry powder

1/4 teaspoon salt

1/8 teaspoon freshly ground black pepper

1. In a medium nonstick saucepan, heat the oil. Add the celery, onion and garlic; cook, stirring as needed, until softened, about 5 minutes.

2. Add the rice, lentils, raisins, curry, salt, pepper and 2 1/2 cups water; bring to a boil, stirring as needed. Reduce the heat and simmer, covered, until the rice and lentils are tender and most of the liquid is absorbed, 40–50 minutes.

3. Remove from the heat and fluff with a fork; cover and let stand 5 minutes.

PER SERVING: 251 Calories, 3 g Total Fat, 0 g Saturated Fat, 0 mg Cholesterol, 154 mg Sodium, 50 g Total Carbohydrate, 4 g Dietary Fiber, 8 g Protein, 37 mg Calcium.

SERVING PROVIDES: 1 Bread, 1 Fruit/Vegetable, 1 Fat.

POINTS PER SERVING: 4.

Cranberry-Basmati Rice

MAKES 4 SERVINGS

Donna-Marie Fieldsa-Fowler
Brooklyn, New York

Determined to serve something different to accompany Thanksgiving dinners, Donna developed this alternative to "plain rice and stuffing": it goes well with poultry any time of year. If you plan to use the fresh juice from the orange in this recipe, remember to zest the orange before juicing it.

1 teaspoon canola oil

1 onion, chopped

1¹/₂ cups low-sodium chicken broth

1 cup basmati rice

¹/₂ cup orange juice

¹/₃ cup dried cranberries

1 teaspoon orange zest

¹/₄ teaspoon dried sage

¹/₄ teaspoon freshly ground black pepper

(See photo.)

1. In a large nonstick saucepan, heat the oil. Add the onion and cook, stirring as needed, until softened, about 5 minutes.

2. Stir in the broth, rice, orange juice, cranberries, orange zest, sage and pepper; bring to a boil, stirring as needed. Reduce the heat and simmer, covered, until most of the liquid is absorbed, about 15 minutes. Remove from the heat and let stand 10 minutes, until all of the liquid is absorbed. Fluff the rice with a fork.

PER SERVING: 229 Calories, 3 g Total Fat, 0 g Saturated Fat, 1 mg Cholesterol, 61 mg Sodium, 49 g Total Carbohydrate, 1 g Dietary Fiber, 6 g Protein, 15 mg Calcium.

SERVING PROVIDES: 2 Breads, 1 Fruit/Vegetable.

POINTS PER SERVING: 5.

Indonesian Rice

MAKES 4 SERVINGS

Leslie Wells
Delta, British Columbia, Canada

Leslie loves to cook spicy food and often serves this dish for company with barbecued chicken or shrimp. It is delicious topped with plain nonfat yogurt, diced apple and currants.

1 tablespoon vegetable oil

1 onion, chopped

1 green bell pepper, seeded and chopped

1 red bell pepper, seeded and chopped

1 celery stalk, chopped

2 tablespoons mango chutney

1 tablespoon reduced-sodium soy sauce

2 teaspoons curry powder, or to taste

4 cups hot cooked brown rice

1. In a large nonstick skillet, heat the oil. Add the onion and cook, stirring as needed, until softened, about 5 minutes.

2. Add the bell peppers, celery, chutney, soy sauce and curry; cook, stirring as needed, until the vegetables are tender, 5–6 minutes. Stir in the rice and fluff with a fork.

PER SERVING: 304 Calories, 5 g Total Fat, 1 g Saturated Fat, 0 mg Cholesterol, 253 mg Sodium, 58 g Total Carbohydrate, 5 g Dietary Fiber, 6 g Protein, 37 mg Calcium.

SERVING PROVIDES: 2 Breads, 1 Fruit/Vegetable, 1 Fat.

POINTS PER SERVING: 5.

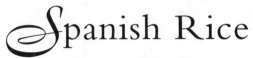panish Rice

MAKES 4 SERVINGS

Patricia A. Colunga
Cypress, California

Patricia took a friend's recipe and modified it by cutting the fat and adding fresh tomato. More healthful? Yes. Better tasting? Absolutely. More visually appealing? For certain!

2 teaspoons olive oil

1⅓ cups brown rice

2 garlic cloves, minced

2 cups low-sodium vegetable broth

One 14½-ounce can diced tomatoes (no salt added)

8 scallions, sliced

1. In a large nonstick saucepan, heat the oil. Add the rice and garlic; cook, stirring as needed, until the rice is lightly browned, about 2 minutes.

2. Add the broth and tomatoes; bring to a boil. Reduce the heat and simmer, covered, until the rice is tender, about 50 minutes, stirring occasionally during the last 15 minutes and adding water if necessary to prevent the rice from sticking to the bottom of the pan. Add the scallions and fluff the mixture with a fork.

PER SERVING: 304 Calories, 4 g Total Fat, 1 g Saturated Fat, 0 mg Cholesterol, 107 mg Sodium, 59 g Total Carbohydrate, 4 g Dietary Fiber, 7 g Protein, 68 mg Calcium.

SERVING PROVIDES: 2 Breads, 1 Fruit/Vegetable, 1 Fat.

POINTS PER SERVING: 6.

Glazed Carrots

MAKES 4 SERVINGS

Lita Saltzman
Denver, Colorado

Subtly sweet and slightly tangy, these pretty glazed carrots liven up any dinner plate.

4 teaspoons reduced-calorie margarine

1/4 red onion, chopped

1 tablespoon fresh lemon juice

2 teaspoons honey

1/8 teaspoon cinnamon

1/8 teaspoon salt

4 carrots, sliced and steamed

In a medium nonstick saucepan, melt the margarine. Add the onion and cook, stirring as needed, until softened, 2–3 minutes. Add the lemon juice, honey, cinnamon and salt; cook, stirring constantly, until heated through and well mixed. Add the carrots; toss to coat.

PER SERVING: 74 Calories, 2 g Total Fat, 0 g Saturated Fat, 0 mg Cholesterol, 151 mg Sodium, 14 g Total Carbohydrate, 3 g Dietary Fiber, 1 g Protein, 32 mg Calcium.

SERVING PROVIDES: 1 Fruit/Vegetable, 1 Fat.

POINTS PER SERVING: 1.

Greek Green Beans

MAKES 4 SERVINGS

Katherine Bernard Furr
Glen Allen, Virginia

Katherine, a registered nurse, swears by this substantial side dish;
the long, slow simmering helps develop the flavors in this classic Greek recipe.
Just add bread and a little reduced-fat cheese and you've got lunch!

1 pound green beans,
  trimmed and halved

One 14½-ounce can diced
  tomatoes (no salt added)

2 onions, coarsely chopped

1 small all-purpose potato,
  cubed

2 teaspoons dried oregano

2 teaspoons extra virgin
  olive oil

¼ teaspoon salt

¼ teaspoon freshly ground
  black pepper

In a large nonstick saucepan, bring the beans, tomatoes, onions, potato, oregano, oil, salt and pepper to a boil. Reduce the heat and simmer, covered, stirring as needed, until the vegetables are tender and the flavors are well blended, about 1 hour.

PER SERVING: 118 Calories, 3 g Total Fat, 0 g Saturated Fat, 0 mg Cholesterol, 158 mg Sodium, 22 g Total Carbohydrate, 4 g Dietary Fiber, 4 g Protein, 88 mg Calcium.

SERVING PROVIDES: 2 Fruit/Vegetables, 1 Fat.

POINTS PER SERVING: 2.

Puree of Butternut Squash

MAKES 8 SERVINGS

Thomas A. Perrino
Yorktown Heights, New York

*This 33-year-old dad lost 33 pounds in nine weeks, thanks to his
favorite vegetable and the new recipe he devised to showcase it.*

2 teaspoons canola oil

3-4 leeks, cleaned and
sliced (about 4 cups)

2 pounds butternut squash,
peeled, seeded and cut
into 2" chunks

³/4 cup low-sodium chicken
broth

¹/2 teaspoon salt

¹/4 teaspoon freshly ground
black pepper

¹/4 teaspoon grated nutmeg

1. In a large nonstick saucepan, heat the oil. Add the leeks and cook, stirring as needed, until softened, about 5 minutes.

2. Stir in the squash, broth, salt, pepper and nutmeg; bring to a boil. Reduce the heat and simmer, covered, until the squash is tender, about 30 minutes. Uncover and simmer until the liquid is reduced to about ¹/4 cup, about 5 minutes.

3. With a slotted spoon, transfer the vegetables to a blender or food processor and puree. Stir the vegetable puree back into the liquid. Increase the heat and cook until heated through, about 2 minutes.

PER SERVING: 88 Calories, 2 g Total Fat, 0 g Saturated Fat, 0 mg Cholesterol, 161 mg Sodium, 19 g Total Carbohydrate, 2 g Dietary Fiber, 2 g Protein, 79 mg Calcium.

SERVING PROVIDES: 1 Bread, 1 Fruit/Vegetable.

POINTS PER SERVING: 2.

$\mathcal{S}$tuffed Tomatoes

MAKES 4 SERVINGS

Alma Wakefield
Scarborough, Ontario, Canada

*As a new member, Alma finds herself thinking more and more about
the nutritional value of whatever she eats. All this thought has led to the development
of this delicious, and healthful, stuffed tomato recipe.*

4 beefsteak tomatoes

2 teaspoons vegetable oil

2 celery stalks, chopped

1 onion, chopped

1 garlic clove, minced

2 slices whole-wheat bread,
made into crumbs

1/2 cup chopped
mushrooms

2 tablespoons minced
parsley

1/2 teaspoon dried sage

1/4 teaspoon salt

1/4 teaspoon freshly ground
black pepper

2 tablespoons grated
Parmesan cheese

1. To prepare the tomato shells, slice off the stem end of each tomato; cut away the stem base and finely chop the usable pulp from the tops. With a grapefruit spoon, carefully scoop out the pulp from the tomatoes; place the tomato pulp in a small bowl. Invert the tomato shells onto a plate; let stand 30 minutes to drain.

2. Preheat the oven to 350° F. Spray a 10 × 6" baking pan with nonstick cooking spray.

3. Meanwhile, in a large nonstick skillet, heat the oil. Add the celery, onion and garlic; cook, stirring as needed, until softened, about 5 minutes. Stir in the bread crumbs, mushrooms, parsley, sage, salt, pepper and the reserved tomato pulp; cook, stirring as needed, until heated through, about 2 minutes.

4. Spoon the filling into the tomato shells; sprinkle the Parmesan cheese on top of each. Place upright in the pan and bake until heated through, about 25 minutes.

PER SERVING: 138 Calories, 5 g Total Fat, 2 g Saturated Fat, 4 mg Cholesterol, 342 mg Sodium, 19 g Total Carbohydrate, 4 g Dietary Fiber, 6 g Protein, 111 mg Calcium.

SERVING PROVIDES: 1 Bread, 2 Fruit/Vegetables, 1 Fat.

POINTS PER SERVING: 2.

Spaghetti Squash Stir-Fry

MAKES 8 SERVINGS

Donna Zinser Clark
Louisville, Kentucky

Don't worry if your skillet or wok isn't big enough;
Donna's flavorsome dish works well in a large Dutch oven, too.

1 spaghetti squash (about 3 pounds)

2 carrots, julienned

2 green bell peppers, seeded and julienned

2 red bell peppers, seeded and julienned

1 cup low-sodium vegetable broth

1 teaspoon dried basil

¼ teaspoon freshly ground black pepper

¼ cup grated Parmesan cheese

(See photo.)

1. Pierce the squash with the tip of a sharp knife in several places; place on a paper plate and microwave on High 20 minutes, until just softened, turning once during cooking. Let stand 5 minutes. Cut the squash in half lengthwise and remove the seeds. Using a fork, scoop out the pulp. Measure out 6 cups squash (reserve any remaining squash for another use).

2. Spray a large nonstick skillet or wok with nonstick cooking spray; heat. Add the carrots and bell peppers; cook, stirring as needed, until tender-crisp, 7–8 minutes.

3. Stir in the spaghetti squash, broth, basil and black pepper; cook until heated through, about 2 minutes. Serve, sprinkled with the cheese.

PER SERVING: 92 Calories, 3 g Total Fat, 1 g Saturated Fat, 4 mg Cholesterol, 144 mg Sodium, 14 g Total Carbohydrate, 3 g Dietary Fiber, 4 g Protein, 118 mg Calcium.

SERVING PROVIDES: 2 Fruit/Vegetables.

POINTS PER SERVING: 1.

Holiday Stuffing

MAKES 12 SERVINGS

Jeannie Applegate
High Point, North Carolina

*A Weight Watchers lifetime member and leader for 20 years, Jeannie has
managed to maintain a 35-pound weight loss, not an easy feat with four hungry children
to feed. At holiday time, the whole family pitches in to make this savory stuffing.*

1 celery stalk, chopped

1 onion, chopped

1/2 cup chopped
  mushrooms

One 8-ounce can sliced
  water chestnuts, drained

3 tablespoons minced
  parsley

1 teaspoon dried sage

One 8-ounce package
  herb-seasoned stuffing
  mix

1. Preheat the oven to 350° F. Spray a 2-quart casserole
with nonstick cooking spray.

2. Spray a large nonstick saucepan with nonstick cooking spray; heat. Add the celery, onion and mushrooms;
cook, stirring as needed, until softened, about 5 minutes.
Stir in the water chestnuts, parsley, sage and 1 1/2 cups
water; bring to a boil. Remove from the heat and stir in
the stuffing mix.

3. Transfer the mixture to the casserole. Bake until heated
through and slightly crispy on top, about 20 minutes.

PER SERVING: 87 Calories, 1 g Total Fat, 0 g Saturated Fat,
0 mg Cholesterol, 277 mg Sodium, 17 g Total Carbohydrate,
0 g Dietary Fiber, 2 g Protein, 32 mg Calcium.

SERVING PROVIDES: 1 Bread.

POINTS PER SERVING: 2.

$\mathscr{L}$emon Caesar Salad

MAKES 6 SERVINGS

Tonya Sarina
Aurora, Colorado

"I love salads but not the commercial low-fat dressings," wrote Tonya. Her solution?
This healthy take on a favorite Caesar dressing replaces the raw egg with
yogurt and sacrifices nothing in terms of creaminess.

1/2 teaspoon grated lemon zest

1 1/2 tablespoons fresh lemon juice

1 large garlic clove

1 teaspoon white wine Worcestershire sauce

1/2 teaspoon Dijon mustard

1/2 teaspoon anchovy paste

2 tablespoons extra virgin olive oil

1/4 cup plain nonfat yogurt

7 cups torn romaine lettuce

One 14-ounce can artichoke hearts, rinsed, drained and halved

One 2-ounce piece Parmesan cheese

18 Melba toast rounds, broken into bite-size pieces

1. In a blender or food processor, puree the lemon zest, lemon juice, garlic, Worcestershire sauce, mustard and anchovy paste. With the motor running, slowly add the olive oil (the mixture will thicken slightly). Add the yogurt; puree until just smooth, about 10 seconds.

2. Place the lettuce and artichoke hearts in a large salad bowl; add the dressing and toss to coat. Using a vegetable peeler, shave the Parmesan into curls; top the salad with the cheese and toast pieces.

PER SERVING: 198 Calories, 9 g Total Fat, 3 g Saturated Fat, 9 mg Cholesterol, 370 mg Sodium, 21 g Total Carbohydrate, 3 g Dietary Fiber, 10 g Protein, 226 mg Calcium.

SERVING PROVIDES: 1 Bread, 2 Fruit/Vegetables, 1 Fat.

POINTS PER SERVING: 4.

Cilantro Caesar Salad

MAKES 4 SERVINGS

Judith Franks
Grass Valley, California

*Like many of us, Judith gets tired of her recipes; she believes that if we keep
sharing our recipes and ideas, we will not get bored with our food programs. That's what this
book is all about, and here is Judith's delicious and healthy contribution.*

4 cups torn romaine lettuce

12 cherry tomatoes, halved

1 cup bean sprouts

¼ cup minced cilantro

2 scallions, thinly sliced

2 tablespoons fat-free
Caesar salad dressing

1 tablespoon fresh lemon
juice

2 tablespoons grated
Parmesan cheese

In a large salad bowl, combine the lettuce, tomatoes, sprouts, cilantro and scallions. Add the dressing and lemon juice; toss to coat. Serve, sprinkled with the cheese.

PER SERVING: 44 Calories, 1 g Total Fat, 1 g Saturated Fat, 2 mg Cholesterol, 131 mg Sodium, 6 g Total Carbohydrate, 2 g Dietary Fiber, 3 g Protein, 63 mg Calcium.

SERVING PROVIDES: 2 Fruit/Vegetables.

POINTS PER SERVING: 1.

Tossed Salad with Mandarin Oranges and Almonds

MAKES 4 SERVINGS

Mary Hatesohl
Leawood, Kansas

Quick and easy to make, this crunchy, colorful salad is a welcome break from the conventional and humdrum. Says Mary: "It keeps me going!"

2 tablespoons minced parsley

2 tablespoons balsamic vinegar

1 tablespoon extra virgin olive oil

1 small garlic clove, minced

1/4 teaspoon sugar

1/4 teaspoon salt

1/4 teaspoon freshly ground black pepper

8 cups torn romaine lettuce

3 celery stalks, sliced

8 scallions, sliced

One 11-ounce can mandarin oranges, drained

2 tablespoons sliced almonds, toasted★

1. In a small jar with a tight-fitting lid or in a small bowl, combine the parsley, vinegar, oil, garlic, sugar, salt, pepper and 1 tablespoon water; cover and shake well or whisk until blended.

2. In a large bowl, combine the lettuce, celery and scallions. Add the dressing; toss to coat. Serve, topped with orange sections and almonds.

PER SERVING: 107 Calories, 6 g Total Fat, 1 g Saturated Fat, 0 mg Cholesterol, 168 mg Sodium, 13 g Total Carbohydrate, 4 g Dietary Fiber, 3 g Protein, 83 mg Calcium.

SERVING PROVIDES: 3 Fruit/Vegetables, 1 Fat.

POINTS PER SERVING: 2.

★*To toast the almonds, place a small nonstick skillet over medium heat. Add the almonds and cook, stirring constantly, until lightly browned, 2–3 minutes.*

Spinach and Sprout Salad

MAKES 8 SERVINGS

Sheryl Boucher
Alliston, Ontario, Canada

*Sheryl is a Weight Watchers member who loves to cook. This healthful salad is
one of her favorites to help her keep on the program.*

2 tablespoons reduced-sodium soy sauce

2 tablespoons fresh lemon juice

1 teaspoon Asian sesame oil

1/4 teaspoon sugar

1/4 teaspoon freshly ground black pepper

8 cups torn cleaned spinach

1 cup sliced mushrooms

1 cup bean sprouts

One 8-ounce can sliced water chestnuts, drained

1 red bell pepper, seeded and julienned

4 scallions, thinly sliced

2 tablespoons sesame seeds, toasted★

1. In a small jar with a tight-fitting lid or in a small bowl, combine the soy sauce, lemon juice, oil, sugar and black pepper; cover and shake well or whisk until blended.

2. In a large salad bowl, combine the spinach, mushrooms, sprouts, water chestnuts, bell pepper and scallions. Add the dressing; toss to coat. Serve, sprinkled with the sesame seeds.

PER SERVING: 53 Calories, 2 g Total Fat, 0 g Saturated Fat, 0 mg Cholesterol, 198 mg Sodium, 8 g Total Carbohydrate, 3 g Dietary Fiber, 3 g Protein, 84 mg Calcium.

SERVING PROVIDES: 1 Fruit/Vegetable.

POINTS PER SERVING: 1.

★*To toast the sesame seeds, place a nonstick skillet over low heat; add the sesame seeds and cook, stirring constantly, until browned, about 3 minutes.*

(See photo.)

*W*hite and Green Bean Salad

MAKES 4 SERVINGS

Sheryl H. Knuth
Omaha, Nebraska

This colorful salad will brighten any meal—indoors or out.
Sheryl especially likes it because it helps encourage good eating habits in her children.
Its refreshing, light and lemony flavor is perfect for hot summer days, and in
cooler weather, it's perfect for rich pork dishes.

1 pound green beans, trimmed and cut into 2" pieces

2 tablespoons red-wine vinegar

1 tablespoon balsamic vinegar

2 teaspoons extra virgin olive oil

1 teaspoon grated lemon zest

1/4 teaspoon freshly ground black pepper

One 19-ounce can cannellini beans, rinsed and drained

1 red bell pepper, seeded and julienned

6 large kalamata olives, pitted and chopped

1. In a large saucepan, steam the green beans until tender-crisp, about 8 minutes.

2. Meanwhile, in a large bowl, combine the vinegars, oil, lemon zest and black pepper. Add both beans, the bell pepper and olives; toss to coat. Serve warm, or refrigerate, covered, until chilled, at least 2 hours.

PER SERVING: 176 Calories, 5 g Total Fat, 1 g Saturated Fat, 0 mg Cholesterol, 302 mg Sodium, 25 g Total Carbohydrate, 8 g Dietary Fiber, 9 g Protein, 70 mg Calcium.

SERVING PROVIDES: 1 Fruit/Vegetable, 2 Protein/Milks, 1 Fat.

POINTS PER SERVING: 2.

Green Bean and Pear Salad

MAKES 6 SERVINGS

Jackie Niedermeier
New Canaan, Connecticut

Jackie is a Weight Watchers staff member working as a receptionist and stock clerk.
She developed this recipe and presented it first for a company dinner.
Since then, it has become her most requested dish.

1 pound green beans,
trimmed

1 tablespoon fresh lemon
juice

1 tablespoon red-wine
vinegar

1 teaspoon olive oil

1 teaspoon Dijon mustard

1/4 teaspoon coarsely
ground black pepper

3 pears, cored and thinly
sliced

1/3 cup crumbled feta
cheese

1 tablespoon pine nuts,
toasted*

1. In a large saucepan, steam the beans until tender-crisp, about 8 minutes.

2. Meanwhile, in a large bowl, combine the lemon juice, vinegar, oil, mustard and pepper. Add the beans, pears, cheese and pine nuts; toss to combine. Serve warm, or refrigerate, covered, until chilled, at least 2 hours.

PER SERVING: 103 Calories, 3 g Total Fat, 1 g Saturated Fat, 7 mg Cholesterol, 107 mg Sodium, 17 g Total Carbohydrate, 3 g Dietary Fiber, 3 g Protein, 71 mg Calcium.

SERVING PROVIDES: 1 Fruit/Vegetable, 1 Fat.

POINTS PER SERVING: 2.

*To toast the pine nuts, place a nonstick skillet over medium heat; add the pine nuts and cook, stirring constantly, until browned, 2–3 minutes.

Tarragon Carrot Salad

MAKES 4 SERVINGS

Sara Schrader
Faribault, Minnesota

*When Sara devised this carrot salad, it was to meet her and
her husband's dietary needs. After trying this vibrant side dish, everyone in
Sara's family, grandchildren included, fell for it big time.*

5 carrots, thinly sliced

1/4 cup orange juice

1 tablespoon minced fresh
tarragon, or 1 teaspoon
dried

1 tablespoon tarragon wine
vinegar

1 teaspoon canola oil

1/4 teaspoon sugar

1/4 teaspoon salt

1/8 teaspoon freshly ground
black pepper

1 onion, coarsely chopped

1 1/2 cups small grapes,
halved

1. In a medium saucepan, bring the carrots and 1/2 cup water to a boil. Reduce the heat and simmer, covered, until tender, about 8 minutes; drain and transfer to a medium bowl.

2. Meanwhile, in a small bowl, combine the orange juice, tarragon, vinegar, oil, sugar, salt and pepper; pour over the carrots. Add the onion; toss to combine. Refrigerate, covered, until the flavors are blended, at least 2 hours. Stir in the grapes and serve.

PER SERVING: 125 Calories, 2 g Total Fat, 0 g Saturated Fat, 0 mg Cholesterol, 182 mg Sodium, 28 g Total Carbohydrate, 5 g Dietary Fiber, 2 g Protein, 53 mg Calcium.

SERVING PROVIDES: 2 Fruit/Vegetables.

POINTS PER SERVING: 2.

Thai Carrot Salad

MAKES 4 SERVINGS

Lita Saltzman
Denver, Colorado

Lita, a businesswoman, avid sports enthusiast and mother of two, adores Thai food.
Try her carrot salad and you'll see why.

4 carrots, shredded

2 serrano chile peppers, seeded, deveined and chopped (wear gloves to prevent irritation)

4 scallions, thinly sliced

2 tablespoons fresh lime juice

2 teaspoons firmly packed light brown sugar

2 teaspoons fish sauce★ or reduced-sodium soy sauce

2 tablespoons unsalted dry-roasted peanuts, coarsely chopped

In a large bowl, combine the carrots, chiles, scallions, lime juice, sugar and fish sauce. Refrigerate, covered, until the flavors are blended, at least 1 hour. Serve, sprinkled with the peanuts.

PER SERVING: 91 Calories, 3 g Total Fat, 0 g Saturated Fat, 0 mg Cholesterol, 137 mg Sodium, 15 g Total Carbohydrate, 4 g Dietary Fiber, 3 g Protein, 38 mg Calcium.

SERVING PROVIDES: 1 Fruit/Vegetable.

POINTS PER SERVING: 1.

★*Fish sauce (also called nam pla, nuoc cham or nuoc mam), a thin brown sauce made from salted and fermented fish, is available in Asian groceries and some supermarkets.*

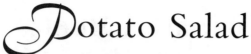 Potato Salad

MAKES 4 SERVINGS

Marline Reinke
Winnipeg, Manitoba, Canada

*Marline loves inventing good recipes that her family enjoys, so they can all eat the same food.
You can serve this excellent potato salad as a side dish to serve four or as a
luncheon dish on a bed of lettuce to serve two.*

¹/₄ cup plain nonfat yogurt

2 tablespoons reduced-calorie mayonnaise

2 teaspoons minced dill

1 teaspoon cider vinegar

¹/₈ teaspoon freshly ground black pepper

1 celery stalk, diced

¹/₂ red bell pepper, seeded and diced

2 hard-cooked eggs, chopped

2 scallions, thinly sliced

2 small red potatoes, cooked and cubed

In a medium bowl, combine the yogurt, mayonnaise, dill, vinegar and black pepper. Add the celery, bell pepper, eggs and scallions; toss to coat. Add the potatoes, toss gently.

PER SERVING: 130 Calories, 5 g Total Fat, 1 g Saturated Fat, 109 mg Cholesterol, 95 mg Sodium, 16 g Total Carbohydrate, 2 g Dietary Fiber, 6 g Protein, 50 mg Calcium.

SERVING PROVIDES: 1 Bread, 1 Fat.

POINTS PER SERVING: 3.

Marinated Beet and Jicama Salad

MAKES 4 SERVINGS

Corri Rochlitz
Scottsdale, Arizona

Corri just moved to Arizona and has created a little sunshine of her own—this bright, crunchy salad.

One 15-ounce can sliced beets, drained

4 scallions, thinly sliced

3 tablespoons fat-free raspberry vinaigrette salad dressing

¹/₂ cup diced jicama★

4 cups torn romaine lettuce

1. In a medium bowl, combine the beets, scallions and salad dressing; refrigerate, covered, until the flavors are blended, at least 1 hour.

2. Stir in the jicama. Place 1 cup of the lettuce on each of 4 plates. Top with the beet mixture.

PER SERVING: 52 Calories, 0 g Total Fat, 0 g Saturated Fat, 0 mg Cholesterol, 237 mg Sodium, 12 g Total Carbohydrate, 3 g Dietary Fiber, 2 g Protein, 41 mg Calcium.

SERVING PROVIDES: 2 Fruit/Vegetables.

POINTS PER SERVING: 0.

★*Jicama (HEE-ca-ma), a crispy, tuberous vegetable similar to water chestnuts in taste and texture, can be found in most supermarkets and Latino grocery stores.*

Cheese and Vegetable Salad

MAKES 4 SERVINGS

Patricia Mele
Homer City, Pennsylvania

*A symphony of color, taste and texture, this Cheese and Vegetable Salad can
go anywhere. At a recent outdoor graduation party, Patricia watched proudly as
guests devoured it. "Nobody knew it was a Weight Watchers recipe; in fact,
it was one of the first dishes to disappear!"*

$1/3$ cup nonfat sour cream

1 tablespoon reduced-
calorie mayonnaise

1 tablespoon fresh lemon
juice

2 cups broccoli florets

2 cups cauliflower florets

1 cup thawed frozen tiny
peas

1 cup shredded nonfat
sharp cheddar cheese

$1/2$ red onion, finely
chopped

3 slices bacon, crisp-cooked
and crumbled

In a large bowl, combine the sour cream, mayonnaise
and lemon juice. Add the broccoli, cauliflower, peas,
cheese and onion; toss to coat. Refrigerate, covered, until
chilled, at least 1–2 hours. Serve, sprinkled with the
bacon.

PER SERVING: 164 Calories, 4 g Total Fat, 1 g Saturated Fat,
8 mg Cholesterol, 407 mg Sodium, 16 g Total Carbohydrate,
5 g Dietary Fiber, 18 g Protein, 329 mg Calcium.

SERVING PROVIDES: 1 Bread, 1 Fruit/Vegetable, 1 Protein/Milk,
40 Bonus Calories.

POINTS PER SERVING: 3.

Coleslaw Supreme

MAKES 8 SERVINGS

Susan Novosiwsky
Vilna, Alberta, Canada

*Susan and her husband own a farm in Alberta, and frequently,
she carries meals out to the fields. This light and easy coleslaw fits in well with her
lifestyle and would brighten any picnic lunch or potluck dinner.*

One 1-pound bag shredded
  cabbage and carrot
  coleslaw blend

2 apples, cored and diced

1/4 cup raisins

1/4 cup reduced-calorie
  mayonnaise

1 tablespoon cider vinegar

1 teaspoon Dijon mustard

In a large bowl, combine the coleslaw blend, apples, raisins, mayonnaise, vinegar and mustard. Refrigerate, covered, until the flavors are blended, at least 1 hour.

PER SERVING: 65 Calories, 2 g Total Fat, 1 g Saturated Fat, 2 mg Cholesterol, 67 mg Sodium, 12 g Total Carbohydrate, 1 g Dietary Fiber, 1 g Protein, 30 mg Calcium.

SERVING PROVIDES: 2 Fruit/Vegetables, 1 Fat.

POINTS PER SERVING: 1.

reek Salad

MAKES 2 SERVINGS

Joan Ritchie-Dewar
Scarborough, Ontario, Canada

*Joan, who works in public relations, has come up with a
vibrant Greek salad that speaks for itself.*

3 cups torn romaine lettuce

1 large tomato, cut into
1" chunks

1/2 cup cucumber, peeled
and sliced

1/2 green bell pepper,
seeded and diced

1/3 cup crumbled feta
cheese

4 scallions, sliced

6 large kalamata olives

2 tablespoons red-wine
vinegar

2 tablespoons minced dill

1 garlic clove, minced

1/4 teaspoon dried oregano

1/4 teaspoon freshly ground
black pepper

2 small whole-wheat pita
breads, warmed

1. In a large salad bowl, combine the lettuce, tomato,
cucumber, bell pepper, cheese, scallions and olives.

2. In a small jar with a tight-fitting lid or in a small
bowl, combine the vinegar, dill, garlic, oregano and black
pepper; cover and shake well or whisk until blended.
Pour over the lettuce mixture; toss to combine. Serve
with the pitas.

PER SERVING: 235 Calories, 10 g Total Fat, 4 g Saturated Fat,
19 mg Cholesterol, 667 mg Sodium, 31 g Total Carbohydrate,
6 g Dietary Fiber, 9 g Protein, 184 mg Calcium.

SERVING PROVIDES: 1 Bread, 3 Fruit/Vegetables, 1 Protein/Milk,
1 Fat.

POINTS PER SERVING: 4.

Orange-Cucumber Salad

MAKES 4 SERVINGS

Mary Lee Berta
Ranchester, Wyoming

A junior high school math teacher, Mary Lee shows—with this vivid fruit and vegetable salad—that she's not only a whiz with numbers, but with flavors, too!

3 oranges, peeled and sliced

1 cucumber, peeled and sliced

1/2 green bell pepper, seeded and cut into 1" strips

1/4 red onion, thinly sliced

3 tablespoons cider vinegar

1 teaspoon canola oil

1/2 teaspoon sugar

1/4 teaspoon salt

In a medium bowl, combine the oranges, cucumber, pepper and onion. Add the vinegar, oil, sugar and salt; toss to coat. Serve at once.

PER SERVING: 66 Calories, 1 g Total Fat, 0 g Saturated Fat, 0 mg Cholesterol, 137 mg Sodium, 14 g Total Carbohydrate, 3 g Dietary Fiber, 1 g Protein, 49 mg Calcium.

SERVING PROVIDES: 1 Fruit/Vegetable.

POINTS PER SERVING: 1.

Tomato-Cucumber Salad

MAKES 4 SERVINGS

Lynn K. Klahm
Cincinnati, Ohio

How versatile is this salad? Lynn likes to snack on it when she comes home from work, just before dinner. It's super as a side dish, too, and great to bring to parties and picnics.

3 tablespoons balsamic vinegar

1/2 teaspoon Italian herb seasoning

1/4 teaspoon sugar

1/4 teaspoon salt

1/4 teaspoon freshly ground black pepper

2 tomatoes, thinly sliced

1 cucumber, peeled and thinly sliced

4 scallions, sliced

1. In a small jar with a tight-fitting lid or in a small bowl, combine the vinegar, Italian seasoning, sugar, salt and pepper; cover and shake well or whisk until blended.

2. On a medium platter, arrange the tomatoes and cucumber in a spiral, alternating the vegetables. Sprinkle with the scallions and drizzle with the dressing.

PER SERVING: 25 Calories, 0 g Total Fat, 0 g Saturated Fat, 0 mg Cholesterol, 147 mg Sodium, 6 g Total Carbohydrate, 1 g Dietary Fiber, 1 g Protein, 14 mg Calcium.

SERVING PROVIDES: 1 Fruit/Vegetable.

POINTS PER SERVING: 0.

Broccoli and Cauliflower Salad

MAKES 8 SERVINGS

Georgia A. Fischer
Mosinee, Wisconsin

Thrilled that she could eat as many vegetables as she liked on Weight Watchers,
Georgia developed this sprightly salad, of which her friends and family can't get enough.

5 tablespoons reduced-
calorie mayonnaise

1 tablespoon cider vinegar

1/2 teaspoon freshly ground
black pepper

4 cups broccoli florets

4 cups cauliflower florets

2 carrots, shredded

1/2 red onion, finely
chopped

In a large bowl, combine the mayonnaise, vinegar and
pepper. Add the broccoli, cauliflower, carrots and onion;
toss to coat.

PER SERVING: 72 Calories, 3 g Total Fat, 1 g Saturated Fat,
3 mg Cholesterol, 86 mg Sodium, 10 g Total Carbohydrate,
4 g Dietary Fiber, 4 g Protein, 51 mg Calcium.

SERVING PROVIDES: 1 Fruit/Vegetable, 1 Fat.

POINTS PER SERVING: 1.

Fusilli Salad with Vegetables and Feta

MAKES 4 SERVINGS

Lynn Bacon
Long Beach, Mississippi

Always a hit at barbecues and picnics, Lynn's festive Greek-accented pasta salad makes good use of the summer garden.

2 cups cooked fusilli

2 medium zucchini, diced

1 cup fresh or thawed frozen corn kernels

1 tomato, diced

1 red onion, chopped

1/4 cup fat-free Italian salad dressing

3/4 cup crumbled feta cheese

In a large bowl, combine the fusilli, zucchini, corn, tomato, onion and dressing; toss to coat. Refrigerate, covered, until chilled, at least 2 hours. Serve, sprinkled with the cheese.

PER SERVING: 217 Calories, 6 g Total Fat, 3 g Saturated Fat, 19 mg Cholesterol, 397 mg Sodium, 34 g Total Carbohydrate, 4 g Dietary Fiber, 9 g Protein, 131 mg Calcium.

SERVING PROVIDES: 2 Breads, 1 Fruit/Vegetable, 1 Protein/Milk.

POINTS PER SERVING: 4.

Waldorf with a Twist

MAKES 4 SERVINGS

Helen Cordon
West Allis, Wisconsin

*After joining Weight Watchers, Helen not only lost 30 pounds and lowered
her cholesterol level by 39 points, she also entered and finished a triathlon. Her fresh new
Waldorf salad—with tangy yogurt instead of mayo—is truly the choice of champions.*

2 apples, cored and diced

1 cup seedless grapes, halved

1 cup plain nonfat yogurt

1 celery stalk, diced

1/4 cup walnuts, chopped

2 tablespoons raisins

1 1/2 teaspoons fresh lemon juice

Ground cinnamon

In a medium bowl, combine the apples, grapes, yogurt, celery, walnuts, raisins and lemon juice; serve, sprinkled with the cinnamon.

PER SERVING: 154 Calories, 5 g Total Fat, 1 g Saturated Fat, 1 mg Cholesterol, 52 mg Sodium, 25 g Total Carbohydrate, 3 g Dietary Fiber, 5 g Protein, 133 mg Calcium.

SERVING PROVIDES: 1 Fruit/Vegetable, 1 Fat.

POINTS PER SERVING: 3.

CHAPTER
5

Poultry

Arroz con Pollo

MAKES 4 SERVINGS

Shannon Hernandez
Gillette, Wyoming

*After joining Weight Watchers in 1991, Shannon was able to lose 52 pounds
and significantly lower her blood pressure. She was also able to take a rather bland
chicken-and-rice recipe and transform it into something bright, spicy
and totally in keeping with her healthful, new lifestyle.*

2 teaspoons olive oil

1 cup long-grain rice

1 onion, chopped

2 garlic cloves, minced

2 cups low-sodium chicken broth

One 10-ounce can tomatoes with green chiles

1 teaspoon dried oregano

1/2 teaspoon ground cumin

2 cups cubed cooked skinless chicken breasts

1 cup thawed frozen green peas

1. In a large nonstick skillet, heat the oil. Add the rice, onion and garlic; cook, stirring as needed, until the onion is softened and the rice is lightly browned, 5–6 minutes.

2. Add the broth, tomatoes, oregano and cumin; bring to a boil. Reduce the heat and simmer, covered, stirring once or twice, until the rice is tender, about 20 minutes.

3. Add the chicken and peas; cook, covered, stirring as needed, until the peas are cooked and the chicken is heated through, 3–4 minutes. Fluff the mixture with a fork before serving.

PER SERVING: 348 Calories, 6 g Total Fat, 1 g Saturated Fat, 50 mg Cholesterol, 423 mg Sodium, 48 g Total Carbohydrate, 4 g Dietary Fiber, 25 g Protein, 66 mg Calcium.

SERVING PROVIDES: 2 Breads, 2 Protein/Milks, 1 Fat.

POINTS PER SERVING: 7.

Garden Pasta Toss

Cranberry-Basmati Rice

Twice-Baked Garlic Potatoes

Spinach and Sprout Salad

Spaghetti Squash Stir-Fry

Grilled Chicken Citrus Salad

Lemon-Tarragon Chicken

Chicken Cacciatore

Chicken Cacciatore

MAKES 4 SERVINGS

Elizabeth J. Gari
Westbury, New York

*Elizabeth remembers her Weight Watchers leader telling the group never
to let on that they're serving a diet recipe. By cooking this slenderized chicken cacciatore,
she fooled even her finicky husband, while at the same time doing
culinary justice to her Italian heritage.*

2 teaspoons olive oil

Four 4-ounce skinless
chicken thighs

1 onion, chopped

3 garlic cloves, minced

3 cups sliced mushrooms

One 14$^{1}/_{2}$-ounce can diced
tomatoes (no salt added)

1 green bell pepper, seeded
and diced

$^{1}/_{4}$ cup tomato paste

1 teaspoon dried oregano

$^{1}/_{4}$ teaspoon freshly ground
black pepper

4 cups hot cooked
spaghetti

(See photo.)

1. In a large nonstick skillet, heat the oil. Add the chicken and brown 2 minutes on each side. Transfer to a plate.

2. In the same skillet, cook the onion and garlic, stirring as needed, until softened, about 5 minutes.

3. Add the mushrooms, tomatoes, bell pepper, tomato paste, oregano and black pepper; bring to a boil, stirring as needed. Return the chicken to the skillet. Reduce heat and simmer, covered, stirring as needed, until the chicken is cooked through, about 25 minutes. Serve the spaghetti, topped with the chicken and sauce.

PER SERVING: 419 Calories, 8 g Total Fat, 2 g Saturated Fat, 94 mg Cholesterol, 245 mg Sodium, 54 g Total Carbohydrate, 5 g Dietary Fiber, 32 g Protein, 73 mg Calcium.

SERVING PROVIDES: 2 Breads, 2 Fruit/Vegetables, 3 Protein/Milks, 1 Fat.

POINTS PER SERVING: 8.

Chicken Marsala

MAKES 4 SERVINGS

Donna Hill
New York, New York

Donna's unorthodox, but delicious, version of Chicken Marsala calls for fresh green grapes.
We think the nutty flavor of brown rice works beautifully with the rich wine sauce.

1 teaspoon canola oil

³/₄ pound skinless boneless chicken breasts, cut into strips

4 shallots, chopped

1 tablespoon all-purpose flour

¹/₂ cup low-sodium chicken broth

¹/₄ cup dry Marsala wine

1 cup seedless green grapes, halved

¹/₄ cup minced parsley

¹/₄ teaspoon freshly ground black pepper

4 cups hot cooked brown rice

1. In a large nonstick skillet, heat the oil. Add the chicken and cook, turning as needed, until lightly browned, 5–6 minutes. Transfer to a plate.

2. Spray the same skillet with nonstick cooking spray; add the shallots and cook, stirring as needed, until softened, about 5 minutes. Add the flour; cook, stirring constantly, until the flour coats the shallots, about 1 minute. Gradually stir in the broth and wine; cook, stirring constantly, until the mixture boils and thickens, about 2 minutes.

3. Stir in the chicken, grapes, parsley and pepper; bring to a boil. Reduce the heat and simmer, covered, until cooked through, about 5 minutes. Serve the rice, topped with the chicken mixture.

PER SERVING: 396 Calories, 5 g Total Fat, 1 g Saturated Fat, 50 mg Cholesterol, 84 mg Sodium, 58 g Total Carbohydrate, 4 g Dietary Fiber, 26 g Protein, 47 mg Calcium.

SERVING PROVIDES: 2 Breads, 1 Fruit/Vegetable, 2 Protein/Milks.

POINTS PER SERVING: 8.

Chicken with Apricot Sauce

MAKES 4 SERVINGS

Lynda Wrigley
McKinney, Texas

"I love the rich sauces that go into the French cooking I used to do," Lynda writes.
She loves to serve this to guests and hear them say that a dish this
lush couldn't possibly be low-calorie.

Four 3-ounce skinless
  boneless chicken breasts

2 cups sliced mushrooms

1 onion, chopped

1 cup low-sodium chicken
  broth

12 dried apricot halves,
  julienned

1/4 teaspoon grated nutmeg

1 tablespoon cornstarch

2 tablespoons brandy (plain
  or apricot-flavored)

4 cups hot cooked spinach
  fettuccine

2 tablespoons pecan halves,
  coarsely chopped

1. Spray a large nonstick skillet with nonstick cooking spray; heat. Add the chicken and cook until browned, about 2 minutes on each side. Transfer to a plate.

2. Spray the same skillet with more nonstick cooking spray. Add the mushrooms and onion; cook, stirring as needed, until softened, about 5 minutes. Add the broth, apricots and nutmeg; cook, scraping up the browned bits, about 1 minute.

3. Return the chicken to the skillet. Reduce the heat and simmer, covered, until cooked through, about 6–8 minutes.

4. In a small bowl, combine the cornstarch and brandy; add to the chicken mixture and cook, stirring constantly, until the mixture boils and thickens, about 1 minute. Serve the fettuccine, topped with the chicken mixture; sprinkle with the pecans.

PER SERVING: 384 Calories, 6 g Total Fat, 1 g Saturated Fat, 91 mg Cholesterol, 117 mg Sodium, 49 g Total Carbohydrate, 6 g Dietary Fiber, 29 g Protein, 54 mg Calcium.

SERVING PROVIDES: 2 Breads, 1 Fruit/Vegetable, 2 Protein/Milks, 1 Fat.

POINTS PER SERVING: 7.

Chicken Tetrazzini

MAKES 2 SERVINGS

Jenny L. Canter
Gallatin, Tennessee

*Jenny—a grandmother who plays piano and teaches Sunday School—has come up
with a chicken casserole full of old-fashioned goodness. What's lacking?
Only the excess fat and calories.*

2 teaspoons unsalted stick
  margarine

2 celery stalks, diced

2 scallions, thinly sliced

1 tablespoon all-purpose
  flour

1 cup skim milk

1/3 cup shredded reduced-
  fat cheddar cheese

1 cup cubed cooked skin-
  less chicken breast

1 cup cooked elbow
  macaroni

1/2 cup frozen green peas

7 fat-free saltine crackers,
  crumbled

1. Preheat the oven to 350° F.

2. In a large nonstick saucepan, melt the margarine. Add
the celery and scallions; cook, stirring as needed, until
softened, about 4 minutes.

3. Add the flour and cook, stirring constantly, until
lightly browned, about 1 minute. Stir in the milk and
cook, stirring constantly, until the mixture boils and
thickens, about 3 minutes. Add the cheese and stir until
melted.

4. Stir in the chicken, macaroni and peas; cook, stirring
as needed, until heated through and the peas are thawed,
about 3 minutes. Transfer to a 1 1/2-quart casserole; top
with the cracker crumbs. Bake until the crackers are
lightly browned, about 10 minutes.

PER SERVING: 406 Calories, 10 g Total Fat, 4 g Saturated Fat,
64 mg Cholesterol, 410 mg Sodium, 43 g Total Carbohydrate,
3 g Dietary Fiber, 34 g Protein, 356 mg Calcium.

SERVING PROVIDES: 2 Breads, 1 Fruit/Vegetable, 3 Protein/Milks,
1 Fat.

POINTS PER SERVING: 8.

Cider-Dijon Chicken

MAKES 4 SERVINGS

Sue Avery
Bow, Washington

*Sue, a Weight Watchers lifetime member, loves to eat out and then go home and
duplicate what she's enjoyed—minus the extra fat and calories, that is.
This chicken dish is the result of a restaurant adventure.*

1 teaspoon canola oil

2 garlic cloves, minced

Four 4-ounce skinless
boneless chicken breasts

2 cups sliced mushrooms

1/2 cup low-sodium chicken
broth

2 tablespoons Dijon
mustard

3 tablespoons all-purpose
flour

1/2 cup apple cider or juice

1/4 cup nonfat sour cream

1/4 cup minced parsley

4 cups hot cooked brown
rice

1. In a large nonstick skillet, heat the oil. Add the garlic and cook, stirring as needed, until lightly browned, about 1 minute.

2. Add the chicken, mushrooms, broth and mustard; bring to a boil. Reduce the heat and simmer, covered, until the chicken is cooked through, 8–10 minutes.

3. In a small bowl, combine the flour with enough of the cider to make a smooth paste; stir in the remaining cider. Add to the chicken mixture; cook, stirring constantly, until the mixture boils and thickens, about 2 minutes. Stir in the sour cream and parsley; cook until heated through, about 1 minute. Serve the rice, topped with the chicken and sauce.

PER SERVING: 421 Calories, 5 g Total Fat, 1 g Saturated Fat, 66 mg Cholesterol, 291 mg Sodium, 56 g Total Carbohydrate, 4 g Dietary Fiber, 34 g Protein, 65 mg Calcium.

SERVING PROVIDES: 2 Breads, 1 Fruit/Vegetable, 3 Protein/Milks.

POINTS PER SERVING: 8.

$\mathcal{L}$emon-Tarragon Chicken

MAKES 4 SERVINGS

Bonnie Sparrow
Kingston, Ontario, Canada

Bonnie is a Weight Watchers lifetime member who developed this recipe using her husband's homemade wine and fresh tarragon from her summer cottage's garden. She likes to serve it with rice and steamed vegetables.

1/4 cup dry white wine

1 tablespoon minced fresh tarragon, or 1 teaspoon dried

1 teaspoon grated lemon zest

2 tablespoons fresh lemon juice

2 garlic cloves, minced

Four 4-ounce skinless boneless chicken breasts

(See photo.)

1. To prepare the marinade, in a gallon-size sealable plastic bag, combine the wine, tarragon, lemon zest, lemon juice and garlic; add the chicken. Seal the bag, squeezing out the air; turn to coat the chicken. Refrigerate 2 hours or overnight, turning the bag occasionally.

2. Spray the broiler or grill rack with nonstick cooking spray; set aside. Preheat the broiler, or prepare the grill.

3. Drain the chicken and discard the marinade. Broil or grill the chicken 5" from the heat, until the chicken is cooked through, about 5 minutes on each side.

PER SERVING: 141 Calories, 1 g Total Fat, 0 g Saturated Fat, 66 mg Cholesterol, 75 mg Sodium, 2 g Total Carbohydrate, 0 g Dietary Fiber, 26 g Protein, 22 mg Calcium.

SERVING PROVIDES: 3 Protein/Milks.

POINTS PER SERVING: 3.

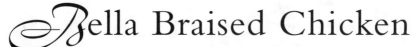Bella Braised Chicken

MAKES 6 SERVINGS

Julie Clawson
Hartford, Connecticut

Seven years ago, Julie, an aspiring opera singer, lost an audition because the director thought she was too heavy for the part. The next day, she joined Weight Watchers. To her surprise, instead of cottage cheese and baked fish, Julie found a whole new world of "real food," out of which evolved this prizewinning recipe. The slow cooking keeps the vegetables firm and the chicken unbelievably moist. Make it for a Sunday supper, and pack any leftovers for lunch the next day.

1 tablespoon unsalted stick margarine

2 onions, chopped

2 celery stalks, diced

1 carrot, diced

2 garlic cloves, minced

3 tablespoons all-purpose flour

1/4 teaspoon freshly ground black pepper

Six 4-ounce skinless boneless chicken breasts

1 tablespoon olive oil

One 14 1/2-ounce can diced tomatoes (no salt added)

1 cup low-sodium chicken broth

1/2 cup dry white wine

2 tablespoons minced parsley, plus more for garnish

1 teaspoon dried thyme leaves

1. Preheat the oven to 325° F.

2. In a large nonstick skillet, melt the margarine. Add the onions, celery, carrot and garlic; cook, stirring as needed, until softened, about 5 minutes. Transfer the vegetables to a 3-quart Dutch oven or casserole.

3. In a gallon-size sealable plastic bag, combine the flour and pepper. Add the chicken; shake to coat.

4. In the same skillet, heat the oil. Add the chicken and brown 2 minutes on each side. Arrange the chicken on top of the vegetables. Return the skillet to the heat; add the tomatoes, broth, wine, parsley and thyme. Cook, scraping up the browned bits from the bottom of the skillet, until the liquid comes to a boil; pour over the chicken. Bake, covered, until the chicken is cooked through and the vegetables are tender, about 1 hour. Serve, sprinkled with additional minced parsley.

PER SERVING: 232 Calories, 6 g Total Fat, 1 g Saturated Fat, 66 mg Cholesterol, 121 mg Sodium, 12 g Total Carbohydrate, 2 g Dietary Fiber, 29 g Protein, 61 mg Calcium.

SERVING PROVIDES: 1 Fruit/Vegetable, 3 Protein/Milks, 1 Fat.

POINTS PER SERVING: 5.

Baked Chicken and Ziti

MAKES 4 SERVINGS

Frances M. Bower
Argyle, New York

After her husband's heart attack, Frances had to rethink her family's eating choices to include more chicken. Now it is a staple protein in her kitchen. "I'm always looking for something new," she says, "and remembered this dish prepared often by my grandmother." Frances serves it with a green salad and has shared it with her Weight Watchers group.

$^1\!/_2$ pound skinless boneless chicken breasts, cut into $^1\!/_4$" strips

1 onion, chopped

2 garlic cloves, minced

One 28-ounce can crushed tomatoes (no salt added)

1 teaspoon Italian herb seasoning

$^1\!/_4$ teaspoon freshly ground black pepper

2 cups ziti or penne

$^2\!/_3$ cup nonfat ricotta cheese

$^1\!/_3$ cup shredded part-skim mozzarella cheese

2 tablespoons grated Parmesan cheese

1. Spray a large nonstick skillet with nonstick cooking spray; heat. Add the chicken and cook, turning as needed, until lightly browned, 5–6 minutes. Transfer to a plate.

2. Preheat the oven to 375° F.

3. Spray the same skillet with more nonstick cooking spray. Add the onion and garlic; cook, stirring as needed, until softened, about 5 minutes. Add the tomatoes, Italian seasoning and pepper; bring to a boil. Reduce the heat and simmer, uncovered, stirring as needed, until the mixture is thickened slightly, 8–10 minutes.

4. Meanwhile, cook the ziti according to package directions. Drain and mix with the ricotta cheese.

5. Pour half of the tomato mixture into a 13 × 9" baking pan, layer with the ziti mixture, the chicken and the remaining tomato mixture. Sprinkle with the cheeses. Bake until hot and bubbling and the cheese is melted, 15–20 minutes.

PER SERVING: 381 Calories, 5 g Total Fat, 2 g Saturated Fat, 40 mg Cholesterol, 209 mg Sodium, 52 g Total Carbohydrate, 3 g Dietary Fiber, 31 g Protein, 371 mg Calcium.

SERVING PROVIDES: 2 Breads, 1 Fruit/Vegetable, 3 Protein/Milks.

POINTS PER SERVING: 7.

Chicken Penne

MAKES 2 SERVINGS

Judith L. Wiseman
Dallas, Texas

*Judy, who lost 30 pounds and increased her aerobic fitness in the course of a year,
first developed this recipe as a super, low-fat way to get vegetables into a meal.
"Now I make it just because it tastes good," she writes.*

1 teaspoon olive oil

1 onion, chopped

1/2 green bell pepper,
  seeded and chopped

1 garlic clove, minced

One 14 1/2-ounce can
  Italian-style stewed
  tomatoes

1/4 pound skinless boneless
  chicken breast, cubed

2 tablespoons dry red wine

1 cup penne or ziti

2 tablespoons grated
  Parmesan cheese

1. In a large nonstick skillet, heat the oil. Add the onion, pepper and garlic; cook, stirring as needed, until softened, about 5 minutes.

2. Add the tomatoes, chicken and wine; bring to a boil. Reduce the heat and simmer, covered, until the chicken is cooked through, 5–6 minutes.

3. Meanwhile, cook the penne according to package directions. Drain and place in a serving bowl. Add the chicken mixture; toss to combine. Serve, sprinkled with the cheese.

PER SERVING: 383 Calories, 5 g Total Fat, 2 g Saturated Fat, 37 mg Cholesterol, 1,036 mg Sodium, 58 g Total Carbohydrate, 6 g Dietary Fiber, 24 g Protein, 131 mg Calcium.

SERVING PROVIDES: 2 Breads, 2 Fruit/Vegetables, 2 Protein/Milks, 1 Fat.

POINTS PER SERVING: 7.

Chicken Enchilada Casserole

MAKES 6 SERVINGS

Dawn Reed
Meriden, Kansas

Dawn, a piano teacher, finds that this substantial Southwestern casserole hits all the right notes, especially with her husband and eight-year-old son.

Ten 6" fat-free corn tortillas, halved

3 cups cubed cooked skinless chicken breasts

1 cup fresh or thawed frozen corn kernels

1 onion, chopped

1/2 green bell pepper, seeded and diced

One 14 1/2-ounce can stewed tomatoes (no salt added)

One 10-ounce can diced tomatoes and green chiles

1 cup shredded reduced-fat cheddar cheese

1. Preheat the oven to 350° F. Spray a 13 × 9" baking pan with nonstick cooking spray.

2. Line the bottom of the pan with half of the tortillas; layer with the chicken, corn, onion, pepper and stewed tomatoes. Cover with the remaining tortillas. Pour the tomatoes and chiles over the top; cover with foil and bake until heated through, about 30 minutes. Uncover and sprinkle with the cheese. Bake, uncovered, until the cheese is melted, about 10 minutes longer.

PER SERVING: 286 Calories, 5 g Total Fat, 1 g Saturated Fat, 51 mg Cholesterol, 628 mg Sodium, 35 g Total Carbohydrate, 7 g Dietary Fiber, 27 g Protein, 274 mg Calcium.

SERVING PROVIDES: 2 Breads, 1 Fruit/Vegetable, 3 Protein/Milks.

POINTS PER SERVING: 5.

Chicken Fajitas

MAKES 2 SERVINGS

Shiela Jones
Jackson, Michigan

Shiela has always had difficulty finding a way to work vegetables into her diet—but not with this lively Southwestern recipe, which is every bit as healthful as it is delicious.

¹/₂ pound skinless boneless chicken breasts, cut into strips

2 tablespoons fat-free Italian salad dressing

1 onion, sliced

¹/₂ green bell pepper, seeded and sliced

¹/₂ red bell pepper, seeded and sliced

Four 6" fat-free flour tortillas

¹/₄ cup salsa

2 tablespoons nonfat sour cream

1. In a gallon-size sealable plastic bag, combine the chicken and salad dressing. Seal the bag, squeezing out the air; turn to coat the chicken. Refrigerate at least 2 hours or overnight, turning the bag occasionally.

2. Spray a large nonstick skillet with nonstick cooking spray; heat. Add the chicken and any remaining marinade; cook, turning as needed, until the chicken is lightly browned, 7–8 minutes. Transfer to a plate and keep warm.

3. Spray the same skillet with more nonstick cooking spray. Add the onion and peppers; cook, stirring as needed, until softened, about 5 minutes.

4. Top the tortillas with the chicken, pepper mixture, salsa and sour cream; roll up and serve.

PER SERVING: 338 Calories, 2 g Total Fat, 0 g Saturated Fat, 66 mg Cholesterol, 865 mg Sodium, 46 g Total Carbohydrate, 3 g Dietary Fiber, 32 g Protein, 44 mg Calcium.

SERVING PROVIDES: 2 Breads, 1 Fruit/Vegetable, 3 Protein/Milks.

POINTS PER SERVING: 6.

Grilled Chicken with Mozzarella and Red Peppers

MAKES 2 SERVINGS

Vivian Elba
Simsbury, Connecticut

*When it's summer-barbecue time, Vivian simply multiplies the quantities
in the recipe to feed whatever size crowd she has.*

1½ teaspoons extra virgin olive oil

1 teaspoon anchovy paste

3 red bell peppers, roasted★ and cut into ¼" slices

⅓ cup cubed part-skim mozzarella cheese

1 plum tomato, cubed

5 pitted small black olives, sliced

2 tablespoons minced flat-leaf parsley

Two 3-ounce skinless boneless chicken breasts

1. Spray the broiler or grill rack with nonstick cooking spray. Preheat the broiler, or prepare the grill.

2. In a medium bowl, combine 1 teaspoon of the oil with the anchovy paste until well blended. Add the peppers, cheese, tomato, olives and parsley; toss lightly.

3. Brush the chicken with the remaining ½ teaspoon of the oil and place on the rack. Broil the chicken 5" from the heat, until cooked through, about 5 minutes on each side. Serve the chicken breasts topped with the pepper mixture.

PER SERVING: 242 Calories, 10 g Total Fat, 1 g Saturated Fat, 66 mg Cholesterol, 249 mg Sodium, 12 g Total Carbohydrate, 3 g Dietary Fiber, 26 g Protein, 86 mg Calcium.

SERVING PROVIDES: 2 Fruit/Vegetables, 3 Protein/Milks, 1 Fat.

POINTS PER SERVING: 5.

★ *To roast the bell peppers, preheat the broiler. Line a baking sheet with foil; place the peppers on the baking sheet. Broil 4–6" from heat, turning frequently with tongs, until the skin is lightly charred on all sides, about 10 minutes. Transfer to a paper bag; fold the bag closed and steam 10 minutes. Peel, seed and devein the peppers over the sink to drain the juices.*

Chicken–Vegetable Stir-Fry

MAKES 8 SERVINGS

Dona Plaza
Fremont, California

"I love to experiment with my old 'fat' recipes," says Dona, "and this is what I came up with for a low-fat stir-fry dish. So far I've lost 55 pounds!" Dona thinks her two-year effort has been worth it, saying, "I'm learning how to eat properly for the rest of my life."

3 tablespoons reduced-sodium soy sauce

3 garlic cloves, minced

1 tablespoon minced peeled gingerroot

1¼ pounds skinless boneless chicken breasts, cut into 1" pieces

3 tablespoons cornstarch

1 teaspoon oyster sauce or fish sauce (optional)

4 teaspoons canola oil

4 carrots, thinly sliced

4 cups broccoli florets

2 onions, sliced

One 8-ounce can sliced water chestnuts, drained

6 cups hot cooked brown rice

1. To prepare the marinade, in a gallon-size sealable plastic bag, combine 2 tablespoons of the soy sauce, the garlic and ginger; add the chicken. Seal the bag, squeezing out the air; turn to coat the chicken. Refrigerate at least 2 hours or overnight, turning the bag occasionally.

2. In a medium bowl, stir the cornstarch, the remaining 1 tablespoon of the soy sauce and the oyster sauce (if using) with ¼ cup water. Add 1¾ cups more water.

3. In a large nonstick wok or skillet, heat the oil. Add the carrots, broccoli and onions; stir-fry until tender-crisp, 10–12 minutes. Transfer to a bowl and keep warm. Add the chicken and marinade to the wok and cook, stirring as needed, until the chicken is cooked through, 8–10 minutes.

4. Return the vegetables to the wok; add the cornstarch mixture and the water chestnuts. Cook, stirring constantly, until the mixture comes to a boil and thickens, 4–5 minutes. Serve the rice, topped with the chicken mixture.

PER SERVING: 336 Calories, 5 g Total Fat, 1 g Saturated Fat, 41 mg Cholesterol, 315 mg Sodium, 50 g Total Carbohydrate, 7 g Dietary Fiber, 24 g Protein, 72 mg Calcium.

SERVING PROVIDES: 2 Breads, 1 Fruit/Vegetable, 2 Protein/Milks, 1 Fat.

POINTS PER SERVING: 6.

Creamy Chicken and Spinach

MAKES 4 SERVINGS

Catherine L. Mundy
Livonia, Michigan

*Creamy, yes, but cream? No way. Catherine says she knows she's succeeded in transforming
old-favorite recipes into healthful versions when nobody in her family asks,
"Is this one of your low-fat recipes, Mom?"*

1 teaspoon canola oil

2 cups sliced mushrooms

1 onion, chopped

2 garlic cloves, minced

1 tablespoon all-purpose flour

1 cup skim milk

1/2 cup low-sodium chicken broth

3/4 pound skinless boneless chicken breasts, cubed

One 10-ounce package frozen chopped spinach, thawed and squeezed dry

1/4 teaspoon freshly ground black pepper

4 cups hot cooked medium pasta shells

2 tablespoons grated Parmesan cheese

1. In a large nonstick skillet, heat the oil. Add the mushrooms, onion and garlic; cook, stirring as needed, until softened, 5–6 minutes.

2. Add the flour and cook, stirring constantly, until the flour is lightly browned, about 1 minute. Gradually stir in the milk and broth; cook, stirring constantly, until the mixture boils and thickens, 2–3 minutes. Stir in the chicken, spinach and pepper; return to a boil, stirring as needed. Reduce the heat and simmer, covered, stirring as needed, until the chicken is cooked, 6–8 minutes.

3. Place the pasta in a serving bowl; add the chicken mixture and toss to combine. Serve, sprinkled with the cheese.

PER SERVING: 231 Calories, 3 g Total Fat, 1 g Saturated Fat, 35 mg Cholesterol, 135 mg Sodium, 29 g Total Carbohydrate, 3 g Dietary Fiber, 21 g Protein, 145 mg Calcium.

SERVING PROVIDES: 2 Breads, 1 Fruit/Vegetable, 3 Protein/Milks.

POINTS PER SERVING: 4.

*C*urried Chicken with Dried Cranberries

MAKES 4 SERVINGS

Robert J. Swek
Detroit, Michigan

When Robert received a gourmet spice kit as a birthday present, he used it, along with some dried cranberries he had on hand, to come up with this colorful Indian-inspired recipe.

2 teaspoons canola oil

Four 3-ounce skinless boneless chicken breasts

2 onions, chopped

2 garlic cloves, minced

2 teaspoons ground cumin

1 teaspoon turmeric

1 teaspoon ground coriander

1 teaspoon ground ginger

1/4 teaspoon crushed red pepper flakes, or to taste

One 14 1/2-ounce can diced tomatoes (no salt added)

2 Granny Smith apples, cored and diced

1/2 cup low-sodium chicken broth

1/4 cup dried cranberries

4 cups hot cooked brown rice

1. In a large nonstick skillet, heat the oil. Add the chicken and cook until lightly browned, 2–3 minutes on each side. Transfer to a plate.

2. Add the onions and cook, stirring as needed, until softened, about 5 minutes. Add the garlic, cumin, turmeric, coriander, ginger and pepper flakes; cook, stirring constantly, until fragrant, about 30 seconds.

3. Add the tomatoes, apples, broth and cranberries; bring to a boil, scraping up the browned bits from the bottom of the skillet. Return the chicken to the skillet; reduce the heat and simmer, covered, until the chicken is cooked through, about 10 minutes. Serve the rice, topped with the chicken breasts and sauce.

PER SERVING: 437 Calories, 6 g Total Fat, 1 g Saturated Fat, 50 mg Cholesterol, 98 mg Sodium, 69 g Total Carbohydrate, 7 g Dietary Fiber, 27 g Protein, 89 mg Calcium.

SERVING PROVIDES: 2 Breads, 2 Fruit/Vegetables, 2 Protein/Milks, 1 Fat.

POINTS PER SERVING: 8.

Chicken and Vegetables

MAKES 4 SERVINGS

Daniel J. Morris
Staten Island, New York

*Daniel, who works in the finance industry, likes to make this chicken
dish for himself and his wife, Eileen, on busy weeknights
when neither of them feels like standing at the stove.*

Four 4-ounce skinless
  boneless chicken breasts

1½ cups sliced mushrooms

1 red bell pepper, seeded
  and cut into 1" strips

1 medium zucchini, sliced

1 onion, coarsely chopped

¼ cup + 2 tablespoons
  barbecue sauce

2 garlic cloves, minced

4 cups hot cooked brown
  rice

1. Preheat the oven to 350° F.

2. Tear off four 12" squares of foil; place 1 chicken breast in the center of each. Top with the mushrooms, pepper, zucchini and onion.

3. In a small bowl, combine the barbecue sauce and garlic; spoon evenly over the chicken and vegetables. Make packets by bringing the 2 sides of the foil up to meet in the center and folding the edges over, then folding the edges of each end together. Allowing room for the packet to expand, crimp the edges. Place the packets on a baking sheet. Bake until the chicken is cooked through and the vegetables are tender, about 40 minutes. Open the packets carefully when testing for doneness, as steam will escape.

4. Place 1 cup rice on each of 4 plates; spoon the contents of 1 packet over each portion.

PER SERVING: 388 Calories, 4 g Total Fat, 1 g Saturated Fat, 66 mg Cholesterol, 278 mg Sodium, 54 g Total Carbohydrate, 5 g Dietary Fiber, 33 g Protein, 53 mg Calcium.

SERVING PROVIDES: 2 Breads, 1 Fruit/Vegetable, 3 Protein/Milks.

POINTS PER SERVING: 7.

*G*arlic-Ginger Chicken and Potatoes

MAKES 2 SERVINGS

Peggy Allen
Pasadena, California

*In the year that she's been a Weight Watchers member, Peggy has lost 112 pounds.
She couldn't have done it without recipes such as this one, which she says,
"has a lot of eye appeal and a lot of flavor."*

1 tablespoon minced
  cilantro

1 tablespoon rice-wine
  vinegar

1 teaspoon reduced-sodium
  soy sauce

1/2 teaspoon minced peeled
  gingerroot

1 garlic clove, minced

Two 4-ounce skinless
  boneless chicken breasts

1 large baking potato,
  scrubbed and cut into
  8 wedges

1. To prepare the marinade, in a gallon-size sealable plastic bag, combine the cilantro, vinegar, soy sauce, ginger and garlic; add the chicken. Seal the bag, squeezing out the air; turn to coat the chicken. Refrigerate 30 minutes.

2. Preheat the oven to 350° F. Spray a 10 × 6" baking pan with nonstick cooking spray.

3. Transfer the chicken and marinade to the pan; add the potato. Bake, covered, until the chicken and potato are partially cooked, about 15 minutes longer. Uncover and bake until the chicken is cooked through and the potato is tender, about 15 minutes longer. Serve the chicken and potato, spooning any remaining pan juices over the chicken.

PER SERVING: 238 Calories, 2 g Total Fat, 0 g Saturated Fat, 66 mg Cholesterol, 184 mg Sodium, 25 g Total Carbohydrate, 3 g Dietary Fiber, 30 g Protein, 34 mg Calcium.

SERVING PROVIDES: 1 Bread, 3 Protein/Milks.

POINTS PER SERVING: 4.

Ginger-Cashew Chicken

MAKES 4 SERVINGS

Katherine Voss
Los Gatos, California

*So very stylish, with its garnish of pickled ginger slices, this fragrant
chicken dish is very much in keeping with the trend toward Asian-influenced fare.
Continuing with the theme, Katherine likes to set her table with wooden chopsticks.*

¾ pound skinless boneless chicken breasts, cut into 1" cubes

2 onions, chopped

2 celery stalks, chopped

3 garlic cloves, minced

1 cup sliced mushrooms

1 cup bean sprouts

1 cup trimmed snow peas

¼ cup unsalted dry-roasted cashews

1 tablespoon minced peeled gingerroot

1 tablespoon reduced-sodium soy sauce

3 cups hot cooked brown rice

Pickled ginger

(See photo.)

1. Spray a large nonstick skillet or wok with nonstick cooking spray; heat. Add the chicken and cook, stirring as needed, until lightly browned, about 3 minutes. Transfer to a plate.

2. Spray the same skillet with more nonstick cooking spray; heat. Add the onions, celery and garlic; cook, stirring as needed, about 5 minutes.

3. Add the mushrooms, bean sprouts, snow peas, cashews, ginger, soy sauce and the chicken; cook, stirring as needed, until the chicken is cooked through and the vegetables are tender, 4–5 minutes. Serve the rice, topped with the chicken mixture; garnish with pickled ginger.

PER SERVING: 361 Calories, 7 g Total Fat, 1 g Saturated Fat, 53 mg Cholesterol, 237 mg Sodium, 47 g Total Carbohydrate, 5 g Dietary Fiber, 29 g Protein, 67 mg Calcium.

SERVING PROVIDES: 2 Breads, 1 Fruit/Vegetable, 3 Protein/Milks, 1 Fat.

POINTS PER SERVING: 7.

Greek Cinnamon Chicken

MAKES 6 SERVINGS

Sharon Stavropoulos
Wilmette, Illinois

Since Sharon cooks for her husband and three grown sons, she is always looking for hearty, satisfying recipes. This dish fits the bill, yet still fits her "program."

1 tablespoon olive oil

2 onions, chopped

4 garlic cloves, minced

Six 4-ounce skinless chicken thighs

One 14½-ounce can diced tomatoes (no salt added)

¼ cup dry white wine

2 bay leaves

1 cinnamon stick

½ teaspoon ground cinnamon

½ teaspoon coarsely ground black pepper

¼ teaspoon salt

6 cups hot cooked couscous

1. In a large nonstick skillet, heat the oil. Add the onions and garlic; cook, stirring as needed, until softened, about 5 minutes.

2. Add the chicken, tomatoes, wine, bay leaves, cinnamon stick, ground cinnamon, pepper and salt; bring to a boil. Reduce the heat and simmer, covered, stirring as needed, until the chicken is cooked through, about 30 minutes. Discard the bay leaves and cinnamon stick. Serve the couscous, topped with the chicken and sauce.

PER SERVING: 392 Calories, 7 g Total Fat, 2 g Saturated Fat, 94 mg Cholesterol, 207 mg Sodium, 48 g Total Carbohydrate, 3 g Dietary Fiber, 30 g Protein, 62 mg Calcium.

SERVING PROVIDES: 2 Breads, 1 Fruit/Vegetable, 3 Protein/Milks, 1 Fat.

POINTS PER SERVING: 8.

Quick Chicken Curry

MAKES 2 SERVINGS

Marguerite J. Barber
Virginia Beach, Virginia

*Marguerite, a special agent with an investigative service, has successfully solved
the mystery of how to make a good chicken curry without excess fat.*

2 teaspoons olive oil

1 onion, chopped

1 tablespoon all-purpose flour

1 tablespoon curry powder

1/2 cup low-sodium chicken broth

1/2 cup unsweetened applesauce

1 apple, cored and diced

2 tablespoons raisins

1 1/2 cups cubed cooked skinless chicken breast

1/4 cup skim milk

2 cups hot cooked brown rice

1. In a large nonstick saucepan, heat the oil. Add the onion and cook, stirring as needed, until softened, about 5 minutes. Add the flour and curry; cook, stirring constantly, until the flour is lightly browned, about 1 minute.

2. Add the broth, applesauce, apple and raisins; bring to a boil, stirring constantly. Reduce the heat and simmer, covered, stirring as needed, until slightly thickened, about 10 minutes.

3. Stir in the chicken and milk; cook until heated through, about 3 minutes. Serve the rice, topped with the chicken curry.

PER SERVING: 538 Calories, 11 g Total Fat, 2 g Saturated Fat, 73 mg Cholesterol, 123 mg Sodium, 77 g Total Carbohydrate, 8 g Dietary Fiber, 35 g Protein, 108 mg Calcium.

SERVING PROVIDES: 2 Breads, 2 Fruit/Vegetables, 3 Protein/Milks, 1 Fat.

POINTS PER SERVING: 10.

Southwest Easy-Oven Chicken

MAKES 6 SERVINGS

C. L. Tree
Oakland, California

C. L. and her husband, Larry Loebig, have put their heads together to come up with this hearty, spicy crowd pleaser that's a cinch to throw together.

1 cup low-sodium chicken broth

One 15-ounce can black beans, rinsed and drained

One 15-ounce can red kidney beans, rinsed and drained

3/4 cup mild salsa

2 garlic cloves, minced

1 pound skinless boneless chicken breasts, cut into 2" pieces

1. Preheat the oven to 350° F.

2. In a 13 × 9" baking pan, combine the broth, the beans, salsa and garlic. Add the chicken and baste with some of the liquid.

3. Bake, stirring once, until the chicken is cooked through and the liquid is reduced, about 45 minutes.

PER SERVING: 241 Calories, 2 g Total Fat, 0 g Saturated Fat, 42 mg Cholesterol, 385 mg Sodium, 29 g Total Carbohydrate, 3 g Dietary Fiber, 27 g Protein, 43 mg Calcium.

SERVING PROVIDES: 2 Breads, 2 Protein/Milks.

POINTS PER SERVING: 4.

Grilled Chicken Citrus Salad

MAKES 4 SERVINGS

Vicki Eckersell
Los Angeles, California

Vicki's family particularly enjoys food with a Southwestern flair, so she created this recipe. "It's very cool and refreshing when the mercury climbs, but we enjoy it year-round," says Vicki, who has lost 18 pounds on the program so far.

¹/₂ cup minced cilantro

¹/₂ cup orange juice

¹/₄ cup fresh lime juice

2 shallots, finely chopped

2 garlic cloves, minced

1 teaspoon chili powder

1 teaspoon ground cumin

1 teaspoon sugar

Four 4-ounce skinless boneless chicken breasts

8 cups torn romaine lettuce

2 navel oranges, peeled and sectioned

2 celery stalks, sliced

4 scallions, sliced

(See photo.)

1. To prepare the marinade and salad dressing, in a medium bowl, combine the cilantro, the juices, shallots, garlic, chili powder, cumin and sugar; pour ¹/₂ cup of this mixture into a gallon-size sealable plastic bag; add the chicken. Seal the bag, squeezing out the air; turn to coat the chicken. Refrigerate at least 2 hours or overnight, turning the bag occasionally. Pour the remaining dressing into a jar and refrigerate, covered, until ready to use.

2. In a large salad bowl, combine the lettuce, oranges, celery and scallions; refrigerate, covered, until ready to use.

3. Preheat the broiler; line the broiler pan with foil. Drain the chicken and discard the marinade. Broil the chicken 5" from the heat, until cooked through, 5–6 minutes on each side. Transfer to a board and slice diagonally.

4. Add the reserved dressing to the salad mixture; toss to coat. Top with the chicken.

PER SERVING: 208 Calories, 2 g Total Fat, 0 g Saturated Fat, 66 mg Cholesterol, 107 mg Sodium, 18 g Total Carbohydrate, 4 g Dietary Fiber, 30 g Protein, 105 mg Calcium.

SERVING PROVIDES: 3 Fruit/Vegetables, 3 Protein/Milks.

POINTS PER SERVING: 4.

Grilled Turkey-Herb Burgers

MAKES 4 SERVINGS

Diane O'Neil
Clinton, Michigan

*Diane, a Weight Watchers leader and the mom of a preschooler, has come up with
a turkey burger that has wonderful flavor. She always keeps a few on
hand in the freezer to cook for a quick and healthful dinner.*

1 pound ground skinless
turkey breast

1 onion, finely chopped

1/4 cup + 2 tablespoons
seasoned dried bread
crumbs

3 tablespoons minced
parsley

3 tablespoons reduced-
calorie mayonnaise

1 tablespoon minced fresh
basil, or 1 teaspoon dried

2 teaspoons Dijon mustard

1/2 teaspoon coarsely
ground black pepper

1. Preheat the broiler.

2. In a large bowl, lightly combine the turkey, onion,
bread crumbs, parsley, mayonnaise, basil, mustard and
pepper. Shape into 4 equal burgers.

3. Spray the broiler rack with nonstick cooking spray;
broil the burgers 5" from the heat, until well done, 4–5
minutes on each side.

PER SERVING: 210 Calories, 4 g Total Fat, 1 g Saturated Fat,
74 mg Cholesterol, 476 mg Sodium, 11 g Total Carbohydrate,
1 g Dietary Fiber, 30 g Protein, 34 mg Calcium.

SERVING PROVIDES: 1 Bread, 3 Protein/Milks, 1 Fat.

POINTS PER SERVING: 4.

Spaghetti-Turkey Pie

MAKES 4 SERVINGS

Sharon Ontiveros
Oxnard, California

Sharon often serves this pie because it appeals to her husband and nine-year-old son.
It's fun to serve and even more fun to eat. A tossed green salad complements the meal perfectly.

6 ounces spaghetti, broken in half

3 egg whites

2 tablespoons grated Parmesan cheese

1 teaspoon olive oil

10 ounces ground skinless turkey breast

1 green bell pepper, seeded and chopped

1 onion, chopped

2 garlic cloves, minced

One 8-ounce can tomato sauce (no salt added)

1 teaspoon dried oregano

¼ teaspoon freshly ground black pepper

⅓ cup shredded part-skim mozzarella cheese

1. Preheat the oven to 350° F. Spray a 9" pie plate with nonstick cooking spray.

2. Cook the spaghetti according to package directions. Rinse under cold water for 30 seconds and drain. Transfer to a medium bowl; stir in the egg whites and Parmesan cheese. Pat into the bottom and up the sides of the plate.

3. In a large nonstick skillet, heat the oil. Add the turkey, bell pepper, onion and garlic; cook, stirring constantly, until the turkey is browned and the vegetables are softened, about 5 minutes. Add the tomato sauce, oregano and black pepper; cook, stirring constantly, until heated through, about 2 minutes.

4. Spread the mixture evenly over the pasta. Bake 25 minutes; sprinkle with the mozzarella cheese and bake until the cheese is melted, about 5 minutes longer. Let stand 5 minutes before serving.

PER SERVING: 334 Calories, 5 g Total Fat, 2 g Saturated Fat, 51 mg Cholesterol, 183 mg Sodium, 41 g Total Carbohydrate, 3 g Dietary Fiber, 30 g Protein, 127 mg Calcium.

SERVING PROVIDES: 2 Breads, 1 Fruit/Vegetable, 3 Protein/Milks.

POINTS PER SERVING: 6.

Turkey-Spinach Scramble

MAKES 4 SERVINGS

Denise N. Mills
Acton, California

*Denise, a nurse-practitioner, puts her Weight Watchers experience to good
use when counseling overweight patients. Her hectic schedule allows little time for
elaborate food preparation, so she came up with this satisfying scramble,
which works especially well stuffed in pita bread.*

1 teaspoon olive oil

10 ounces ground skinless
turkey breast

3 garlic cloves, minced

One 10-ounce package
frozen chopped spinach,
thawed and squeezed dry

2 tomatoes, chopped

1/2 teaspoon salt

1/2 teaspoon freshly ground
black pepper

4 small whole-wheat pita
breads, halved

1. In a large nonstick skillet, heat the oil. Add the turkey and garlic; cook, stirring constantly, until the turkey is browned, about 5 minutes.

2. Add the spinach, tomatoes, salt and pepper; cook, stirring as needed, until the spinach is wilted and tomatoes are softened, about 5 minutes. Spoon 1/2 cup of the turkey mixture into each pita half.

PER SERVING: 201 Calories, 3 g Total Fat, 0 g Saturated Fat, 44 mg Cholesterol, 519 mg Sodium, 23 g Total Carbohydrate, 5 g Dietary Fiber, 23 g Protein, 101 mg Calcium.

SERVING PROVIDES: 1 Bread, 1 Fruit/Vegetable, 2 Protein/Milks.

POINTS PER SERVING: 3.

Spicy Turkey-Bean Chili

MAKES 12 SERVINGS

Joanie Kensil-Bradsher
Tempe, Arizona

*Joanie's favorite way to serve this chili is stuffed in flour tortillas and topped
with shredded lettuce and nonfat sour cream. The chili makes
great leftovers, and it freezes well, too.*

1 tablespoon olive oil

1 pound ground skinless
turkey breast

3 green bell peppers,
seeded and diced

4 onions, chopped

6 garlic cloves, minced

1 tablespoon ground cumin

2 teaspoons dried oregano

½ teaspoon cayenne
pepper

3 bay leaves

One 28-ounce can crushed
tomatoes (no salt added)

Two 15-ounce cans black
beans, rinsed and drained

One 15-ounce can fat-free
refried beans

One 4-ounce can diced
green chiles, rinsed and
drained

One 4-ounce can sliced
jalapeño peppers, rinsed
and drained

1. In a large nonstick saucepan or Dutch oven, heat the oil. Add the turkey, bell peppers, onions, garlic, cumin, oregano, cayenne and bay leaves; cook, stirring as needed, until the turkey is browned and the vegetables are softened, 6–8 minutes.

2. Add the tomatoes, the beans, chiles and jalapeños; bring to a boil. Reduce the heat and simmer, covered, stirring as needed, until the flavors are well blended, about 45 minutes. Discard the bay leaves.

PER SERVING: 202 Calories, 2 g Total Fat, 0 g Saturated Fat, 22 mg Cholesterol, 298 mg Sodium, 29 g Total Carbohydrate, 5 g Dietary Fiber, 18 g Protein, 77 mg Calcium.

SERVING PROVIDES: 2 Breads, 1 Fruit/Vegetable, 1 Protein/Milk.

POINTS PER SERVING: 3.

Turkey-Eggplant Casserole

MAKES 8 SERVINGS

Marjorie F. Kohler
Phoenix, Arizona

*Marjorie, a retired teacher, often cooks and freezes meals in individual
portions to microwave later. She likes to serve this savory casserole with a
green salad and French bread, followed, perhaps, by a baked apple for dessert.*

1¼ pounds ground skinless turkey breast

1 onion, chopped

3 garlic cloves, minced

1 large (1½-pound) eggplant, cubed

One 28-ounce can crushed tomatoes (no salt added)

1 green bell pepper, seeded and diced

1 red bell pepper, seeded and diced

¾ cup seasoned dried bread crumbs

1 teaspoon dried basil

¼ cup grated Parmesan cheese

1. Preheat the oven to 350° F. Spray a 13 × 9" baking pan with nonstick cooking spray.

2. Spray a large nonstick saucepan or Dutch oven with nonstick cooking spray; heat. Add the turkey, onion and garlic; cook, stirring as needed, until the turkey is browned and the onion is softened, 5–6 minutes.

3. Add the eggplant, tomatoes, peppers, bread crumbs and basil; bring to a boil, stirring as needed.

4. Transfer the turkey mixture to the pan and bake, covered, until the vegetables are tender, 45–50 minutes; uncover and sprinkle with the cheese. Bake until the cheese is lightly browned, about 15 minutes longer. Let stand 5 minutes before serving.

PER SERVING: 189 Calories, 2 g Total Fat, 1 g Saturated Fat, 46 mg Cholesterol, 397 mg Sodium, 21 g Total Carbohydrate, 3 g Dietary Fiber, 22 g Protein, 127 mg Calcium.

SERVING PROVIDES: 1 Bread, 1 Fruit/Vegetable, 2 Protein/Milks.

POINTS PER SERVING: 3.

Turkey Lasagna

MAKES 8 SERVINGS

Jean Carlton
Minnetonka, Minnesota

Jean's family loves her Turkey Lasagna, and as a Weight Watchers leader, she has shared her recipe with many members. They all give it rave reviews and agree that it belongs in their own favorite-recipes cookbook.

2 teaspoons olive oil

10 ounces ground skinless turkey breast

1 onion, chopped

One 28-ounce can whole tomatoes (no salt added), coarsely chopped

One 6-ounce can tomato paste (no salt added)

1/4 cup grated Parmesan cheese

1 teaspoon dried basil

1 teaspoon dried oregano

1/2 teaspoon sugar

12 no-boil lasagna noodles

2 cups nonfat cottage cheese

1 cup shredded part-skim mozzarella cheese

1. Preheat the oven to 350° F.

2. In a large nonstick saucepan or Dutch oven, heat the oil. Add the turkey and onion; cook, stirring as needed, until the turkey is browned and the onion is softened, about 5 minutes.

3. Stir in the tomatoes, tomato paste, Parmesan cheese, basil, oregano and sugar; bring to a boil. Reduce the heat and simmer, uncovered, until the flavors are blended, about 5 minutes.

4. Spoon one-third of the sauce in the bottom of a 13 × 9" baking pan; top with 3 of the noodles; spread with half of the cottage cheese, and top with 3 more noodles. Repeat the layering once more, ending with the sauce. Sprinkle the mozzarella cheese evenly on top.

5. Bake, covered, 1 hour; uncover and bake until cooked through and golden, about 10 minutes longer. Let stand 10 minutes before serving.

PER SERVING: 275 Calories, 5 g Total Fat, 2 g Saturated Fat, 37 mg Cholesterol, 359 mg Sodium, 31 g Total Carbohydrate, 2 g Dietary Fiber, 26 g Protein, 202 mg Calcium.

SERVING PROVIDES: 1 Bread, 1 Fruit/Vegetable, 3 Protein/Milks.

POINTS PER SERVING: 6.

urkey Soft Tacos

MAKES 4 SERVINGS

Karen Jackson
Little Rock, Arkansas

*Karen, who lost 70 pounds on Weight Watchers, has been at her goal
weight since 1987! What's kept her there? "A balanced diet and exercise I enjoy."
Try Karen's spicy turkey tacos, and you'll understand how she's had
no trouble maintaining her goal weight all these years.*

³/₄ pound ground skinless turkey breast

1 onion, chopped

2 garlic cloves, minced

1 cup canned black beans, rinsed and drained

1 green bell pepper, seeded and diced

One 8-ounce can tomato sauce (no salt added)

1 jalapeño pepper, seeded, deveined and chopped (wear gloves to prevent irritation)

2 teaspoons ground cumin

2 teaspoons chili powder

¹/₂ teaspoon dried oregano

Eight 6" fat-free flour tortillas, warmed

2 cups shredded lettuce

1 tomato, chopped

1. Spray a large nonstick skillet with nonstick cooking spray; heat. Add the turkey, onion and garlic; cook, stirring as needed, until the turkey is browned and the onion is softened, about 5 minutes.

2. Add the beans, bell pepper, tomato sauce, jalapeño, cumin, chili powder and oregano; bring to a boil. Reduce the heat and simmer, uncovered, stirring as needed, until the flavors are blended, 10–15 minutes.

3. Top the tortillas with the turkey mixture, lettuce and tomato; roll up and serve.

PER SERVING: 432 Calories, 2 g Total Fat, 0 g Saturated Fat, 53 mg Cholesterol, 756 mg Sodium, 71 g Total Carbohydrate, 6 g Dietary Fiber, 33 g Protein, 67 mg Calcium.

SERVING PROVIDES: 2 Breads, 1 Fruit/Vegetable, 3 Protein/Milks.

POINTS PER SERVING: 8.

Turkey Tortilla Casserole

MAKES 4 SERVINGS

Pat Unger
Wausau, Wisconsin

Pat, her husband and daughter follow the Weight Watchers food plan. Because of dishes like this hearty Southwestern turkey casserole, everybody's succeeding with their weight loss efforts and nobody feels deprived.

2 teaspoons canola oil

1 green bell pepper, seeded and chopped

1 onion, chopped

1/2 pound ground skinless turkey breast

One 14 1/2-ounce can Cajun-style stewed tomatoes

1 cup fat-free refried beans

One 4-ounce can chopped green chiles, rinsed and drained

Six 6" corn tortillas, quartered

1/3 cup shredded reduced-fat Monterey Jack cheese

1. Preheat the oven to 350° F.

2. In a large nonstick skillet, heat the oil. Add the pepper and onion; cook, stirring as needed, until softened, about 5 minutes.

3. Add the turkey and cook, stirring as needed, until browned, about 5 minutes. Stir in the tomatoes, beans and chiles; bring to boil. Reduce the heat and simmer, uncovered, stirring frequently, until slightly thickened, about 5 minutes.

4. Spoon one-third of the turkey mixture onto the bottom of a 10 × 6" baking pan. Arrange half of the tortillas evenly over the top. Repeat the layering once more, ending with the turkey mixture. Sprinkle evenly with the cheese. Bake, covered, 20 minutes. Uncover and bake until heated through and golden, about 10 minutes longer.

PER SERVING: 291 Calories, 5 g Total Fat, 2 g Saturated Fat, 42 mg Cholesterol, 774 mg Sodium, 38 g Total Carbohydrate, 6 g Dietary Fiber, 24 g Protein, 202 mg Calcium.

SERVING PROVIDES: 2 Breads, 1 Fruit/Vegetable, 3 Protein/Milks, 1 Fat.

POINTS PER SERVING: 5.

Vegetable-Turkey Pizza

MAKES 8 SERVINGS

Maria Stavropoulos
Windsor, Connecticut

As an attorney with a hectic lifestyle, Maria was too busy to notice the pounds creep up on her. Once she did, however, she joined Weight Watchers and made some serious changes. "This recipe," she writes, "evolved out of my desire to incorporate more vegetables into my main meals, while keeping things simple yet tasty."

¼ pound ground skinless turkey breast

1 onion, thinly sliced

4 garlic cloves, minced

One 9-ounce package frozen artichoke hearts, thawed

1½ cups sliced mushrooms

One 8-ounce can tomato sauce (no salt added)

1 green bell pepper, seeded and diced

1 tablespoon rinsed drained capers

1 teaspoon dried basil

1 teaspoon dried oregano

One 12" baked pizza crust shell

1½ cups shredded nonfat mozzarella cheese

1. Preheat the oven to 375° F.

2. Spray a large nonstick skillet with nonstick cooking spray; heat. Add the turkey, onion and garlic; cook, stirring as needed, until the turkey is browned and the onion is softened, about 5 minutes.

3. Add the artichokes, mushrooms, tomato sauce, pepper, capers, basil and oregano; bring to a boil. Reduce the heat and simmer, uncovered, stirring as needed, until the vegetables are softened, 8–10 minutes.

4. Place the pizza crust shell on a baking sheet. With a slotted spoon, transfer the turkey-vegetable mixture to the flatbread. Cook the liquid remaining in the skillet 2 minutes, until it reduces to about 2 tablespoons; pour the liquid evenly over the vegetables. Sprinkle evenly with the cheese, and bake until the cheese is melted, 15–18 minutes.

PER SERVING: 215 Calories, 2 g Total Fat, 0 g Saturated Fat, 11 mg Cholesterol, 477 mg Sodium, 35 g Total Carbohydrate, 5 g Dietary Fiber, 16 g Protein, 173 mg Calcium.

SERVING PROVIDES: 2 Breads, 1 Fruit/Vegetable, 1 Protein/Milk.

POINTS PER SERVING: 3.

One-Dish Turkey with Stuffing

MAKES 4 SERVINGS

Lana M. Wraith
N. Massapequa, New York

Lana came up with this festive turkey dish so that she could
"eat something really good for my body instead of shoveling in fast food."

Four 3-ounce skinless
  boneless turkey cutlets

3 tablespoons fat-free
  Italian salad dressing

2 celery stalks, sliced

2 onions, chopped

One 8-ounce package
  herb-seasoned stuffing
  mix

2 apples, cored and diced

¼ cup raisins

1. In a gallon-size sealable plastic bag, combine the turkey and salad dressing. Seal the bag, squeezing out the air; turn to coat the turkey. Refrigerate at least 2 hours or overnight, turning the bag occasionally.

2. Preheat the oven to 350° F. Spray a 12 × 8" baking pan with nonstick cooking spray.

3. Spray a large nonstick saucepan with nonstick cooking spray; heat. Add the turkey and marinade; cook until lightly browned, about 3 minutes on each side. Transfer to a plate.

4. Spray the same saucepan with more nonstick cooking spray. Add the celery and onions; sauté until softened, about 5 minutes. Stir in the stuffing mix, apples, raisins, and 1½ cups hot water. Transfer to the pan and top with the turkey. Bake, covered, 15 minutes. Uncover and bake until heated through, about 5 minutes longer.

PER SERVING: 400 Calories, 4 g Total Fat, 0 g Saturated Fat, 53 mg Cholesterol, 986 mg Sodium, 64 g Total Carbohydrate, 3 g Dietary Fiber, 28 g Protein, 111 mg Calcium.

SERVING PROVIDES: 2 Breads, 2 Fruit/Vegetables, 2 Protein/Milks.

POINTS PER SERVING: 8.

Turkey Cordon Bleu

MAKES 4 SERVINGS

Rose Marie Cullen
Springfield, Ohio

A master leader for Weight Watchers for almost 20 years, Rose Marie reached
her own weight goal more than 25 years ago. Turkey Cordon Bleu is
one favorite way of maintaining her target weight.

1 tablespoon all-purpose flour

1/4 teaspoon freshly ground black pepper

1/4 teaspoon poultry seasoning

Four 3-ounce skinless boneless turkey breast cutlets

1 tablespoon olive oil

1 cup thinly sliced mushrooms

1 onion, chopped

1/4 cup chopped lean ham

Two 3/4-ounce part-skim mozzarella cheese slices, halved

1/4 cup canned pimientos, julienned

1. Preheat the oven to 350° F. Spray an 8" square baking pan with nonstick cooking spray.

2. In a gallon-size sealable plastic bag, combine the flour, pepper and poultry seasoning. Add the turkey; shake to coat.

3. In a large nonstick skillet, heat the oil. Add the turkey and cook until lightly browned, about 2 minutes on each side. Transfer to the baking pan.

4. In the same skillet, combine the mushrooms, onion and ham; cook, stirring constantly, until softened, about 5 minutes. Spoon evenly over the turkey; top each cutlet with a cheese slice. Bake until the turkey is cooked through, about 15 minutes. Serve, garnished with the pimiento strips.

PER SERVING: 186 Calories, 6 g Total Fat, 2 g Saturated Fat, 63 mg Cholesterol, 180 mg Sodium, 5 g Total Carbohydrate, 1 g Dietary Fiber, 26 g Protein, 85 mg Calcium.

SERVING PROVIDES: 3 Protein/Milks, 1 Fat.

POINTS PER SERVING: 4.

Turkey Pie

MAKES 4 SERVINGS

Mary C. Hansen
St. Louis, Missouri

Mary, an active grandmother, won first prize from a local newspaper with the original recipe for this turkey pie. Her updated version, revised according to Weight Watchers guidelines, turned out to be the hit of a recent potluck shower she attended.

6 sheets phyllo dough (about 4 ounces), thawed if frozen

1 teaspoon unsalted stick margarine

1 onion, chopped

3 tablespoons all-purpose flour

2 cups skim milk

One 1-pound package frozen mixed vegetables (broccoli, cauliflower and carrots), thawed

2 cups diced cooked skinless turkey breast

1 cup sliced mushrooms

1 packet instant low-sodium chicken broth and seasoning mix

1/3 cup shredded nonfat cheddar cheese

(See photo.)

1. Preheat the oven to 375° F. Cover the phyllo dough with a damp towel and plastic wrap to prevent drying.

2. In a large nonstick saucepan, melt the margarine. Add the onion and cook, stirring as needed, until softened, about 5 minutes.

3. Add the flour and cook, stirring constantly, until the onion is coated with the flour, about 1 minute. Gradually stir in the milk; cook, stirring constantly, until the mixture boils and thickens, 4–5 minutes. Add the mixed vegetables, turkey, mushrooms and broth mix; return to a boil, stirring as needed. Remove from the heat and stir in the cheese.

4. Pour the mixture into a 9" square baking pan. Fold each phyllo sheet in half and place, one at a time, on top of the mixture, spraying each sheet lightly with nonstick cooking spray, including the top layer. Tuck under the overlapping edges. Bake until golden, about 30 minutes. Let stand 10 minutes before serving.

PER SERVING: 294 Calories, 4 g Total Fat, 1 g Saturated Fat, 51 mg Cholesterol, 334 mg Sodium, 35 g Total Carbohydrate, 4 g Dietary Fiber, 29 g Protein, 287 mg Calcium.

SERVING PROVIDES: 1 Bread, 1 Fruit/Vegetable, 3 Protein/Milks.

POINTS PER SERVING: 5.

Hawaiian Turkey Stir-Fry

MAKES 4 SERVINGS

Kim Berge
Wetaskiwin, Alberta, Canada

Have some leftover turkey you don't know what to do with? Try this vibrant stir-fry dish, which Kim created out of a recipe she found. "I had few of the main ingredients, so I took what I had in the fridge and made something better and healthier!"

1 teaspoon canola oil

2 carrots, julienned

2 celery stalks, sliced

2 onions, chopped

2 tablespoons all-purpose flour

1 cup low-sodium chicken broth

2 cups cubed cooked skinless turkey breasts

2 cups sliced mushrooms

One 20-ounce can unsweetened pineapple chunks (reserve juice)

1 teaspoon dried thyme leaves

1/4 teaspoon dried sage

4 cups hot cooked brown rice

1. In a large nonstick skillet, heat the oil. Add the carrots, celery and onions; cook, stirring as needed, until softened, 6–8 minutes.

2. In a small bowl, combine the flour with 2 tablespoons cold water; mix to a smooth paste. Stir in the broth; mix until smooth and pour into the skillet. Cook, stirring constantly, until the mixture boils and thickens, 2–3 minutes. Stir in the turkey, mushrooms, pineapple and its juice, the thyme and sage; bring to a boil. Reduce the heat and simmer, covered, until heated through, 3–4 minutes. Serve the rice, topped with the turkey mixture.

PER SERVING: 460 Calories, 4 g Total Fat, 1 g Saturated Fat, 48 mg Cholesterol, 101 mg Sodium, 82 g Total Carbohydrate, 7 g Dietary Fiber, 26 g Protein, 88 mg Calcium.

SERVING PROVIDES: 2 Breads, 3 Fruit/Vegetables, 2 Protein/Milks.

POINTS PER SERVING: 8.

Penne with Broccoli Rabe and Hot Turkey Sausage

MAKES 4 SERVINGS

Marie A. Geocos
Dumont, New Jersey

Mama mia, has Marie ever come up with one spicy pasta sauce!
Here's authentic Italian flavor rich enough to satisfy even a native Neapolitan.
Complete the meal with a Caesar salad with reduced-calorie dressing.

2 teaspoons olive oil

4 hot Italian turkey
  sausages, casings removed

2 garlic cloves, minced

1 cup low-sodium chicken
  broth

1/4 teaspoon crushed red
  pepper flakes

1 bunch broccoli rabe,
  cleaned and chopped
  (about 8 cups)

4 cups hot cooked penne

2 tablespoons grated
  Parmesan cheese

1. In a large nonstick skillet, heat the oil. Add the sausages and garlic; cook, stirring as needed, until the sausages are browned and crumbled, 6–8 minutes.

2. Add the broth and pepper flakes; bring to a boil, scraping up the browned bits from the bottom of the skillet. Stir in the broccoli rabe; reduce the heat and simmer, covered, stirring as needed, until the broccoli rabe is wilted, 5–6 minutes. Serve the penne, topped with the sausage mixture; sprinkle with the cheese.

PER SERVING: 370 Calories, 11 g Total Fat, 3 g Saturated Fat, 33 mg Cholesterol, 514 mg Sodium, 49 g Total Carbohydrate, 6 g Dietary Fiber, 22 g Protein, 162 mg Calcium.

SERVING PROVIDES: 2 Breads, 2 Fruit/Vegetables, 2 Protein/Milks, 1 Fat.

POINTS PER SERVING: 7.

Noodles with Turkey Sausage and Cabbage

MAKES 4 SERVINGS

Gile M. Kirk
Corona, California

*This hearty, flavor-rich noodle dish is much
more than the mere sum of its parts.*

4 hot or sweet Italian
turkey sausages, cut
into 1" pieces

1 carrot, chopped

1 onion, chopped

1 celery stalk, thinly sliced

2 garlic cloves, minced

3 cups chopped cabbage

One 14½-ounce can diced
tomatoes (no salt added)

1 cup low-sodium chicken
broth

¼ teaspoon freshly ground
black pepper

2 cups hot cooked egg
noodles

1. Spray a large nonstick skillet with nonstick cooking spray; heat. Add the sausages and cook, stirring as needed, until almost cooked through, about 5 minutes. Add the carrot, onion, celery and garlic; cook, stirring as needed, until softened, about 5 minutes.

2. Add the cabbage, tomatoes, broth and pepper; bring to a boil. Reduce the heat and simmer, covered, until the sausages are cooked through and the vegetables are tender, about 10 minutes. Serve the noodles, topped with the sausage and vegetable mixture.

PER SERVING: 235 Calories, 8 g Total Fat, 2 g Saturated Fat, 49 mg Cholesterol, 443 mg Sodium, 28 g Total Carbohydrate, 4 g Dietary Fiber, 15 g Protein, 96 mg Calcium.

SERVING PROVIDES: 1 Bread, 2 Fruit/Vegetables, 1 Protein/Milk.

POINTS PER SERVING: 5.

$\mathcal{L}$inguine with Turkey Sausage

MAKES 4 SERVINGS

Katherine J. Newman
Zionsville, Indiana

"The first time I joined Weight Watchers, I had just had my first baby; I joined the first Monday of the new year. That baby will soon be 27 and has three siblings," writes Katherine, who credits Weight Watchers with helping her through those busy years. This tasty and easy dish springs from her experience and creativity.

2 teaspoons olive oil

4 hot or sweet Italian turkey sausages, casings removed

1 onion, chopped

One 14^1/$_2$-ounce can Italian-style stewed tomatoes

1 green bell pepper, seeded and diced

2 celery stalks, chopped

4 cups hot cooked linguine

2 tablespoons grated Parmesan cheese

1. In a large nonstick skillet, heat the oil. Add the sausages and onion; cook, stirring as needed, until the sausages are browned and crumbled and the onion is softened, 6–8 minutes.

2. Add the tomatoes, pepper and celery; bring to a boil. Reduce the heat and simmer, covered, stirring as needed, until the flavors are blended and the vegetables are tender, about 10 minutes. Serve the linguine, topped with the sausage mixture; sprinkle with the cheese.

PER SERVING: 353 Calories, 9 g Total Fat, 2 g Saturated Fat, 30 mg Cholesterol, 837 mg Sodium, 51 g Total Carbohydrate, 5 g Dietary Fiber, 17 g Protein, 52 mg Calcium.

SERVING PROVIDES: 2 Breads, 1 Fruit/Vegetable, 2 Protein/Milks, 1 Fat.

POINTS PER SERVING: 7.

CHAPTER
6

Seafood

Florentine Orange Roughy

MAKES 6 SERVINGS

Barbara M. Friedrich
Santa Barbara, California

*Barbara, a diabetic, has difficulty finding recipes that fit her regimen. This flavorful entrée
fits in with her dietary needs and works beautifully served with brown rice.*

18 cherry tomatoes, halved

8 scallions, sliced

¹/₄ cup fresh lemon juice

3 cups sliced mushrooms

3 garlic cloves, minced

One 10-ounce package
frozen chopped spinach,
thawed and squeezed dry

2 tablespoons minced dill

¹/₄ teaspoon salt

Six 4-ounce orange roughy
or flounder fillets

12 lemon slices

1. Preheat the oven to 425° F. In a medium bowl, combine the tomatoes, scallions and lemon juice.

2. Spray a large nonstick skillet with nonstick cooking spray; heat. Add the mushrooms and garlic; cook, stirring constantly, until softened, about 5 minutes. Remove from the heat and stir in the spinach, dill and salt.

3. Divide the spinach mixture among 6 double layers of foil. Place 1 piece of fish on top of each spinach mound; top with the tomato mixture and the lemon slices. Make packets by bringing the 2 sides of the foil up to meet in the center and folding the edges over, then folding the edges of each end together. Allowing room for the packet to expand, crimp the edges. Place the packets on a baking sheet and bake until the fish is opaque, 18–20 minutes. Open the packets carefully when testing for doneness, as steam will escape.

PER SERVING: 182 Calories, 9 g Total Fat, 0 g Saturated Fat, 23 mg Cholesterol, 203 mg Sodium, 9 g Total Carbohydrate, 2 g Dietary Fiber, 20 g Protein, 79 mg Calcium.

SERVING PROVIDES: 1 Fruit/Vegetable, 2 Protein/Milks.

POINTS PER SERVING: 4.

$\mathcal{G}$reek Baked Fish with Vegetables

MAKES 4 SERVINGS

Sharon Stavropoulos
Wilmette, Illinois

"This Plaki—a traditional dish from Salonica—is an adaptation of a classical way to cook fish in Greece," writes Sharon, whose husband was born in that country. "Enjoy this great-tasting dish and imagine dining at a harborside taverna on a Greek island!"

1 tablespoon olive oil

2 onions, chopped

5 garlic cloves, minced

One 28-ounce can whole tomatoes (no salt added), coarsely chopped

4 carrots, thinly sliced

1 green bell pepper, seeded and chopped

1/4 cup dry white wine

2 teaspoons dried oregano

1/2 cup minced flat-leaf parsley

1 1/4 pounds fish fillets (perch, orange roughy, cod or flounder)

Freshly ground black pepper, to taste

1. Preheat the oven to 400° F.

2. In a large nonstick saucepan or Dutch oven, heat the oil. Add the onions and garlic; cook, stirring as needed, until softened, about 5 minutes.

3. Add the tomatoes, carrots, bell pepper, wine and oregano; bring to a boil. Reduce the heat and simmer, uncovered, stirring as needed, until the sauce is slightly thickened, about 20 minutes. Stir in the parsley.

4. Ladle half of the sauce into a 2 1/2-quart casserole; top with the fish. Ladle the remaining sauce on top. Bake until the fish is opaque, 15–20 minutes. Serve, sprinkled with the black pepper.

PER SERVING: 283 Calories, 6 g Total Fat, 1 g Saturated Fat, 128 mg Cholesterol, 155 mg Sodium, 26 g Total Carbohydrate, 6 g Dietary Fiber, 31 g Protein, 230 mg Calcium.

SERVING PROVIDES: 2 Fruit/Vegetables, 2 Protein/Milks, 1 Fat.

POINTS PER SERVING: 5.

Grilled Halibut with Nectarine Salsa

MAKES 4 SERVINGS

Diane Barnette
Sparks, Nevada

"This dish is terrific on hot summer days and reminds me of the wonderful restaurant grills along the California coast," says Diane, whose home is in the Nevada desert.

3 nectarines, pitted and diced

¼ red onion, chopped

1 jalapeño pepper, seeded, deveined and chopped (wear gloves to prevent irritation)

2 tablespoons minced cilantro

1 tablespoon fresh lemon juice

1 teaspoon honey

Four 6-ounce halibut steaks

½ teaspoon freshly ground black pepper

Cilantro sprigs

1. Spray the broiler or grill rack with nonstick cooking spray; set aside. Preheat the broiler, or prepare the grill.

2. In a medium nonreactive bowl, combine the nectarines, onion, jalapeño, minced cilantro, lemon juice and honey; toss to combine.

3. Sprinkle both sides of the halibut steaks with the black pepper. Broil or grill the halibut steaks 5" from the heat until the fish is opaque, 5–6 minutes on each side. Serve, topped with the nectarine salsa; garnish with the cilantro.

PER SERVING: 236 Calories, 4 g Total Fat, 1 g Saturated Fat, 54 mg Cholesterol, 93 mg Sodium, 12 g Total Carbohydrate, 1 g Dietary Fiber, 36 g Protein, 88 mg Calcium.

SERVING PROVIDES: 1 Fruit/Vegetable, 3 Protein/Milks.

POINTS PER SERVING: 5.

Poached Fillet of Sole

MAKES 2 SERVINGS

Donna-Marie Fieldsa-Fowler
Brooklyn, New York

Donna-Marie and her husband have drastically cut down on meat in their diets.
They love this simple, flavorful fish dish, which they usually enjoy over
rice and with a fresh green salad.

2 teaspoons olive oil

1/2 onion, finely chopped

3 shallots, thinly sliced

1 garlic clove, minced

1/4 cup dry white wine

2 teaspoons fresh lemon
   juice

1 teaspoon dried tarragon

1 bay leaf

1/8 teaspoon freshly ground
   black pepper

Two 4-ounce sole or
   flounder fillets

1 1/2 tomatoes, chopped

1. In a large nonstick skillet, heat the oil. Add the onion, shallots and garlic; cook, stirring as needed, until softened, about 5 minutes.

2. Add the wine, lemon juice, tarragon, bay leaf and pepper. Add the fish, gently spooning the onion mixture over the fillets. Reduce the heat and simmer, until partially cooked, about 3 minutes.

3. Gently stir in the tomatoes; simmer, covered, until the fish is opaque and flakes easily when tested with a fork, 2–3 minutes. Discard the bay leaf. Serve, topped with the sauce.

PER SERVING: 254 Calories, 7 g Total Fat, 1 g Saturated Fat, 68 mg Cholesterol, 132 mg Sodium, 13 g Total Carbohydrate, 2 g Dietary Fiber, 29 g Protein, 64 mg Calcium.

SERVING PROVIDES: 1 Fruit/Vegetable, 2 Protein/Milks, 1 Fat.

POINTS PER SERVING: 5.

Peppered Lemon Swordfish Steaks

MAKES 4 SERVINGS

Theresa Sylvester
Columbus, Ohio

*Fragrant with fresh herbs, this delicious swordfish is good served with a
rice dish and a green salad. Theresa gives this dish proudly to her "civilian" friends
("those who don't have to worry about their weight"), and they just gobble it up.
The packets can be prepared early in the day or the day before and
kept in the refrigerator.*

1¼ pounds swordfish steak
(1" thick), cut into
4 equal pieces

2 lemons, thinly sliced

½ red onion, thinly sliced

2 tablespoons minced fresh
rosemary leaves, or 2 teaspoons dried

1 tablespoon minced fresh
thyme leaves, or 1 tea-
spoon dried

1 teaspoon coarsely ground
black pepper

¼ teaspoon salt

(See photo.)

1. Preheat the oven to 500° F, or prepare the grill.

2. Place each piece of fish on the center of 4 double layers of foil. Top each evenly with the lemons, onion, rosemary, thyme, pepper and salt. Make packets by bringing
the 2 sides of the foil up to meet in the center and folding the edges over, then folding the edges of each end
together. Allowing room for the packets to expand,
crimp the edges. If baking, place the packets on a baking sheet. Bake or grill until the fish is opaque, 10–12
minutes. Open the packets carefully when testing for
doneness, as steam will escape.

PER SERVING: 189 Calories, 6 g Total Fat, 2 g Saturated Fat,
55 mg Cholesterol, 266 mg Sodium, 7 g Total Carbohydrate,
0 g Dietary Fiber, 29 g Protein, 57 mg Calcium.

SERVING PROVIDES: 2 Protein/Milks.

POINTS PER SERVING: 4.

$\mathcal{S}$almon with Herb-Shrimp Sauce

MAKES 4 SERVINGS

Marilyn Guild
Orinda, California

This savory salmon recipe fits in with Marilyn's weight-loss program, yet fills her husband and daughter's quotient for healthful, flavorsome fare.

One 12-ounce salmon fillet

¼ cup dry white wine

2 teaspoons reduced-calorie margarine

2 tablespoons all-purpose flour

¾ cup low-sodium chicken broth

2 tablespoons fresh lemon juice

¼ pound cooked peeled small shrimp

1 tablespoon minced fresh oregano, or ½ teaspoon dried

1 tablespoon minced fresh rosemary leaves, or ½ teaspoon dried

½ teaspoon coarsely ground black pepper

Fresh rosemary sprigs

1. Preheat the oven to 350° F. Spray an 8" square baking pan with nonstick cooking spray.

2. Place the salmon in the pan; add the wine. Bake until the fish is opaque and flakes easily when tested with a fork, 15–20 minutes.

3. In a medium nonstick saucepan, melt the margarine. Add the flour and cook, stirring constantly, about 1 minute. Gradually stir in the broth and lemon juice; cook, stirring constantly, until the mixture boils and thickens, 2–3 minutes. Add the shrimp, oregano, rosemary and pepper; cook, stirring as needed, until heated through, about 2 minutes.

4. Place the salmon on a platter. Pour the juices from the baking pan into the sauce; cook, stirring as needed, until heated through, about 1 minute. Pour the sauce over the salmon and serve, garnished with the rosemary.

PER SERVING: 192 Calories, 7 g Total Fat, 1 g Saturated Fat, 103 mg Cholesterol, 144 mg Sodium, 4 g Total Carbohydrate, 0 g Dietary Fiber, 24 g Protein, 33 mg Calcium.

SERVING PROVIDES: 2 Protein/Milks.

POINTS PER SERVING: 4.

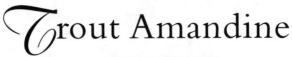rout Amandine

MAKES 2 SERVINGS

Estelle Sassaman
Waldoboro, Maine

Estelle, a writing teacher at the University of Maine at Augusta, has composed a super version of a classic. "I created it on a whim," she says, "but it's a keeper!"

Two ¹/₂-pound whole trout, cleaned

2 tablespoons fresh lemon juice

1 teaspoon reduced-calorie margarine

¹/₂ teaspoon paprika

2 tablespoons minced flat-leaf parsley

1 tablespoon sliced unblanched almonds, toasted★

2 lemon wedges

1. Preheat the oven to 350° F. Spray a 13 × 9" baking pan with nonstick cooking spray.

2. Place the trout, skin-side down, in the pan. Sprinkle with the lemon juice; dot with the margarine and sprinkle with the paprika. Bake, covered, about 5 minutes. Uncover and bake until the fish is opaque, about 5 minutes longer. Sprinkle with the parsley and almonds; serve, garnished with the lemon.

PER SERVING: 290 Calories, 14 g Total Fat, 2 g Saturated Fat, 99 mg Cholesterol, 114 mg Sodium, 4 g Total Carbohydrate, 0 g Dietary Fiber, 36 g Protein, 97 mg Calcium.

SERVING PROVIDES: 2 Protein/Milks, 1 Fat.

POINTS PER SERVING: 7.

★*To toast the almonds, place a small nonstick skillet over medium heat. Add the almonds and cook, stirring constantly, until lightly browned, 2–3 minutes.*

Zesty Flounder

MAKES 2 SERVINGS

Pauline Philipps-Zabel
Evanston, Illinois

Pauline likes to serve this simple, savory fish dish with
Spanish rice and steamed green beans.

2 tablespoons minced
cilantro

2 tablespoons Dijon
mustard

¼ cup + 2 tablespoons
plain dried bread crumbs

Two 8-ounce flounder or
sole fillets

3 tablespoons salsa

2 tablespoons grated
Parmesan cheese

1. Preheat the oven to 350° F. Spray a 12 × 8" baking pan with nonstick cooking spray.

2. On a dinner plate, combine the cilantro, mustard and 2 tablespoons water. Place the bread crumbs on a second dinner plate. Dip each fillet in the mustard mixture, then in the bread crumbs, coating both sides.

3. Place the fillets in the pan. Top each with the salsa, and sprinkle with the cheese. Bake until the fish is opaque, about 20 minutes.

PER SERVING: 335 Calories, 6 g Total Fat, 2 g Saturated Fat, 113 mg Cholesterol, 917 mg Sodium, 16 g Total Carbohydrate, 1 g Dietary Fiber, 47 g Protein, 157 mg Calcium.

SERVING PROVIDES: 1 Bread, 3 Protein/Milks.

POINTS PER SERVING: 7.

Curried Shrimp

MAKES 4 SERVINGS

Leo Berg
Atascadero, California

*Leo and his wife, both caterers, once served this recipe at a wedding reception
for 200 guests. To nobody's surprise, it was a huge hit.*

2 teaspoons vegetable oil

1 green bell pepper, seeded
  and chopped

1 onion, chopped

1 garlic clove, minced

2 tablespoons all-purpose
  flour

1 tablespoon curry powder,
  or to taste

1/4 teaspoon ground ginger

1/4 teaspoon salt

1 1/2 cups low-sodium
  chicken broth

1 pound cooked peeled
  medium shrimp

4 cups hot cooked brown
  rice

1. In a large nonstick saucepan, heat the oil. Add the pepper, onion and garlic; cook, stirring as needed, until softened, about 5 minutes.

2. Add the flour, curry, ginger and salt; cook, stirring constantly, until fragrant, about 30 seconds. Add the broth; cook, stirring constantly, until the mixture comes to a boil and thickens, about 2 minutes.

3. Add the shrimp and cook, stirring as needed, until heated through, about 3 minutes. Serve the rice, topped with the shrimp mixture.

PER SERVING: 395 Calories, 6 g Total Fat, 1 g Saturated Fat, 223 mg Cholesterol, 441 mg Sodium, 53 g Total Carbohydrate, 5 g Dietary Fiber, 31 g Protein, 86 mg Calcium.

SERVING PROVIDES: 2 Breads, 1 Fruit/Vegetable, 2 Protein/Milks, 1 Fat.

POINTS PER SERVING: 7.

Ginger Shrimp Stir-Fry

MAKES 4 SERVINGS

Toni Gerdes
Shawnee Mission, Kansas

When Toni cooks, she likes flavors that are assertive and clear. This bright shrimp stir-fry dish brings a definite taste of Asia into the kitchen.

1 teaspoon olive oil

1¼ pounds medium shrimp, peeled and deveined

2 carrots, julienned

2 tablespoons minced peeled gingerroot

3 garlic cloves, minced

2 cups trimmed snow peas

½ cup low-sodium chicken broth

2 teaspoons reduced-sodium soy sauce

1 teaspoon Asian sesame oil

4 cups hot cooked brown rice

2 tablespoons sesame seeds, toasted★

(See photo.)

1. In a large nonstick skillet, heat the olive oil. Add the shrimp; cook, stirring as needed, until pink, about 3 minutes. Transfer to a plate and keep warm.

2. Add the carrots to the skillet; cook, stirring as needed, until tender-crisp, 4–5 minutes. Add the ginger and garlic; cook, stirring constantly, until the garlic is lightly browned, about 1 minute. Reduce the heat and simmer, covered, until heated through, about 1 minute longer.

3. Add the shrimp, snow peas, broth, soy sauce, and sesame oil; bring to a boil, stirring as needed. Reduce the heat and simmer, covered, until heated through, about 1 minute longer. Serve the rice, topped with the shrimp mixture; sprinkle with the sesame seeds.

PER SERVING: 446 Calories, 9 g Total Fat, 1 g Saturated Fat, 175 mg Cholesterol, 315 mg Sodium, 59 g Total Carbohydrate, 7 g Dietary Fiber, 32 g Protein, 175 mg Calcium.

SERVING PROVIDES: 2 Breads, 1 Fruit/Vegetable, 2 Protein/Milks, 1 Fat.

POINTS PER SERVING: 8.

★*To toast the sesame seeds, place a small nonstick skillet over medium heat. Add the sesame seeds and cook, stirring constantly, until lightly browned, 2–3 minutes.*

Penne with Shrimp and Mushrooms

MAKES 4 SERVINGS

Koreena M. Taylor
Albuquerque, New Mexico

"I truly love seafood and had to find a way for shrimp to fit my new way of eating right," Koreena writes. Well, she did it!

1 tablespoon unsalted stick margarine

1 onion, chopped

4 garlic cloves, minced

1¼ pounds medium shrimp, peeled and deveined

4 cups sliced mushrooms

½ cup minced parsley

2 tablespoons fresh lemon juice

¼ teaspoon coarsely ground black pepper

4 cups hot cooked penne

1. In a large nonstick skillet, melt the margarine. Add the onion and garlic; cook, stirring as needed, until softened, about 5 minutes.

2. Add the shrimp and mushrooms; cook, stirring as needed, until the shrimp turn pink and the mushrooms have released their liquid, 6–8 minutes. Stir in the parsley, lemon juice and pepper. Serve the penne, topped with the shrimp mixture.

PER SERVING: 379 Calories, 6 g Total Fat, 1 g Saturated Fat, 174 mg Cholesterol, 178 mg Sodium, 48 g Total Carbohydrate, 4 g Dietary Fiber, 32 g Protein, 94 mg Calcium.

SERVING PROVIDES: 2 Breads, 1 Fruit/Vegetable, 2 Protein/Milks, 1 Fat.

POINTS PER SERVING: 7.

Shrimp and Penne with Bell Pepper Sauce

MAKES 4 SERVINGS

Joel Riley
Paso Robles, California

*"I added different spices until I was happy with the taste," says Joel.
Serve this zesty shrimp sauce over any tubular pasta and smile!*

4 red bell peppers, roasted★
¹/₂ cup parsley leaves
¹/₄ cup dry white wine
2 garlic cloves
1 teaspoon dried oregano
1 pound large shrimp, peeled and deveined
4 cups hot cooked penne
Freshly ground black pepper, to taste

1. In a blender or food processor, puree the bell peppers, parsley, wine, garlic and oregano.

2. Pour the bell pepper mixture into a medium saucepan; bring to a boil. Add the shrimp. Reduce the heat and simmer, covered, stirring as needed, until the shrimp turn pink, 3–5 minutes. Serve the penne, topped with the shrimp mixture; sprinkle with the black pepper.

PER SERVING: 336 Calories, 3 g Total Fat, 0 g Saturated Fat, 140 mg Cholesterol, 143 mg Sodium, 48 g Total Carbohydrate, 4 g Dietary Fiber, 26 g Protein, 86 mg Calcium.

SERVING PROVIDES: 2 Breads, 1 Fruit/Vegetable, 1 Protein/Milk.

POINTS PER SERVING: 6.

★*To roast the bell peppers, preheat the broiler. Line a baking sheet with foil; place the peppers on the baking sheet. Broil peppers 4-6" from heat, turning frequently with tongs, until the skin is lightly charred on all sides, about 10 minutes. Transfer to a paper bag; fold the bag closed and steam 10 minutes. Peel, seed and devein the peppers over the sink to drain the juices.*

Shrimp with Feta and Tomatoes

MAKES 4 SERVINGS

Bill Spence
Sebastopol, California

Math teacher Bill Spence juggled the numbers to come up with this festive low-fat seafood dish, a streamlined version of a fattening favorite from a local restaurant.

1 teaspoon olive oil

4 scallions, sliced

2 garlic cloves, minced

3 tomatoes, chopped

1/4 cup dry white wine

1 tablespoon fresh lemon juice

1/2 teaspoon dried oregano

1/4 teaspoon freshly ground black pepper

1 pound large shrimp, peeled and deveined

1/3 cup feta cheese, crumbled

1/4 cup minced flat-leaf parsley

4 cups hot cooked brown basmati rice

1. In a large nonstick skillet, heat the oil. Add the scallions and garlic; cook, stirring as needed, until softened, 2–3 minutes.

2. Add the tomatoes, wine, lemon juice, oregano and pepper; cook, stirring as needed, until the tomatoes are just softened, about 2 minutes. Add the shrimp; reduce the heat and simmer, covered, until the shrimp turn pink, 3–5 minutes. Remove from the heat and stir in the cheese and parsley. Serve the rice, topped with the shrimp mixture.

PER SERVING: 395 Calories, 7 g Total Fat, 3 g Saturated Fat, 150 mg Cholesterol, 284 mg Sodium, 53 g Total Carbohydrate, 5 g Dietary Fiber, 27 g Protein, 146 mg Calcium.

SERVING PROVIDES: 2 Breads, 1 Fruit/Vegetable, 2 Protein/Milks.

POINTS PER SERVING: 7.

Shrimp and Vegetable Creole

MAKES 6 SERVINGS

Contessa N. Skelton
Amarillo, Texas

*Inspired by the seasonal bounty at the market, Contessa put together this
colorful shrimp and vegetable all-in-one dish. Having almost reached her goal weight, she says,
"With recipes like this, anyone can do it!"*

1 tablespoon vegetable oil

2 onions, chopped

1 celery stalk, chopped

1/2 green bell pepper,
seeded and chopped

1/2 red bell pepper, seeded
and chopped

1/2 yellow bell pepper,
seeded and chopped

2 garlic cloves, minced

One 14 1/2-ounce can diced
tomatoes (no salt added)

One 8-ounce can tomato
sauce (no salt added)

2 teaspoons Worcestershire
sauce

1 teaspoon dried oregano

1/2 teaspoon dried thyme
leaves

1/8–1/4 teaspoon cayenne
pepper

1 pound medium shrimp,
peeled and deveined

3 medium zucchini, sliced

6 cups hot cooked white
rice

1. In a large nonstick saucepan or Dutch oven, heat the oil. Add the onions, celery, bell peppers and the garlic; cook, stirring as needed, until softened, 6–8 minutes.

2. Add the tomatoes, tomato sauce, Worcestershire sauce, oregano, thyme and cayenne; bring to a boil. Reduce the heat and cook, stirring as needed, until the sauce is slightly thickened, about 10 minutes.

3. Add the shrimp and zucchini; return to a boil. Reduce the heat and simmer, covered, stirring as needed, until the shrimp turn pink, 5–7 minutes. Serve the rice, topped with the shrimp mixture.

PER SERVING: 423 Calories, 5 g Total Fat, 1 g Saturated Fat, 108 mg Cholesterol, 154 mg Sodium, 72 g Total Carbohydrate, 3 g Dietary Fiber, 23 g Protein, 111 mg Calcium.

SERVING PROVIDES: 2 Breads, 2 Fruit/Vegetables, 1 Protein/Milk, 1 Fat.

POINTS PER SERVING: 8.

Shrimp with Vegetables and Farfalle

MAKES 4 SERVINGS

Kathleen M. Correia
Pawtucket, Rhode Island

*After losing 69 pounds and reaching her goal weight, Kathleen has become
a lifetime member. She enjoys the support and tips she gets from meetings; one tip
she uses often is to adapt her old favorite recipes to fit the Weight Watchers program.
Here is one delicious conversion.*

1 tablespoon olive oil

2 onions, chopped

3 garlic cloves, minced

1 pound shrimp, peeled and deveined

3 medium zucchini, sliced

1 cup low-sodium chicken broth

1 tablespoon dried oregano

1/2 teaspoon freshly ground black pepper

4 cups hot cooked farfalle

2 tomatoes, cut in wedges

2 tablespoons grated Parmesan cheese

1. In a large nonstick skillet, heat the oil. Add the onions and garlic; cook, stirring as needed, until softened, about 5 minutes.

2. Add the shrimp, zucchini, broth, oregano and pepper; bring to a boil. Reduce the heat and simmer, uncovered, stirring as needed, until the shrimp turn pink, 3–5 minutes.

3. Stir in the farfalle and tomatoes; cook, stirring as needed, until heated through, 2–3 minutes. Serve, sprinkled with the cheese.

PER SERVING: 406 Calories, 9 g Total Fat, 2 g Saturated Fat, 135 mg Cholesterol, 269 mg Sodium, 54 g Total Carbohydrate, 5 g Dietary Fiber, 30 g Protein, 186 mg Calcium.

SERVING PROVIDES: 2 Breads, 2 Fruit/Vegetables, 2 Protein/Milks, 1 Fat.

POINTS PER SERVING: 8.

Quick Shrimp Broil

MAKES 2 SERVINGS

Marie A. Geocos
Dumont, New Jersey

Marie is married and has two young children. In her efforts to keep off the pounds, she has created this supereasy, flavorful low-fat version of a favorite shrimp dish she enjoys at a local restaurant. It is perfect with crusty French bread and a green salad.

1 teaspoon extra virgin olive oil

2 garlic cloves, minced

1/2 pound large shrimp, peeled and deveined

1 tomato, coarsely chopped

1/4 cup dry white wine

1/3 cup shredded part-skim mozzarella cheese

1. Preheat the broiler.

2. In a medium ovenproof skillet, heat the oil. Add the garlic and cook, stirring constantly, until lightly browned, about 1 minute.

3. Add the shrimp and tomato; cook, stirring as needed, until the shrimp turn pink, 3–5 minutes. Add the wine and cook 1 minute longer.

4. Sprinkle evenly with the cheese and broil until the cheese is melted and golden, 2–3 minutes.

PER SERVING: 207 Calories, 7 g Total Fat, 3 g Saturated Fat, 152 mg Cholesterol, 234 mg Sodium, 6 g Total Carbohydrate, 1 g Dietary Fiber, 24 g Protein, 181 mg Calcium.

SERVING PROVIDES: 1 Fruit/Vegetable, 2 Protein/Milks, 1 Fat.

POINTS PER SERVING: 5.

*C*rab Enchiladas

MAKES 4 SERVINGS

Angela J. Stanfel
San Bruno, California

*Angela, a businesswoman who coaches a girls' basketball team in her spare time,
makes this dish for friends who love Mexican fare and seafood. So, have the whole enchilada—
two, in fact. You might want to top it with a dab of nonfat sour cream
and serve a salsa-topped salad alongside.*

2 teaspoons canola oil

1 onion, thinly sliced

2 garlic cloves, minced

3/4 pound cooked crab-
meat, picked over and
flaked

One 14 1/2-ounce can diced
tomatoes (no salt added)

1 cup salsa

1/4 teaspoon freshly ground
black pepper

Eight 6" fat-free flour
tortillas

3/4 cup shredded nonfat
cheddar cheese

3/4 cup shredded nonfat
Monterey Jack cheese

1. Preheat the oven to 350° F.

2. In a large nonstick skillet, heat the oil. Add the onion
and garlic; cook, stirring as needed, until softened, about
5 minutes.

3. Stir in the crabmeat, tomatoes, salsa and pepper; bring
to a boil. Reduce the heat and simmer, uncovered, until
the flavors are blended, about 3 minutes.

4. Spread about 1/2 cup of the crab mixture evenly in
the bottom of a 10 × 6" baking pan. Place about 1/3 cup
of the crab mixture on each of the tortillas; roll up and
place them, seam-side down, in the pan. Spoon the
remaining crab mixture evenly on top; sprinkle with the
cheeses. Bake, covered, 25 minutes; uncover and bake
until hot and bubbling and the cheese is golden, about
10 minutes longer.

PER SERVING: 382 Calories, 4 g Total Fat, 0 g Saturated Fat,
87 mg Cholesterol, 1,349 mg Sodium, 48 g Total Carbohydrate,
3 g Dietary Fiber, 36 g Protein, 310 mg Calcium.

SERVING PROVIDES: 2 Breads, 1 Fruit/Vegetable, 2 Protein/Milks,
1 Fat.

POINTS PER SERVING: 7.

Fettuccine with Crab and Tomatoes

MAKES 4 SERVINGS

Jane Szumanski
Las Vegas, Nevada

Jane, a Weight Watchers receptionist in Las Vegas, doesn't gamble when it comes to maintaining her 50-pound weight loss. She hit the jackpot when she came up with this flavorsome pasta recipe, which she serves with a generous salad and some of her husband's homemade fat-free French bread. This dish is especially attractive when it is made with spinach fettuccine.

¹/₂ cup low-sodium chicken broth

1 onion, chopped

3 garlic cloves, minced

8 small plum tomatoes, quartered

¹/₄ cup tomato paste (no salt added)

¹/₄ cup dry white wine

1 teaspoon dried basil

¹/₄ teaspoon freshly ground black pepper

¹/₈ teaspoon cayenne pepper

³/₄ pound cooked crabmeat, picked over and flaked

¹/₄ cup minced parsley

6 ounces fettuccine

4 scallions, sliced

2 tablespoons grated Parmesan cheese

1. In a large nonstick skillet, bring the broth, onion and garlic to a boil. Reduce the heat and simmer, uncovered, stirring as needed, until the onion is softened and most of the liquid has evaporated, about 5 minutes.

2. Add the tomatoes, tomato paste, wine, basil, black pepper and cayenne; cook, stirring as needed, until the tomatoes are softened, 5–6 minutes. Add the crab and parsley; cook, stirring as needed, until heated through, 2–3 minutes.

3. Meanwhile, cook the fettuccine according to package directions. Drain, reserving ¹/₂ cup of the cooking liquid; place the fettuccine in a serving bowl. Immediately add the crab mixture and the cooking liquid; toss to coat. Serve, sprinkled with the scallions and cheese.

PER SERVING: 311 Calories, 3 g Total Fat, 1 g Saturated Fat, 88 mg Cholesterol, 320 mg Sodium, 41 g Total Carbohydrate, 3 g Dietary Fiber, 26 g Protein, 169 mg Calcium.

SERVING PROVIDES: 2 Breads, 1 Fruit/Vegetable, 2 Protein/Milks.

POINTS PER SERVING: 6.

Seafood-Pasta Salad

MAKES 4 SERVINGS

Mary Lewis
Stafford, Texas

*Mary's husband and two young sons enjoy taste-testing her experiments in
new weight-conscious recipes. This creamy pasta salad, which Mary serves
with Melba toast, is one of their favorites.*

¼ cup plain nonfat yogurt

¼ cup nonfat sour cream

1 tablespoon fresh lemon
juice

1 garlic clove, minced

¼ teaspoon freshly ground
black pepper

4 cups cold cooked penne

½ pound cooked crab-
meat, picked over and
flaked

2 cups broccoli florets

1 carrot, diced

4 scallions, thinly sliced

10 pitted small black olives,
sliced

1 teaspoon rinsed drained
capers

1. In a large bowl, combine the yogurt, sour cream, lemon juice, garlic and pepper.

2. Add the penne, crab, broccoli, carrot, scallions, olives and capers; toss to combine. Refrigerate, covered, until chilled, at least 1 hour.

PER SERVING: 317 Calories, 3 g Total Fat, 0 g Saturated Fat, 57 mg Cholesterol, 298 mg Sodium, 49 g Total Carbohydrate, 5 g Dietary Fiber, 23 g Protein, 167 mg Calcium.

SERVING PROVIDES: 2 Breads, 1 Fruit/Vegetable, 1 Protein/Milk.

POINTS PER SERVING: 6.

Seafood Fra Diavolo

MAKES 8 SERVINGS

Tina Marie Fiorito
Wellington, Florida

Tina, a Weight Watchers leader, proudly displays her Italian heritage in this bold and forthright seafood pasta. If fresh crab is beyond your pocketbook, use canned; avoid surimi, since it doesn't hold up well.

2 teaspoons olive oil

4 onions, chopped

4 large garlic cloves, minced

One 28-ounce can crushed tomatoes (no salt added)

Two 8-ounce cans tomato sauce (no salt added)

One 6-ounce can tomato paste (no salt added)

¼ cup dry red wine

1 teaspoon crushed red pepper flakes, or to taste

1 teaspoon dried basil

¼ teaspoon dried oregano

⅛ teaspoon freshly ground black pepper

1 pound bay scallops

¾ pound large shrimp, peeled and deveined

½ pound cooked crabmeat, picked over and flaked

One 12-ounce box capellini (angel-hair pasta)

¼ cup minced parsley

1. In a large Dutch oven, heat the oil. Add the onions and garlic; cook, stirring as needed, until softened, about 5 minutes.

2. Add the tomatoes, tomato sauce, tomato paste, wine, pepper flakes, basil, oregano, black pepper and 1 cup water; bring to a boil. Reduce the heat and simmer, uncovered, until slightly thickened, about 15 minutes.

3. Add the scallops, shrimp and crab; cook, stirring as needed, until the shrimp turn pink, 8–10 minutes.

4. Meanwhile, cook the capellini according to package directions. Serve, topped with the sauce; sprinkle with the parsley.

PER SERVING: 375 Calories, 4 g Total Fat, 1 g Saturated Fat, 112 mg Cholesterol, 306 mg Sodium, 51 g Total Carbohydrate, 5 g Dietary Fiber, 32 g Protein, 146 mg Calcium.

SERVING PROVIDES: 2 Breads, 2 Fruit/Vegetables, 2 Protein/Milks.

POINTS PER SERVING: 7.

Seafood Linguine

MAKES 4 SERVINGS

Edna Stewart
Indianapolis, Indiana

*"Someday," Edna writes, "I will write my own cookbook." If this seafood pasta
is any indication of the caliber of recipes she can devise, we can hardly wait!*

1 tablespoon extra virgin
olive oil

8 scallions, thinly sliced

3 garlic cloves, minced

1/2 pound cooked peeled
medium shrimp

1/2 pound cooked crab-
meat, picked over and
flaked

2 tablespoons dry white
wine

1 tablespoon fresh lemon
juice

1/4 teaspoon crushed red
pepper flakes

1/4 teaspoon dried thyme
leaves

1/4 teaspoon salt

4 cups hot cooked linguine

(See photo.)

1. In a large nonstick skillet, heat the oil. Add the scallions and garlic; cook, stirring constantly, until softened,
2–3 minutes.

2. Add the shrimp, crab, wine, lemon juice, pepper
flakes, thyme and salt; cook, stirring constantly, until
heated through, about 3 minutes. Serve the linguine,
topped with the seafood mixture.

PER SERVING: 356 Calories, 6 g Total Fat, 1 g Saturated Fat,
167 mg Cholesterol, 425 mg Sodium, 42 g Total Carbohydrate,
3 g Dietary Fiber, 30 g Protein, 109 mg Calcium.

SERVING PROVIDES: 2 Breads, 2 Protein/Milks, 1 Fat.

POINTS PER SERVING: 7.

Pasta with Seafood in Lemon Dill Sauce

MAKES 4 SERVINGS

Kimberly Holl
Portola Valley, California

Kimberly loves bicycling—so much so that she cycled from Paris to Rome. She also loves seafood and shares this favorite recipe with us. Don't forget to zest the lemon before you juice it.

2 teaspoons reduced-calorie margarine

2 shallots, finely chopped

1 tablespoon all-purpose flour

1 cup skim milk

10 ounces bay scallops

1/2 pound cooked crab-meat, picked over and flaked

1/4 pound cooked peeled shrimp

2 tablespoons minced dill

1 tablespoon fresh lemon juice

1 teaspoon lemon zest

4 cups hot cooked medium pasta shells

Dill sprigs

1. In a medium nonstick saucepan, melt the margarine. Add the shallots and cook, stirring as needed, until softened, about 2 minutes. Add the flour and cook, stirring constantly, 1 minute. Gradually add the milk and cook, stirring constantly, until the mixture boils and thickens, about 3 minutes.

2. Add the scallops, crab, shrimp, minced dill, lemon juice and zest; cook, stirring as needed, until the scallops are opaque, about 5 minutes. Serve the pasta, topped with the seafood mixture; garnish with the dill sprigs.

PER SERVING: 354 Calories, 4 g Total Fat, 1 g Saturated Fat, 137 mg Cholesterol, 394 mg Sodium, 40 g Total Carbohydrate, 2 g Dietary Fiber, 37 g Protein, 182 mg Calcium.

SERVING PROVIDES: 2 Breads, 3 Protein/Milks.

POINTS PER SERVING: 7.

Scallops and Vegetables over Penne

MAKES 6 SERVINGS

Pirita Krobisch
Suffern, New York

"Some of our best times have been around the dining-room table," Pirita writes,
adding that she first developed this recipe to feed 12 people at her brother's summer home
in Maine. When scallops are too costly, she substitutes shrimp, fish or even chicken.

2 tablespoons olive oil

3 onions, chopped

3 garlic cloves, minced

One 28-ounce can crushed
    tomatoes (no salt added)

2 green bell peppers,
    seeded and chopped

1 medium zucchini,
    chopped

2 pounds sea scallops

1/2 cup low-sodium chicken
    broth

1/4 cup minced basil

2 tablespoons fresh lemon
    juice

6 cups hot cooked penne

1/4 cup minced parsley

1. In a large nonstick skillet, heat the oil. Add the onions and garlic; cook, stirring as needed, until softened, about 5 minutes. Add the tomatoes, peppers and zucchini; bring to a boil. Reduce the heat and simmer, uncovered, until slightly thickened, about 5 minutes.

2. Add the scallops, broth, basil and lemon juice; bring to a boil. Reduce the heat and simmer, stirring as needed, until the scallops are opaque, about 5 minutes.

3. Place the pasta in a large serving bowl. Add the scallop mixture and parsley; toss to coat.

PER SERVING: 423 Calories, 7 g Total Fat, 1 g Saturated Fat, 47 mg Cholesterol, 259 mg Sodium, 56 g Total Carbohydrate, 5 g Dietary Fiber, 33 g Protein, 114 mg Calcium.

SERVING PROVIDES: 2 Breads, 1 Fruit/Vegetable, 2 Protein/Milks, 1 Fat.

POINTS PER SERVING: 8.

Easy Clam Linguine

MAKES 4 SERVINGS

Connie Lyndon
Calgary, Alberta, Canada

*After a 10-month solo world tour, Connie used the self-confidence she gained
to lose 60 pounds. This delicious pasta is an adaptation of
a dish from her favorite Italian restaurant.*

8 scallions, sliced

2 garlic cloves, minced

1/4 teaspoon crushed red pepper flakes

Two 6 1/2-ounce cans chopped clams, drained (reserve the liquid)

One 14 1/2-ounce can stewed tomatoes (no salt added)

1/4 cup dry white wine

2 tablespoons minced fresh basil, or 2 teaspoons dried

1 teaspoon dried oregano

4 cups hot cooked linguine

2 tablespoons grated Parmesan cheese

1. Spray a large nonstick skillet with nonstick cooking spray; heat. Add the scallions, garlic and pepper flakes; cook, stirring as needed, until softened, 2–3 minutes.

2. Add the clams, the reserved liquid, the tomatoes, wine, basil and oregano; bring to a boil. Reduce the heat and simmer, uncovered, until the liquid is reduced by one-third, 10–12 minutes.

3. Place the linguine in a large serving bowl; add the clam sauce and toss to coat. Serve, sprinkled with the cheese.

PER SERVING: 341 Calories, 4 g Total Fat, 1 g Saturated Fat, 33 mg Cholesterol, 303 mg Sodium, 53 g Total Carbohydrate, 6 g Dietary Fiber, 22 g Protein, 208 mg Calcium.

SERVING PROVIDES: 2 Breads, 1 Fruit/Vegetable, 1 Protein/Milk.

POINTS PER SERVING: 6.

Tuna-Macaroni Salad

MAKES 4 SERVINGS

Linda Fogg
Columbus, Ohio

*After Linda broke her thumb skiing, she found cooking difficult. That's when
she came up with this "throw-together" salad, a quick and easy dish
that proves how adversity can be turned into advantage.*

1½ cups elbow macaroni

One 1-pound package
frozen mixed vegetables
(cauliflower, carrots and
snow pea pods), thawed

Two 6-ounce cans water-
packed tuna, drained and
flaked

4 scallions, sliced

¼ cup minced flat-leaf
parsley

3 tablespoons fat-free
Italian salad dressing

2 tablespoons balsamic
vinegar

2 teaspoons dried basil

¼ teaspoon crushed red
pepper flakes

(See photo.)

1. In a large pot of boiling water, cook the macaroni 6 minutes, until almost tender. Add the mixed vegetables; return the water to a boil, then cook until the pasta and vegetables are just tender, about 1 minute longer. Drain and then rinse under cold running water.

2. Meanwhile, in a large bowl, combine the tuna, scallions, parsley, salad dressing, vinegar, basil and pepper flakes. Add the pasta and vegetables; toss well. Refrigerate, covered, until chilled, at least 2 hours.

PER SERVING: 291 Calories, 1 g Total Fat, 0 g Saturated Fat, 32 mg Cholesterol, 417 mg Sodium, 39 g Total Carbohydrate, 4 g Dietary Fiber, 30 g Protein, 75 mg Calcium.

SERVING PROVIDES: 2 Breads, 1 Fruit/Vegetable, 1 Protein/Milk.

POINTS PER SERVING: 5.

Turkey Pie

Tuna-Macaroni Salad

una Patties

MAKES 4 SERVINGS

Nikki Howard
Richmond, British Columbia, Canada

"Our meetings are not only educational, they're fun," says Nikki of her
Saturday morning Weight Watchers group. We think that making these tuna patties
can be fun, too, but eating them is even better.

Two 6-ounce cans water-packed tuna, drained and flaked

3 egg whites

3 tablespoons seasoned dried bread crumbs

4 scallions, thinly sliced

2 tablespoons minced parsley

1/4 teaspoon freshly ground black pepper

1. In a medium bowl, combine the tuna, egg whites, bread crumbs, scallions, parsley and pepper. Shape the mixture into 4 equal patties.

2. Spray a large nonstick skillet with nonstick cooking spray; heat. Add the patties and cook until golden brown, about 5 minutes on each side.

PER SERVING: 137 Calories, 1 g Total Fat, 0 g Saturated Fat, 32 mg Cholesterol, 462 mg Sodium, 5 g Total Carbohydrate, 1 g Dietary Fiber, 26 g Protein, 24 mg Calcium.

SERVING PROVIDES: 1 Protein/Milk.

POINTS PER SERVING: 3.

Salmon, Papaya and Rice Salad

MAKES 4 SERVINGS

Jane Shaddy
Spokane, Washington

Jane, who lost 40 pounds on the Weight Watchers program, credits her husband with this exciting tropical salad; he has, she says, "a natural ability to identify compatible flavors." Pick out any skin from the salmon, but leave in the bones (mash them with a fork)—they're a great source of calcium.

One 14³/₄-ounce can red or pink salmon, drained and flaked

2 cups cold cooked brown rice

1 large papaya, peeled, seeded and diced

¹/₄ cup minced parsley

2 tablespoons fresh lime juice

1 tablespoon cider vinegar

¹/₂ teaspoon coarsely ground black pepper

12 romaine lettuce leaves

1. In a large bowl, combine the salmon, rice, papaya, parsley, lime juice, vinegar and pepper. Refrigerate, covered, until chilled, at least 2 hours.

2. Fluff the salad mixture with a fork. Arrange 3 lettuce leaves on each of 4 plates; top with the salad.

PER SERVING: 305 Calories, 7 g Total Fat, 2 g Saturated Fat, 37 mg Cholesterol, 470 mg Sodium, 39 g Total Carbohydrate, 4 g Dietary Fiber, 21 g Protein, 264 mg Calcium.

SERVING PROVIDES: 1 Bread, 1 Fruit/Vegetable, 3 Protein/Milks.

POINTS PER SERVING: 6.

CHAPTER

7

Vegetarian

Angel Hair Pasta with Plum Tomatoes and Fresh Basil

MAKES 4 SERVINGS

Sarah, Duchess of York
London, England

The Duchess' secret to this simple pasta dish? "Just a hint of balsamic vinegar for extra zing. I truly believe a person's taste buds need to be cultivated. Little things can help tremedously, like a hint of Tabasco or a squeeze of fresh lime juice." Since she has been on the program, not only has the Duchess' palate changed: "I've found the whole Weight Watchers experience—the meetings, the food plan and, most importantly, the people—to be an incredible, fun adventure."

6 ounces angel hair pasta

1 tablespoon extra virgin olive oil

1 garlic clove, crushed

6 plum tomatoes, peeled, seeded and chopped

1/2 cup minced fresh basil

1/2 teaspoon salt

Freshly ground pepper, to taste

2 teaspoons balsamic vinegar

1 1/2 ounces Parmesan cheese, shaved

1. Cook the pasta according to package directions. Drain; set aside and keep warm.

2. In a large nonstick skillet, heat the oil. Add the garlic and sauté until fragrant, about 30 seconds. Add the tomatoes and cook, stirring as needed, until softened, about 5 minutes. Stir in the basil, salt, and pepper; cook until the tomatoes are very soft, about 5 minutes. Pour over the pasta; toss with the vinegar. Serve, topped with the Parmesan.

PER SERVING: 268 Calories, 8 g Total Fat, 3 mg Saturated Fat, 8 mg Cholesterol, 504 mg Sodium, 39 g Total Carbohydrate, 3 g Dietary Fiber, 11 g Protein, 170 mg Calcium.

SERVING PROVIDES: 2 Breads, 1 Fruit/1 Vegetable, 1 Fat.

POINTS PER SERVING: 5.

$\mathscr{A}$lfredo Pizza

MAKES 8 SERVINGS

Roberta (Bobbi) Dannar
Dickinson, Texas

Who doesn't love pizza? This popular dish takes on extra appeal thanks to Bobbi's special version for Weight Watchers, which combines great taste with sensible eating.

1 cup skim milk

1 tablespoon all-purpose flour

1 onion, chopped

2 whole cloves

¼ teaspoon grated nutmeg

¼ teaspoon freshly ground black pepper

6 cups trimmed cleaned spinach

¼ cup grated Parmesan cheese

1 pound refrigerated ready-made pizza crust dough

3 large plum tomatoes, sliced

2 cups shredded part-skim mozzarella cheese

(See photo.)

1. Preheat the oven to 450° F. Spray a 15" pizza pan with nonstick cooking spray.

2. In a large nonstick saucepan, combine 2 tablespoons of the milk with the flour; stir until smooth. Stir in the remaining milk, the onion, cloves, nutmeg and pepper. Cook over medium heat, stirring constantly, until the mixture boils and thickens, about 4 minutes. Remove from the heat; discard the cloves. Add the spinach and Parmesan cheese; stir until the spinach is moistened and slightly wilted.

3. Press the pizza dough into the bottom of the pan; pinch the edge to form a rim. Spread the spinach mixture evenly over the dough. Top with the tomatoes and the mozzarella cheese. Bake until the crust is browned and the cheese is golden, 12–15 minutes.

PER SERVING: 261 Calories, 8 g Total Fat, 4 g Saturated Fat, 19 mg Cholesterol, 542 mg Sodium, 33 g Total Carbohydrate, 2 g Dietary Fiber, 15 g Protein, 301 mg Calcium.

SERVING PROVIDES: 2 Breads, 1 Fruit/Vegetable, 2 Protein/Milks.

POINTS PER SERVING: 5.

Chalupas

MAKES 2 SERVINGS

Linda Wise
Arlington, Texas

*Chalupa, which means "boat" in Spanish, is a corn tortilla dough formed
into a boat shape that is typically filled with chicken, beans, vegetables and cheese.
Linda has produced her own quick vegetarian chalupa, using store-bought taco shells.
Be sure to arm yourself with extra napkins before serving.*

Two ³/₄-ounce rectangular taco shells

¹/₂ cup fat-free refried beans

3 tablespoons shredded nonfat cheddar cheese

1 tomato, chopped

¹/₂ cup shredded lettuce

2 tablespoons nonfat sour cream

2 tablespoons salsa

1 tablespoon rinsed drained canned chopped green chiles (optional)

(See photo.)

1. Preheat the oven to 350° F.

2. Place the taco shells on a baking sheet; spread the beans evenly in the bottoms of the shells. Top each with half of the cheese. Bake until hot and the cheese is melted, about 8 minutes.

3. Top each chalupa with half of the tomato, lettuce, sour cream, salsa and chiles (if using).

PER SERVING: 200 Calories, 5 g Total Fat, 1 g Saturated Fat, 1 mg Cholesterol, 510 mg Sodium, 30 g Total Carbohydrate, 6 g Dietary Fiber, 10 g Protein, 191 mg Calcium.

SERVING PROVIDES: 1 Bread, 1 Fruit/Vegetable, 1 Protein/Milk.

POINTS PER SERVING: 3.

Creamy Fettuccine Primavera

MAKES 4 SERVINGS

Debbie Price
Battle Creek, Michigan

*As a Weight Watchers leader for three years, Debbie often comes
up with recipes for her members. Creamy Fettuccine Primavera
is one such recipe that met with great success.*

1 teaspoon olive oil

1 onion, chopped

2 cups broccoli florets

1/2 cup evaporated
skimmed milk

1 teaspoon dried basil

1/4 teaspoon freshly ground
black pepper

1 tomato, coarsely chopped

4 cups hot cooked
fettuccine

1/2 cup grated Parmesan
cheese

1. In a large nonstick skillet, heat the oil. Add the onion and cook, stirring as needed, until softened, about 5 minutes.

2. Add the broccoli, milk, basil and pepper; cook, covered, until the broccoli is tender-crisp, about 3 minutes. Add the tomato and cook until heated through, about 1 minute.

3. Place the fettuccine in a medium serving bowl. Top with the broccoli mixture and the cheese; toss to coat.

PER SERVING: 330 Calories, 7 g Total Fat, 3 g Saturated Fat, 62 mg Cholesterol, 254 mg Sodium, 51 g Total Carbohydrate, 7 g Dietary Fiber, 17 g Protein, 292 mg Calcium.

SERVING PROVIDES: 2 Breads, 1 Fruit/Vegetable, 1 Protein/Milk.

POINTS PER SERVING: 6.

Roasted Red Pepper Pasta

MAKES 2 SERVINGS

Vivian Elba
Simsbury, Connecticut

*With two children and three jobs, Vivian has a schedule that is packed
with demands. This lively pasta dish meets several of them—it's quick, flavorful
and can satisfy a hungry husband, as well as the most finicky child.*

4 red bell peppers, roasted★
and coarsely chopped

1 tomato, chopped

1/3 cup diced part-skim
mozzarella cheese

1/4 cup minced flat-leaf
parsley

5 pitted small black olives,
sliced

1 teaspoon extra virgin
olive oil

1/2 teaspoon coarsely
ground black pepper

3 ounces fettuccine

2 lemon wedges

1. In a medium bowl, combine the bell peppers, tomato, cheese, parsley, olives, oil and black pepper.

2. Cook the fettuccine according to package directions. Drain and place in a serving bowl. Immediately add the bell pepper mixture and toss to coat. Serve, garnished with the lemon.

PER SERVING: 311 Calories, 9 g Total Fat, 3 g Saturated Fat, 51 mg Cholesterol, 172 mg Sodium, 49 g Total Carbohydrate, 6 g Dietary Fiber, 13 g Protein, 181 mg Calcium.

SERVING PROVIDES: 2 Breads, 3 Fruit/Vegetables, 1 Protein/Milk, 1 Fat.

POINTS PER SERVING: 6.

★ *To roast the bell peppers, preheat the broiler. Line a baking sheet with foil; place the peppers on the baking sheet. Broil 4-6" from heat, turning frequently with tongs, until the skin is lightly charred on all sides, about 10 minutes. Transfer to a paper bag; fold the bag closed and let steam 10 minutes. Peel, seed and devein peppers over the sink to drain the juices.*

Greek Spinach and Rice

MAKES 4 SERVINGS

Irene J. Walker
Gloucester, Ontario, Canada

*"My whole life should be like this recipe—
easy, healthy and interesting!" writes Irene.*

1 teaspoon vegetable oil

4 onions, chopped

One 28-ounce can crushed
tomatoes (no salt added)

One 10-ounce package
frozen chopped spinach,
thawed

1¹/₃ cups long-grain white
rice

1 cup low-sodium veg-
etable broth

¹/₄ teaspoon freshly ground
black pepper

³/₄ cup crumbled feta
cheese

10 pitted small black olives,
halved

4 lemon slices

1. Preheat the oven to 350° F.

2. In a large flameproof casserole or Dutch oven, heat
the oil. Add the onions and cook, stirring as needed,
until softened, 6–8 minutes.

3. Add the tomatoes, spinach, rice, broth and pepper;
bring to a boil, stirring as needed. Bake, covered, until
the rice is tender and most of the liquid is absorbed,
about 1 hour.

4. Serve the rice mixtures topped with the cheese and
olives; garnish with the lemon.

PER SERVING: 384 Calories, 8 g Total Fat, 4 g Saturated Fat,
19 mg Cholesterol, 403 mg Sodium, 69 g Total Carbohydrate,
5 g Dietary Fiber, 12 g Protein, 286 mg Calcium.

SERVING PROVIDES: 2 Breads, 2 Fruit/Vegetables, 1 Protein/Milk,
1 Fat.

POINTS PER SERVING: 7.

Pasta with Eggplant and Sun-Dried Tomatoes

MAKES 6 SERVINGS

Amy Goodman
Millville, Utah

*Amy, a bon vivant whose interests range from weight lifting to philosophy,
had fun coming up with this colorful, flavor-intense pasta.
Lots of vegetables make for large, filling portions.*

½ cup boiling water

14 sun-dried tomato halves (not oil-packed)

4 teaspoons olive oil

1 medium (1¼-pound) eggplant, diced

4 garlic cloves, minced

One 10-ounce package frozen chopped spinach, thawed and squeezed dry

2 tomatoes, chopped

1 cup low-sodium vegetable broth

3 tablespoons pine nuts

2 tablespoons minced fresh basil, or 2 teaspoons dried

¼ teaspoon freshly ground black pepper

4½ cups hot cooked rigatoni

¼ cup grated Parmesan cheese

1. In a small bowl, pour the boiling water over the sun-dried tomatoes; set aside until softened, about 20 minutes.

2. In a large nonstick saucepan or Dutch oven, heat the oil. Add the eggplant and cook, stirring constantly, until it softens and releases some liquid, about 5 minutes. Add the garlic and cook, stirring constantly, until the garlic is lightly browned, about 1 minute.

3. Add the spinach, chopped tomatoes, broth, pine nuts, basil, pepper and the sun-dried tomatoes with the liquid; bring to a boil. Reduce the heat and simmer, covered, stirring as needed, until the vegetables are softened, about 5 minutes. Place the rigatoni in a serving bowl; top with the eggplant mixture and toss to coat. Serve, sprinkled with the cheese.

PER SERVING: 287 Calories, 7 g Total Fat, 2 g Saturated Fat, 3 mg Cholesterol, 125 mg Sodium, 46 g Total Carbohydrate, 6 g Dietary Fiber, 12 g Protein, 158 mg Calcium.

SERVING PROVIDES: 2 Breads, 2 Fruit/Vegetables, 1 Fat.

POINTS PER SERVING: 5.

Penne alla Vodka

MAKES 8 SERVINGS

Mary Ann Palestino
Brooklyn , New York

*Mary Ann developed this recipe for her boyfriend, who wanted something
low-fat and luscious. What could be more romantic than
two people enjoying a healthful dinner together?*

2 teaspoons olive oil

1 onion, chopped

2 garlic cloves, minced

One 28-ounce can whole
tomatoes in puree,
coarsely chopped

1/4 teaspoon crushed red
pepper flakes, or to taste

1/2 cup minced parsley

1/2 cup evaporated
skimmed milk

2 tablespoons vodka

8 cups hot cooked penne

1. In a large nonstick saucepan, heat the oil. Add the onion and garlic; cook, stirring as needed, until softened, about 5 minutes.

2. Stir in the tomatoes and pepper flakes; bring to a boil. Reduce the heat and simmer, uncovered, until the sauce is slightly thickened, about 10 minutes.

3. Stir in the parsley, milk and vodka; cook until heated through, about 1 minute. Place the penne in a large serving bowl; add the tomato mixture and toss to coat.

PER SERVING: 261 Calories, 2 g Total Fat, 0 g Saturated Fat, 1 mg Cholesterol, 179 mg Sodium, 49 g Total Carbohydrate, 3 g Dietary Fiber, 9 g Protein, 99 mg Calcium.

SERVING PROVIDES: 2 Breads, 1 Fruit/Vegetable.

POINTS PER SERVING: 5.

Vegetarian Rice Casserole

MAKES 6 SERVINGS

Vima Dubyna
Las Vegas, Nevada

Seventeen years ago, Vima came up with this wild-rice recipe to serve to her vegetarian aunt and uncle. It still works today, and you don't have to be a vegetarian to appreciate its savory goodness.

1 tablespoon olive oil

2 onions, chopped

2 celery stalks, chopped

1/2 green bell pepper, seeded and chopped

One 14 1/2-ounce can diced tomatoes (no salt added)

1/2 cup minced flat-leaf parsley

1 teaspoon dried thyme leaves

1/4 teaspoon freshly ground black pepper

2 1/2 cups cooked brown rice

2 cups cooked wild rice

1 cup shredded reduced-fat cheddar cheese

1. Preheat the oven to 350° F.

2. In a large nonstick skillet, heat the oil. Add the onions, celery and bell pepper; cook, stirring as needed, until softened, 5–6 minutes.

3. Add the tomatoes, parsley, thyme and black pepper; bring to a boil. Stir in the rices; transfer to a 3-quart casserole. Cover with foil and bake 10 minutes; uncover and sprinkle with the cheese. Bake until the cheese is melted, about 3 minutes longer.

PER SERVING: 235 Calories, 5 g Total Fat, 0 g Saturated Fat, 3 mg Cholesterol, 326 mg Sodium, 38 g Total Carbohydrate, 3 g Dietary Fiber, 10 g Protein, 202 mg Calcium.

SERVING PROVIDES: 2 Breads, 1 Fruit/Vegetable, 1 Protein/Milk, 1 Fat.

POINTS PER SERVING: 5.

$\mathcal{W}$hite Whisper Pasta

MAKES 4 SERVINGS

Joan Jernigan
Kelseyville, California

"It tastes too good to be diet food," is the response Joan usually gets when she
serves this luxurious pasta with its elegant white sauce.

2 teaspoons olive oil

2 cups sliced mushrooms

3 garlic cloves, minced

1/2 cup skim milk

1/3 cup nonfat cottage
cheese

3 tablespoons basil leaves

3 tablespoons parsley leaves

2 tablespoons all-purpose
flour

1 teaspoon dried oregano

1/4 cup grated Parmesan
cheese

2 tablespoons grated Asiago
cheese

4 cups fusilli

1/2 pound green beans,
trimmed and cut into
2" pieces

1. In a large nonstick skillet, heat the oil. Add the mushrooms and garlic; cook, stirring as needed, until the mushrooms release their liquid, 4–5 minutes.

2. In a blender or food processor, puree the milk, cottage cheese, basil, parsley, flour and oregano. Add to the mushroom mixture; stir in the Parmesan and the Asiago cheeses and cook, stirring as needed, until heated through, about 2 minutes.

3. Meanwhile, cook the pasta according to package directions, adding the green beans during the last 4 minutes of cooking. Drain and transfer to a large bowl. Immediately top with the mushroom sauce; toss to coat.

PER SERVING: 326 Calories, 8 g Total Fat, 4 g Saturated Fat, 16 mg Cholesterol, 383 mg Sodium, 44 g Total Carbohydrate, 2 g Dietary Fiber, 18 g Protein, 300 mg Calcium.

SERVING PROVIDES: 2 Breads, 1 Fruit/Vegetable, 1 Protein/Milk, 1 Fat.

POINTS PER SERVING: 7.

ean Quesadillas

MAKES 2 SERVINGS

Jill Diewald
Billerica, Massachusetts

Jill, a mother of two who also works full time, finds that this piquant quesadilla recipe delivers a lot of gusto in return for a minimum of fuss.

Four 6" fat-free flour tortillas

1/2 cup canned fat-free refried beans

1 tomato, diced

4 scallions, thinly sliced

1/3 cup shredded reduced-fat cheddar cheese

2 tablespoons salsa

2 tablespoons nonfat sour cream

1. Spread each tortilla evenly with the beans. Top 2 of the tortillas evenly with the tomato, scallions and cheese. Place the remaining 2 tortillas, bean-side down, on top of them; press gently to help them stick together.

2. Spray a large nonstick skillet with nonstick cooking spray; heat. Cook the quesadillas until lightly browned, about 3 minutes on each side. Cut each quesadilla into quarters. Serve with the salsa and sour cream.

PER SERVING: 302 Calories, 4 g Total Fat, 2 g Saturated Fat, 13 mg Cholesterol, 930 mg Sodium, 51 g Total Carbohydrate, 6 g Dietary Fiber, 16 g Protein, 220 mg Calcium.

SERVING PROVIDES: 2 Breads, 1 Fruit/Vegetable, 1 Protein/Milk.

POINTS PER SERVING: 5.

Beans and Rice Olé

MAKES 4 SERVINGS

Mary Ann Hazen
Rochester Hills, Michigan

Mary Ann, a professor of management, finds it a cinch to manage her busy lifestyle, her vegetarian diet and her new husband's hearty appetite: Just cook something as nutritious, easy and filling as this flavorsome rice and bean dish.

One 19-ounce can red
  kidney beans, rinsed
  and drained
2 cups cooked brown rice
3/4 cup salsa
1/4 cup minced parsley
3/4 cup shredded nonfat
  cheddar cheese

1. Preheat the oven to 350° F.

2. In a medium bowl, combine the beans, rice, salsa and parsley; transfer to a 2-quart casserole. Sprinkle with the cheese and bake, uncovered, until the mixture is heated through and the cheese is melted, about 20 minutes.

PER SERVING: 302 Calories, 1 g Total Fat, 0 g Saturated Fat, 2 mg Cholesterol, 646 mg Sodium, 53 g Total Carbohydrate, 6 g Dietary Fiber, 20 g Protein, 234 mg Calcium.

SERVING PROVIDES: 1 Bread, 2 Protein/Milks.

POINTS PER SERVING: 5.

*B*eans and Greens

MAKES 4 SERVINGS

Christine Damiano
Syracuse, New York

*"I am an Italian mother who loves to cook," writes Christine.
She came up with this recipe, which does justice to her rich culinary heritage
and still adheres to her program of losing weight. Don't let your kids be put off by the
color—they'll love the creamy "comfort food" texture and peppery flavor. Serve it
with brown rice, pasta or whole-wheat Italian bread for a light supper.*

2 teaspoons olive oil

1 onion, chopped

2 garlic cloves, minced

One 19-ounce can cannellini or red kidney beans, rinsed and drained

$\frac{1}{2}$ cup low-sodium vegetable broth

2 tablespoons minced parsley

$\frac{1}{4}$ teaspoon salt

$\frac{1}{4}$ teaspoon freshly ground black pepper

1 bunch escarole, cleaned and coarsely chopped (about 8 cups)

1. In a large nonstick skillet, heat the oil. Add the onion and garlic; cook, stirring as needed, until softened, about 5 minutes.

2. Add the beans, broth, parsley, salt and pepper; bring to a boil, stirring as needed. Place the escarole on top; reduce the heat and simmer, covered, stirring once, until the escarole is wilted, about 5 minutes. Serve hot.

PER SERVING: 197 Calories, 3 g Total Fat, 0 g Saturated Fat, 0 mg Cholesterol, 170 mg Sodium, 33 g Total Carbohydrate, 7 g Dietary Fiber, 12 g Protein, 95 mg Calcium.

SERVING PROVIDES: 2 Fruit/Vegetables, 2 Protein/Milks, 1 Fat.

POINTS PER SERVING: 3.

Brown Rice, Lentil and Barley Pilaf

MAKES 8 SERVINGS

Nancy Knowlton
Reno, Nevada

*This recipe can be cut in half to serve four, or make the full batch;
refrigerate any extra in a covered container and reheat as needed in the microwave.
It's incredibly versatile: Nancy serves it as a vegetarian entrée or as a side dish for meat
or poultry—she wraps it in tortillas and tops them with salsa.*

4 carrots, diced

4 cups low-sodium vegetable broth

1¹/₃ cups brown rice

2 onions, chopped

¹/₂ cup lentils, rinsed and drained

¹/₂ cup pearl barley

2 cups broccoli florets

¹/₄ cup minced parsley

1. In a large nonstick saucepan or Dutch oven, combine the carrots, broth, rice, onions, lentils and barley; bring to a boil. Reduce the heat and simmer, covered, until the grains are softened, 30–40 minutes.

2. Add the broccoli and parsley; simmer, covered, until the grains are tender and the broccoli is tender-crisp, about 10 minutes.

PER SERVING: 255 Calories, 2 g Total Fat, 0 g Saturated Fat, 0 mg Cholesterol, 67 mg Sodium, 53 g Total Carbohydrate, 8 g Dietary Fiber, 9 g Protein, 51 mg Calcium.

SERVING PROVIDES: 1 Bread, 1 Fruit/Vegetable.

POINTS PER SERVING: 4.

$\mathcal{L}$entil Chili

MAKES 8 SERVINGS

Christine Jarussi
Columbiana, Ohio

As a corporate food service director and dietitian, Chris certainly knows how to make healthful food taste great. She loves to serve this zesty Lentil Chili at luncheon parties and dinners, and she always gets rave reviews.

1 pound lentils, picked over, rinsed and drained

One 14½-ounce can diced tomatoes (no salt added)

1 green bell pepper, seeded and chopped

1 cup low-sodium vegetable broth

One 6-ounce can tomato paste (no salt added)

1 carrot, chopped

1 onion, chopped

2 tablespoons red-wine vinegar

2 teaspoons dried oregano

2 teaspoons ground cumin

2 garlic cloves, minced

¼ teaspoon crushed red pepper flakes

¼ teaspoon salt

1. In a large nonstick saucepan or Dutch oven, bring the lentils and 5 cups water to a boil. Reduce the heat and simmer, covered, until the lentils are slightly softened, about 20 minutes.

2. Add the tomatoes, bell pepper, broth, tomato paste, carrot, onion, vinegar, oregano, cumin, garlic, pepper flakes and salt; bring to a boil. Reduce the heat and simmer, covered, until the lentils are tender, about 40 minutes.

PER SERVING: 231 Calories, 1 g Total Fat, 0 g Saturated Fat, 0 mg Cholesterol, 109 mg Sodium, 42 g Total Carbohydrate, 8 g Dietary Fiber, 17 g Protein, 69 mg Calcium.

SERVING PROVIDES: 1 Fruit/Vegetable, 2 Protein/Milks.

POINTS PER SERVING: 3.

$\mathcal{L}$entil Lasagna

MAKES 4 SERVINGS

Jocelyn Kalajian
Mahtomedi, Minnesota

Jocelyn, a professional singer and voice teacher, sings praises for this anything-but-ho-hum lasagna. Lentils, instead of ground beef, take center stage.

2 teaspoons olive oil

1 onion, chopped

3 garlic cloves, minced

One 14^1/$_2$-ounce can diced tomatoes (no salt added)

1 cup lentils, rinsed and drained

One 6-ounce can tomato paste (no salt added)

1 teaspoon ground cumin

^{1}/$_4$ teaspoon freshly ground black pepper

^{1}/$_8$ teaspoon cayenne pepper

5–6 cooked lasagna noodles

1 cup nonfat ricotta cheese

2 tablespoons grated Parmesan cheese

1. Preheat the oven to 350° F. Spray a 9" square baking pan with nonstick cooking spray.

2. In a large nonstick skillet, heat the oil. Add the onion and garlic; cook, stirring as needed, until softened, about 5 minutes.

3. Add the tomatoes, lentils, tomato paste, cumin, black pepper, cayenne and 1 cup water; bring to a boil. Reduce the heat and simmer, covered, until the lentils are tender, 30–35 minutes.

4. Cut the noodles in half crosswise. In the pan, spread one-quarter of the lentil mixture; top with one-third of the noodles and one-third of the ricotta cheese. Repeat the layering 2 more times, ending with the lentil mixture. Sprinkle evenly with the Parmesan cheese. Bake, covered, 25 minutes. Uncover and bake until the cheese is golden and the lasagna is bubbling around the edges, about 10 minutes longer. Let stand 10 minutes before serving.

PER SERVING: 434 Calories, 5 g Total Fat, 1 g Saturated Fat, 2 mg Cholesterol, 167 mg Sodium, 69 g Total Carbohydrate, 9 g Dietary Fiber, 30 g Protein, 420 mg Calcium.

SERVING PROVIDES: 2 Breads, 1 Fruit/Vegetable, 3 Protein/Milks, 1 Fat.

POINTS PER SERVING: 7.

Spinach and White Bean Lasagna

MAKES 6 SERVINGS

Janine Bologna
Arlington, Virginia

Guests at Janine's dinner parties love the zesty and colorful lasagna she serves. It was inspired by her grandmother's recipe, which Janine has slimmed down and revved up with flavor.

1 tablespoon olive oil

2 carrots, diced

2 onions, chopped

6 garlic cloves, minced

Two 14½-ounce cans stewed tomatoes (no salt added)

3 cups sliced mushrooms

One 19-ounce can cannellini beans, rinsed and drained

One 10-ounce package frozen chopped spinach, thawed and squeezed dry

9 no-boil lasagna noodles

¼ cup + 2 tablespoons grated Parmesan cheese

1. Preheat the oven to 350° F.

2. In a large nonstick saucepan or Dutch oven, heat the oil. Add the carrots, onions and garlic; cook, stirring as needed, until softened, about 5 minutes.

3. Stir in the tomatoes, mushrooms, beans and spinach; bring to a boil. Reduce the heat and simmer, covered, until the vegetables are tender, about 15 minutes.

4. Spoon one-fourth of the tomato mixture in the bottom of a 13 × 9" baking pan; top with 3 lasagna noodles. Repeat the layering three more times, ending with the tomato mixture. Sprinkle the cheese evenly on top. Bake, covered, 35 minutes. Uncover and bake, until bubbling and golden, about 10 minutes longer. Let stand 10 minutes before serving.

PER SERVING: 285 Calories, 5 g Total Fat, 1 g Saturated Fat, 4 mg Cholesterol, 280 mg Sodium, 48 g Total Carbohydrate, 10 g Dietary Fiber, 15 g Protein, 208 mg Calcium.

SERVING PROVIDES: 1 Bread, 2 Fruit/Vegetables, 2 Protein/Milks, 1 Fat.

POINTS PER SERVING: 4.

$\mathscr{S}$tuffed Peppers

MAKES 2 SERVINGS

Carolyn Webb
Sault Ste. Marie, Ontario, Canada

Carolyn, a Weight Watchers lifetime member, relies upon this easy, attractive dish whenever she needs to throw a meatless dinner together quickly. Served with a tossed salad, it's a meal.

1 red bell pepper, halved lengthwise and seeded

1 yellow bell pepper, halved lengthwise and seeded

2 teaspoons unsalted stick margarine

1 celery stalk, diced

1 onion, chopped

1 cup quick-cooking brown rice

1 cup low-sodium mixed vegetable juice

1 cup drained rinsed canned chickpeas

1/4 cup minced fresh parsley

Dash cayenne pepper

1/3 cup shredded part-skim mozzarella cheese

(See photo.)

1. Place the bell pepper halves, cut-side up, in a 2-quart microwavable casserole; add 2 tablespoons water. Microwave, covered, on High until softened, 4 minutes; invert the peppers and drain.

2. Meanwhile, in a large nonstick saucepan, melt the margarine. Add the celery and onion; cook, stirring as needed, until softened, about 5 minutes.

3. Add the rice and vegetable juice; bring to a boil, stirring as needed. Reduce the heat and simmer, covered, until the rice is tender, about 8 minutes. Stir in the chickpeas, parsley and cayenne; cook, stirring as needed, until heated through, about 2 minutes.

4. Divide the rice mixture evenly among the pepper halves; sprinkle evenly with the cheese. Return the peppers to the casserole; microwave, covered, on High until the cheese is melted, 4 minutes.

PER SERVING: 494 Calories, 12 g Total Fat, 3 g Saturated Fat, 12 mg Cholesterol, 231 mg Sodium, 81 g Total Carbohydrate, 9 g Dietary Fiber, 21 g Protein, 241 mg Calcium.

SERVING PROVIDES: 2 Breads, 2 Fruit/Vegetables, 3 Protein/Milks, 1 Fat.

POINTS PER SERVING: 9.

$\mathcal{V}$egetarian Chili

MAKES 8 SERVINGS

Alison R. Greene
Framingham, Massachusetts

*Alison says the terrific thing about this recipe is that it can be put together quickly
with ingredients kept on hand in the kitchen. She likes to serve it with
corn bread and tops it with nonfat plain yogurt to cut the spiciness.*

4 teaspoons olive oil

3 onions, chopped

One 28-ounce can crushed tomatoes (no salt added)

2 cups low-sodium vegetable broth

1 1/2 cups bulgur (cracked wheat)

One 19-ounce can red kidney beans, rinsed and drained

One 19-ounce can cannellini beans, rinsed and drained

2 cups fresh or thawed frozen corn kernels

1 green bell pepper, seeded and chopped

4 teaspoons chili powder, or to taste

1/2 teaspoon salt

1/4 teaspoon cayenne pepper, or to taste

1. In a large nonstick saucepan or Dutch oven, heat the oil. Add the onions and cook, stirring as needed, until softened, about 5 minutes.

2. Stir in the tomatoes, broth and bulgur; bring to a boil. Reduce the heat and simmer, covered, stirring as needed, until the bulgur is tender, about 10 minutes.

3. Add the kidney beans, cannellini beans, corn, bell pepper, chili powder, salt and cayenne; bring to a boil. Reduce the heat and simmer, uncovered, stirring as needed, until heated through and slightly thickened, about 10 minutes.

PER SERVING: 285 Calories, 4 g Total Fat, 0 g Saturated Fat, 0 mg Cholesterol, 359 mg Sodium, 52 g Total Carbohydrate, 13 g Dietary Fiber, 13 g Protein, 77 mg Calcium.

SERVING PROVIDES: 2 Breads, 1 Fruit/Vegetable, 2 Protein/Milks, 1 Fat.

POINTS PER SERVING: 3.

Open Tofu Burritos

MAKES 4 SERVINGS

Deborah A. Ciupak
Minneapolis, Minnesota

*Having decided to eliminate meat from her diet,
Deborah incorporated tofu into her favorite type of food, Tex-Mex,
and came up with this winning combination.*

2 teaspoons canola oil

1 green bell pepper, seeded and chopped

1 onion, chopped

4 garlic cloves, minced

One 28-ounce can crushed tomatoes (no salt added)

2 tablespoons chili powder

2 teaspoons dried basil

1 teaspoon dried oregano

1/4 teaspoon salt

1/4 teaspoon cayenne pepper (optional)

1 pound firm reduced-fat tofu, cubed

Eight 6" fat-free flour tortillas, warm

3/4 cup shredded nonfat cheddar cheese

1. In a large nonstick saucepan or Dutch oven, heat the oil. Add the bell pepper, onion and garlic; cook, stirring as needed, until softened, about 5 minutes.

2. Stir in the tomatoes, chili powder, basil, oregano, salt and cayenne (if using); bring to a boil. Reduce the heat and simmer, uncovered, stirring as needed, until the flavors are blended, about 10 minutes.

3. Add the tofu and cook, stirring as needed, until heated through, about 3 minutes. Top each tortilla with the tofu mixture and serve, sprinkled with the cheese.

PER SERVING: 334 Calories, 5 g Total Fat, 1 g Saturated Fat, 2 mg Cholesterol, 947 mg Sodium, 53 g Total Carbohydrate, 5 g Dietary Fiber, 22 g Protein, 325 mg Calcium.

SERVING PROVIDES: 2 Breads, 1 Fruit/Vegetable, 2 Protein/Milks, 1 Fat.

POINTS PER SERVING: 6.

Tofu-Spaghetti Sauce

MAKES 4 SERVINGS

Marcy Lynn Fenton
Aurora, Ohio

*Marcy, a vegetarian and young newlywed, has developed a repertoire
of healthful, satisfying meatless dishes. This tomato sauce more than fits into her lifestyle.
"Everyone loves it," she writes enthusiastically. And no wonder, it's delicious!*

8 garlic cloves, minced

Two 14½-ounce cans
stewed tomatoes
(no salt added)

2 teaspoons dried basil

1 teaspoon dried oregano

½ teaspoon crushed red
pepper flakes

¼ teaspoon salt

1 pound firm reduced-fat
tofu, cubed

4 cups hot cooked
spaghetti

1. Spray a large nonstick skillet with nonstick cooking spray; heat. Add the garlic and cook, stirring constantly, until lightly browned, about 1 minute.

2. Add the tomatoes, basil, oregano, pepper flakes and salt; bring to a boil. Reduce the heat and simmer until the sauce thickens slightly, about 5 minutes. Gently stir in the tofu and simmer until the tofu is heated through, about 5 minutes. Serve the spaghetti, topped with the tofu mixture.

PER SERVING: 313 Calories, 3 g Total Fat, 0 g Saturated Fat, 0 mg Cholesterol, 268 mg Sodium, 57 g Total Carbohydrate, 7 g Dietary Fiber, 16 g Protein, 152 mg Calcium.

SERVING PROVIDES: 2 Breads, 1 Fruit/Vegetable, 2 Protein/Milks.

POINTS PER SERVING: 5.

CHAPTER
8

$\mathcal{M}$eat

Beef in a Leaf

MAKES 4 SERVINGS

Tonya Sarina
Aurora, Colorado

*"Inspired by Vietnamese cuisine, I created this attractive and fresh entrée,"
writes enthusiastic Weight Watchers leader Tonya. We love the intriguing blend of flavors
and the contrasting texture the crunchy lettuce provides. Although this is a messy dish, it's a
great way to get kids to eat greens, and it forces you to eat slowly. Breaking the pasta
into thirds before you cook it (or using rice) would make it
a little neater—but not as much fun.*

2 teaspoons olive oil

1 pound lean sirloin steak,
   cut into 2 × ¼" strips

2 tablespoons reduced-
   sodium soy sauce

2 tablespoons balsamic
   vinegar

2 tablespoons honey

½ teaspoon crushed red
   pepper flakes, or to taste

4 cups cooked capellini
   (angel-hair pasta)

1 head (1¼ pounds) red
   leaf lettuce, separated,
   washed and patted dry

(See photo.)

1. In a large nonstick skillet, heat the oil. Add the beef and cook, turning as needed, until browned, 5–6 minutes.

2. Add the soy sauce, vinegar, honey and pepper flakes; cook, stirring constantly, about 1 minute. Add the pasta and toss to coat; cook until the pasta is heated through, about 1 minute longer. Transfer to a serving dish.

3. Arrange the lettuce leaves on a large platter; place the serving dish in the center. Spoon about ¼ cup of the beef mixture onto each lettuce leaf; roll up and eat with your hands.

PER SERVING: 429 Calories, 9 g Total Fat, 2 g Saturated Fat, 69 mg Cholesterol, 381 mg Sodium, 54 g Total Carbohydrate, 4 g Dietary Fiber, 33 g Protein, 117 mg Calcium.

SERVING PROVIDES: 2 Breads, 2 Fruit/Vegetables, 3 Protein/Milks, 1 Fat.

POINTS PER SERVING: 8.

Beef Stroganoff

MAKES 4 SERVINGS

Donna Presberg
Agoura Hills, California

Donna, a Weight Watchers lifetime member, tinkered with this generations-old family recipe. Now, it's revised and ready to fit into her healthful new lifestyle.

2 teaspoons vegetable oil

1 pound lean round steak, trimmed and cut into 2 × 1/4" strips

2 onions, chopped

2 garlic cloves, minced

1 tablespoon all-purpose flour

2 cups sliced mushrooms

1 cup low-sodium mixed vegetable juice

1 cup low-sodium beef broth

1 tablespoon Worcestershire sauce

1/4 cup minced parsley

1/4 cup nonfat sour cream

4 cups hot cooked egg noodles

1. In a large nonstick skillet, heat the oil. Add the beef and cook, turning as needed, until browned, about 5 minutes; transfer to a plate.

2. Spray the same skillet with nonstick cooking spray; heat. Add the onions and garlic; cook, stirring as needed, until softened, about 5 minutes. Add the flour and cook, stirring constantly, until the flour is lightly browned, about 1 minute.

3. Return the beef to the skillet and stir in the mushrooms, vegetable juice, broth and Worcestershire sauce; bring to a boil. Reduce the heat and simmer, covered, stirring as needed, until the beef is tender, about 45 minutes.

4. Stir in the parsley and sour cream; cook, stirring as needed, until heated through, about 2 minutes. Serve the noodles, topped with the beef mixture.

PER SERVING: 450 Calories, 10 g Total Fat, 3 g Saturated Fat, 114 mg Cholesterol, 189 mg Sodium, 52 g Total Carbohydrate, 5 g Dietary Fiber, 35 g Protein, 68 mg Calcium.

SERVING PROVIDES: 2 Breads, 1 Fruit/Vegetable, 3 Protein/Milks, 1 Fat.

POINTS PER SERVING: 9.

Braised Steak with Vegetables

MAKES 4 SERVINGS

Frances Libbrecht
Marshall, Michigan

Frances is savvy about what she eats. This hearty, vegetable-enriched dish works well in her diet; serve it with a baked potato and you've got a meal.

Four 4-ounce cubed steaks

2 onions, sliced

2 tablespoons all-purpose flour

One 14½-ounce can stewed tomatoes (no salt added)

½ cup dry red wine

3 carrots, thinly sliced

2 cups sliced mushrooms

2 bay leaves

¼ teaspoon freshly ground black pepper

2 medium zucchini, sliced

1. Spray a large nonstick saucepan with nonstick cooking spray; heat. Brown the steaks, about 2 minutes on each side. Transfer to a plate.

2. Spray the same saucepan with more nonstick cooking spray; sauté the onions until softened, about 5 minutes. Add the flour, stirring constantly, until the flour is lightly browned, about 1 minute. Stir in the tomatoes and wine. Add the carrots, mushrooms, bay leaves, pepper and steaks; bring to a boil. Reduce the heat and simmer, covered, stirring as needed, until the steak and vegetables are tender, 30–40 minutes.

3. Add the zucchini; return to a boil. Reduce the heat and simmer, covered, 5–6 minutes. Discard the bay leaves. Serve the steaks, topped with the vegetable mixture.

PER SERVING: 293 Calories, 7 g Total Fat, 2 g Saturated Fat, 66 mg Cholesterol, 116 mg Sodium, 26 g Total Carbohydrate, 6 g Dietary Fiber, 29 g Protein, 89 mg Calcium.

SERVING PROVIDES: 2 Fruit/Vegetables, 3 Protein/Milks, 40 Bonus Calories.

POINTS PER SERVING: 5.

$\mathscr{M}$ushroom-Stuffed Beef

MAKES 6 SERVINGS

Marsha Thomas
Reno, Nevada

*Marsha, who runs an advertising agency, doesn't have to work hard
to sell folks on this savory dish. Just one forkful says it all—delicious.*

1 cup reconstituted dried
mushrooms

1 cup sliced fresh
mushrooms

1 onion, finely chopped

1/2 red bell pepper, seeded
and chopped

2 garlic cloves, minced

1/2 cup seasoned dried
bread crumbs

1/4 cup minced parsley

1 teaspoon dried thyme
leaves

1 1/2 pounds London broil

1 tablespoon vegetable oil

1/4 cup dry red wine

1. Preheat the oven to 325° F.

2. In a medium bowl, combine the dried and fresh
mushrooms, the onion, bell pepper, garlic, bread crumbs,
parsley and thyme.

3. As though you were cutting a loaf of French bread,
cut the beef lengthwise almost all the way through;
spread open. Spread the mushroom mixture evenly over
the inside of the beef. Starting from one short end, roll
up jelly-roll style; tie the beef roll together securely with
kitchen string.

4. In a nonstick Dutch oven or flameproof casserole,
heat the oil. Add the beef and cook, turning as needed,
until browned, about 10 minutes. Add the wine. Bake,
covered, until the beef is cooked through and tender,
about 1 hour. Serve with the sauce.

PER SERVING: 230 Calories, 6 g Total Fat, 2 g Saturated Fat,
65 mg Cholesterol, 328 mg Sodium, 12 g Total Carbohydrate,
2 g Dietary Fiber, 28 g Protein, 30 mg Calcium.

SERVING PROVIDES: 1 Bread, 1 Fruit/Vegetable, 3 Protein/Milks,
1 Fat.

POINTS PER SERVING: 5.

Big Beef and Veggie Burgers

MAKES 6 SERVINGS

Tonya Sarina
Aurora, Colorado

"This feeds my appetite for big food," said Tonya, who received rave reviews for these juicy burgers at a July 4th barbecue.

1 pound lean ground beef (10% or less fat)

2 medium zucchini, shredded

1 onion, finely chopped

2 tablespoons minced dill

2 teaspoons dry mustard

1 jalapeño pepper, deveined and minced (wear gloves to prevent irritation), optional

1/4 teaspoon freshly ground black pepper

3 small whole-wheat pita breads, halved crosswise

1 1/2 cups torn romaine lettuce

2 tomatoes, sliced

1. Spray the broiler or grill rack with nonstick cooking spray; set aside. Preheat the broiler, or prepare the grill.

2. In a large bowl, thoroughly combine the beef, zucchini, onion, dill, mustard, jalapeño (if using) and black pepper. Form into 6 patties.

3. Arrange the patties on the rack; broil 5" from the heat 4–5 minutes on each side (medium to well-done). Place a hamburger in each pita and top with the lettuce and tomatoes.

PER SERVING: 189 Calories, 8 g Total Fat, 3 g Saturated Fat, 44 mg Cholesterol, 135 mg Sodium, 14 g Total Carbohydrate, 2 g Dietary Fiber, 17 g Protein, 27 mg Calcium.

SERVING PROVIDES: 1 Bread, 1 Fruit/Vegetable, 2 Protein/Milks.

POINTS PER SERVING: 4.

Beef and Vegetable Chili

MAKES 6 SERVINGS

Sarah J. Egan
Hunt Valley, Maryland

For Christmas, Sarah gave her husband a membership to Weight Watchers.
She joined, too. Now, the whole family, including their 12-year-old son, enjoys a healthier,
more active lifestyle. This lively chili is filling enough to satisfy Sarah's husband,
a man with a big appetite.

1 tablespoon canola oil

1/2 pound lean ground beef (10% or less fat)

1 green bell pepper, seeded and chopped

1 onion, chopped

One 14 1/2-ounce can chili-style tomatoes

1 1/2 cups fresh or thawed frozen corn kernels

One 15-ounce can red kidney beans, rinsed and drained

2 teaspoons chili powder

1/4 teaspoon crushed red pepper flakes

1/8 teaspoon ground cumin

3 cups fusilli

1. In a large nonstick skillet, heat the oil. Add the beef, bell pepper and onion; cook, stirring as needed, until the beef is browned and the vegetables are softened, 5–6 minutes.

2. Add the tomatoes, corn, beans, chili powder, pepper flakes and cumin; bring to a boil, stirring as needed. Reduce the heat and simmer, covered, stirring as needed, until the flavors are blended, about 20 minutes.

3. Meanwhile, cook the pasta according to package directions. Serve, topped with the beef mixture.

PER SERVING: 408 Calories, 8 g Total Fat, 2 g Saturated Fat, 23 mg Cholesterol, 521 mg Sodium, 64 g Total Carbohydrate, 6 g Dietary Fiber, 21 g Protein, 34 mg Calcium.

SERVING PROVIDES: 2 Breads, 1 Fruit/Vegetable, 2 Protein/Milks, 1 Fat.

POINTS PER SERVING: 7.

ℋamburger Nests

MAKES 4 SERVINGS

Lydia J. Goatcher
Edmonton, Alberta, Canada

*Lydia, a full-time microbiologist, seeks simplicity and versatility in planning
her meals. These nifty hamburger nests can be served for dinner one night and microwaved
for lunch the following afternoon. Kids not only love to eat these,
but they also have a grand time making them.*

12 slices reduced-calorie
  oatmeal bread

1/2 pound lean ground beef
  (10% or less fat)

1 onion, chopped

3 tablespoons seasoned
  dried bread crumbs

1 egg, lightly beaten

2 garlic cloves, minced

1/4 teaspoon freshly ground
  black pepper

1/4 cup barbecue sauce

1/3 cup shredded nonfat
  cheddar cheese

1. Preheat the oven to 350° F. Spray twelve 2 3/4" muffin cups with nonstick cooking spray. Place 1 slice of bread in each muffin cup, pressing firmly to mold into the shape of the cup.

2. In a medium bowl, combine the beef, onion, bread crumbs, egg, garlic and pepper. Spoon evenly into the bread-lined muffin cups. Top each with 1 teaspoon of the barbecue sauce and an even sprinkling of the cheese.

3. Bake until the beef is cooked through and browned, about 25 minutes.

PER SERVING: 322 Calories, 11 g Total Fat, 3 g Saturated Fat, 90 mg Cholesterol, 667 mg Sodium, 39 g Total Carbohydrate, 1 g Dietary Fiber, 23 g Protein, 184 mg Calcium.

SERVING PROVIDES: 2 Breads, 2 Protein/Milks.

POINTS PER SERVING: 7.

*O*ven Beef Stew

Colleen Uehlein
Grafton, Ohio

"Life is great!" says Colleen, a lifetime member who has lost 60 pounds with
Weight Watchers over the past two years. Her beef stew, homey and old-fashionedly delicious,
has what it takes to make an optimist out of anyone.

1½ pounds lean round steak, cut into 1½" cubes

6 small all-purpose potatoes, scrubbed and quartered

3 carrots, sliced

2 celery stalks, sliced

2 onions, chopped

1 cup low-sodium mixed vegetable juice

½ cup low-sodium beef broth

¼ cup red-wine vinegar

2 tablespoons tapioca or brown rice

2 tablespoons Worcestershire sauce

1 tablespoon paprika

½ cup minced parsley

(See photo.)

1. Preheat the oven to 325° F.

2. In a Dutch oven or flameproof casserole, combine the beef, potatoes, carrots, celery, onions, vegetable juice, broth, vinegar, tapioca, Worcestershire sauce and paprika. Bake, covered, until the beef and vegetables are tender, about 3 hours. Stir in the parsley and serve.

PER SERVING: 325 Calories, 4 g Total Fat, 1 g Saturated Fat, 65 mg Cholesterol, 202 mg Sodium, 40 g Total Carbohydrate, 5 g Dietary Fiber, 31 g Protein, 50 mg Calcium.

SERVING PROVIDES: 1 Bread, 1 Fruit/Vegetable, 3 Protein/Milks.

POINTS PER SERVING: 6.

*M*exican Potato Casserole

MAKES 4 SERVINGS

Laurie Love
Midland, Texas

*Laurie, who hails from the Lone Star State, has come up with this hearty
Southwestern casserole for Texas-size appetites.*

1 teaspoon olive oil

$^1/_2$ pound lean ground beef
(10% or less fat)

2 green bell peppers,
seeded and chopped

8 scallions, sliced

2 tomatoes, chopped

1 tablespoon chili powder

1 tablespoon ground cumin

1 tablespoon garlic powder

$^1/_2$ teaspoon freshly ground
black pepper

$^1/_4$ teaspoon salt

2 large baking potatoes,
scrubbed and thinly
sliced

$^3/_4$ cup nonfat cheddar
cheese, shredded

1. Preheat the oven to 350° F. Spray a 13 × 9" baking
dish with nonstick cooking spray; set aside.

2. In a large nonstick skillet, heat the oil. Add the beef,
bell peppers and scallions; cook, stirring as needed, until
the beef is browned and the vegetables are softened, 6–8
minutes.

3. Add the tomatoes, chili powder, cumin, garlic powder, black pepper and salt; cook, stirring as needed, until
the flavors are blended, about 5 minutes.

4. Arrange alternate layers of the potatoes and beef
mixture in the baking dish. Cover with foil and bake
40 minutes; uncover and sprinkle evenly with the
cheese. Bake until the potatoes are cooked through and
the cheese is melted, about 10 minutes longer.

PER SERVING: 327 Calories, 10 g Total Fat, 3 g Saturated Fat,
46 mg Cholesterol, 386 mg Sodium, 37 g Total Carbohydrate,
6 g Dietary Fiber, 27 g Protein, 248 mg Calcium.

SERVING PROVIDES: 1 Bread, 1 Fruit/Vegetable, 2 Protein/Milks.

POINTS PER SERVING: 6.

$\mathcal{S}$assy Meatloaf

MAKES 6 SERVINGS

Odette Maloney
Washington, Pennsylvania

While losing more than 30 pounds on the Fat & Fiber Plan, Odette learned to cook low-fat foods with big flavor for her family. This meatloaf gets the sassiness from the salsa, and nobody in Odette's family is complaining.

1 pound lean ground beef (10% or less fat)

1¼ cups low-sodium salsa

¾ cup quick-cooking oatmeal

1 carrot, shredded

2 plum tomatoes, diced

½ cup coarsely chopped mushrooms

1. Preheat the oven to 350° F. Spray a loaf pan with nonstick cooking spray.

2. In a large bowl, combine the beef, salsa, oatmeal, carrot, tomatoes and mushrooms. Shape the mixture into a loaf.

3. Place the loaf in the pan. Bake until browned and a knife inserted in the center comes out clean and hot, about 1 hour and 5 minutes. Let stand about 10 minutes before slicing.

PER SERVING: 183 Calories, 8 g Total Fat, 3 g Saturated Fat, 44 mg Cholesterol, 61 mg Sodium, 12 g Total Carbohydrate, 2 g Dietary Fiber, 16 g Protein, 11 mg Calcium.

SERVING PROVIDES: 1 Bread, 1 Fruit/Vegetable, 2 Protein/Milks.

POINTS PER SERVING: 4.

Spectacular Spaghetti

MAKES 8 SERVINGS

Sandra Irwin
Pasadena, California

*Sandra, a business attorney, really means business in the kitchen.
The sauce for this recipe is richly flavored: "The secret to the wonderful taste is the
cloves and the hint of sugar," she writes. And for an added bonus, it freezes
beautifully. Serve with garlic bread to complete the meal.*

2 onions, chopped

4 garlic cloves, minced

1¹/₄ pounds lean ground
beef (10% or less fat)

3 cups sliced mushrooms

One 28-ounce can crushed
tomatoes (no salt added)

One 6-ounce can tomato
paste (no salt added)

¹/₂ cup minced fresh basil,
or 2 tablespoons dried

¹/₄ cup dry red wine

1 tablespoon minced fresh
marjoram, or 1 teaspoon
dried

1 tablespoon minced fresh
oregano, or 1 teaspoon
dried

1 teaspoon sugar

¹/₂ teaspoon coarsely
ground black pepper

¹/₄ teaspoon ground cloves

8 cups hot cooked
spaghetti

1. Spray a large nonstick saucepan or Dutch oven with nonstick cooking spray; heat. Add the onions and garlic; cook, stirring as needed, until softened, about 5 minutes. Add the beef and mushrooms; cook, stirring as needed, until the beef is browned and the mushrooms have released their liquid, 5–6 minutes.

2. Stir in the tomatoes, tomato paste, basil, wine, marjoram, oregano, sugar, pepper and cloves; bring to a boil. Reduce the heat and simmer, uncovered, stirring as needed, until the flavors are blended, about 20 minutes. Serve the spaghetti, topped with the beef mixture.

PER SERVING: 386 Calories, 9 g Total Fat, 3 g Saturated Fat, 44 mg Cholesterol, 82 mg Sodium, 53 g Total Carbohydrate, 5 g Dietary Fiber, 24 g Protein, 81 mg Calcium.

SERVING PROVIDES: 2 Breads, 1 Fruit/Vegetable, 2 Protein/Milks.

POINTS PER SERVING: 8.

Mexican Pork Chops

MAKES 4 SERVINGS

Julie Hessenflow
Prairie Village, Kansas

A healthy recipe, such as this one, keeps Julie from "straying" off her diet.
If you like hot and spicy Mexican flavors, use hot salsa or
Mexican-style stewed tomatoes in this family pleaser.

Four 4-ounce boneless
  pork loin cutlets
1 green bell pepper, seeded
  and chopped
1 onion, chopped
One 14¹/₂-ounce can
  stewed tomatoes (no salt
  added)
2 cups fresh or thawed
  frozen corn kernels
¹/₂ cup salsa
1¹/₂ teaspoons dried
  oregano
¹/₂ teaspoon ground cumin

1. Preheat the oven to 350° F.

2. Spray a large nonstick skillet with nonstick cooking spray; heat. Add the pork and brown 2 minutes on each side; transfer to a 3-quart casserole.

3. Spray the same skillet with more nonstick cooking spray. Add the pepper and onion; cook, stirring as needed, until softened, about 5 minutes. Add the tomatoes, corn, salsa, oregano and cumin; cook, stirring as needed, until heated through, about 2 minutes.

4. Pour the corn mixture evenly over the pork. Bake, covered, until the pork is tender, about 45 minutes.

PER SERVING: 286 Calories, 8 g Total Fat, 2 g Saturated Fat, 67 mg Cholesterol, 230 mg Sodium, 27 g Total Carbohydrate, 6 g Dietary Fiber, 28 g Protein, 72 mg Calcium.

SERVING PROVIDES: 1 Bread, 1 Fruit/Vegetable, 3 Protein/Milks.

POINTS PER SERVING: 5.

Oven-Barbecued Pork Roast

MAKES 6 SERVINGS

Margo Johnson
Dublin, California

*Margo, a grandmother of six, has traveled the world and enjoys camping,
sewing and volunteer work. She likes "simple, on-the-program fun food," like this
barbecued pork roast, which keeps the family happy, dazzles company
and has helped her in her efforts to lose 70 pounds.*

One 1½-pound boneless pork loin

2 Red Delicious apples, peeled, cored and chopped

1 cup fresh or frozen cranberries

¼ cup barbecue sauce

2 tablespoons firmly packed light brown sugar

1. Preheat the oven to 325° F.

2. Place the pork on a rack in a shallow roasting pan. Roast until the pork is browned and the center reaches 165° F on a meat thermometer, about 1 hour and 20 minutes.

3. Meanwhile, in a medium saucepan, combine the apples, cranberries, barbecue sauce, sugar and ¼ cup water; bring to a boil. Reduce the heat and simmer, uncovered, stirring as needed, until the cranberries pop and the sauce is slightly thickened, about 15 minutes. Place the pork on a serving platter and slice. Spoon the sauce over the pork slices.

PER SERVING: 217 Calories, 7 g Total Fat, 2 g Saturated Fat, 67 mg Cholesterol, 146 mg Sodium, 13 g Total Carbohydrate, 1 g Dietary Fiber, 25 g Protein, 29 mg Calcium.

SERVING PROVIDES: 1 Fruit/Vegetable, 3 Protein/Milks.

POINTS PER SERVING: 5.

Baked Pork Chops with Potatoes and Vegetables

MAKES 4 SERVINGS

Kathleen Rushmore
Grand Rapids, Michigan

Kathleen works full-time and travels whenever she can, so an easy and satisfying recipe like this one fits perfectly into her hectic schedule.

2 large baking potatoes, scrubbed and thinly sliced

2 cups sliced mushrooms

2 onions, thinly sliced

1/4 cup minced basil

1/2 teaspoon salt

1/4 teaspoon freshly ground black pepper

Four 4-ounce boneless pork loin cutlets

One 14 1/2-ounce can stewed tomatoes (no salt added)

1. Preheat the oven to 325° F. Spray a 13 × 9" baking dish with nonstick cooking spray.

2. Place the potatoes, mushrooms, onions, basil, salt and pepper in the dish; toss to combine. Place the pork cutlets over the vegetable mixture; pour the tomatoes over all. Bake, covered, until the pork and potatoes are fork-tender, about 1 1/2 hours.

PER SERVING: 330 Calories, 7 g Total Fat, 2 g Saturated Fat, 67 mg Cholesterol, 368 mg Sodium, 38 g Total Carbohydrate, 7 g Dietary Fiber, 30 g Protein, 116 mg Calcium.

SERVING PROVIDES: 1 Bread, 1 Fruit/Vegetable, 3 Protein/Milks.

POINTS PER SERVING: 6.

Sweet-and-Sour Gingered Pork

MAKES 4 SERVINGS

Beverly Jean Cyr
Windsor, Ontario, Canada

*"Finding ways of cutting out the fat in family favorites and developing new
and interesting tastes makes it fun, not frustrating, to be in the kitchen again," writes Beverly,
a retired home economics teacher and current Weight Watchers leader.*

1 teaspoon canola oil

3/4 pound lean pork tender-
loin, cut into 1" cubes

2 carrots, chopped

2 celery stalks, diced

1 green bell pepper, seeded
and chopped

1 onion, chopped

2 garlic cloves, minced

1/4 cup chili sauce

1/4 cup grape spreadable
fruit

1 teaspoon chopped crys-
tallized ginger

4 cups hot cooked brown
rice

1. In a large nonstick skillet, heat the oil. Add the pork and cook, turning as needed, until browned, about 5 minutes.

2. Add the carrots, celery, pepper, onion and garlic; cook, stirring as needed, until the pork is cooked through and the vegetables are tender-crisp, 6–8 minutes.

3. Add the chili sauce, spreadable fruit, ginger and 1/2 cup water; cook, stirring constantly, until heated through, about 3 minutes. Serve the rice, topped with the pork mixture.

PER SERVING: 434 Calories, 6 g Total Fat, 1 g Saturated Fat, 55 mg Cholesterol, 313 mg Sodium, 70 g Total Carbohydrate, 6 g Dietary Fiber, 24 g Protein, 59 mg Calcium.

SERVING PROVIDES: 2 Breads, 2 Fruit/Vegetables, 2 Protein/Milks.

POINTS PER SERVING: 8.

*B*raised Lamb Shanks

MAKES 4 SERVINGS

Marilyn Mehling
Bakersfield, California

Just the thing to take the chill out of a winter's evening, Marilyn's hearty, homey recipe for lamb is as easy to make as it is to enjoy.

One 28-ounce can crushed tomatoes (no salt added)

2 onions, coarsely chopped

1/4 cup dry red wine

4 garlic cloves, minced

1 teaspoon dried oregano

1/2 teaspoon cinnamon

1/4 teaspoon grated nutmeg

1/4 teaspoon freshly ground black pepper

Three 12-ounce lamb shanks, trimmed

4 cups hot cooked brown rice

1. Preheat the oven to 350° F.

2. In a large nonstick Dutch oven or flameproof casserole, combine the tomatoes, onions, wine, garlic, oregano, cinnamon, nutmeg and pepper; bring to a boil. Remove from the heat and add the lamb. Bake, covered, until the meat almost falls off the bone, about 1 1/2 hours. Let cool until the shanks are comfortable to handle, about 30 minutes.

3. Cut the meat from the bone; discard the gristle and bones. Return the meat to the tomato mixture and cook over medium heat until heated through, about 10 minutes. Serve the rice, topped with the meat and sauce.

PER SERVING: 443 Calories, 8 g Total Fat, 2 g Saturated Fat, 74 mg Cholesterol, 94 mg Sodium, 59 g Total Carbohydrate, 6 g Dietary Fiber, 32 g Protein, 103 mg Calcium.

SERVING PROVIDES: 2 Breads, 1 Fruit/Vegetable, 3 Protein/Milks.

POINTS PER SERVING: 8.

$\mathscr{L}$amb and Vegetable Stew with Rosemary

MAKES 8 SERVINGS

Jay Broyles
Orange, California

*Offer this hearty dish as a thick soup or as an entrée—it's your call.
When she's pressed for time, Jay makes this versatile stew with bags of precut
vegetables from the supermarket produce department.*

4 teaspoons olive oil

2 pounds lean lamb, cut into 1" cubes

3 onions, chopped

3 garlic cloves, minced

5 carrots, cut into 1" chunks

One 28-ounce can crushed tomatoes (no salt added)

5 celery stalks, cut into 1" chunks

1 cup low-sodium beef broth

1 cup dry red wine

1 tablespoon dried rosemary leaves, crumbled

1/2 teaspoon freshly ground black pepper

8 small red potatoes, scrubbed and cut into 1" chunks

8 small pearl onions, peeled

1/2 cup minced parsley

1. In a large nonstick saucepan or Dutch oven, heat the oil. Add the lamb and cook, turning as needed, until browned, 6–8 minutes. Add the chopped onions and garlic; cook, stirring as needed, until the onions are softened, about 5 minutes.

2. Add the carrots, tomatoes, celery, broth, wine, rosemary and pepper; bring to a boil, stirring as needed. Reduce the heat and cook, covered, until the lamb is partly cooked through, about 30 minutes.

3. Add the potatoes and pearl onions; cook, covered, stirring as needed, until the lamb and vegetables are tender, about 45 minutes. Stir in the parsley.

PER SERVING: 353 Calories, 9 g Total Fat, 3 g Saturated Fat, 70 mg Cholesterol, 147 mg Sodium, 36 g Total Carbohydrate, 6 g Dietary Fiber, 27 g Protein, 90 mg Calcium.

SERVING PROVIDES: 1 Bread, 2 Fruit/Vegetables, 3 Protein/Milks, 1 Fat.

POINTS PER SERVING: 7.

Cajun Ham and Potato Bake

MAKES 2 SERVINGS

Vicky Stroup
Sioux Falls, South Dakota

*Vicky's hobby has always been cooking. She thought after joining Weight Watchers
she would have to find a new one, but discovered it's still just as much
fun to cook low-fat, healthful food.*

1 tablespoon red-wine
  vinegar

1 tablespoon Dijon mustard

2 teaspoons chili powder

1/4 teaspoon ground cumin

1/4 teaspoon cayenne
  pepper

2 small all-purpose pota-
  toes, scrubbed and thinly
  sliced

1 onion, thinly sliced

3/4 cup diced turkey ham

1. Preheat the oven to 350° F. Spray a 9" square baking
pan with nonstick cooking spray.

2. In a medium bowl, combine the vinegar, mustard,
chili powder, cumin and cayenne. Add the potatoes,
onion and ham; toss to coat. Transfer to the pan.

3. Bake, covered, until the potatoes are almost tender,
about 35 minutes; uncover and bake until the potatoes
are tender and browned, about 10 minutes longer.

PER SERVING: 204 Calories, 3 g Total Fat, 1 g Saturated Fat,
26 mg Cholesterol, 639 mg Sodium, 31 g Total Carbohydrate,
4 g Dietary Fiber, 12 g Protein, 32 mg Calcium.

SERVING PROVIDES: 1 Bread, 1 Protein/Milk.

POINTS PER SERVING: 4.

Bellisimo Sausage and Penne

MAKES 4 SERVINGS

Kimberly Holl
Portola Valley, California

Kimberly, a reading specialist and sports enthusiast, traveled on a tandem bicycle from Paris to Rome. You can taste the flavor of the Italian countryside in this savory pasta dish.

2 hot or sweet Italian pork sausages, casings removed

1 green bell pepper, seeded and diced

1 red bell pepper, seeded and diced

1 onion, chopped

One 9-ounce package frozen artichoke hearts, thawed

Half 10-ounce package frozen leaf spinach, thawed

8 sun-dried tomato halves (not oil-packed), chopped

4 cups hot cooked penne, farfalle or medium pasta shells

3 tablespoons pine nuts

1. Spray a large nonstick skillet with nonstick cooking spray; heat. Add the sausages and cook, stirring as needed, until browned, about 6 minutes. Add the bell peppers and the onion; cook, stirring as needed, until the vegetables are softened, 6–8 minutes.

2. Add the artichoke hearts, spinach and tomatoes; cook, stirring constantly, until heated through, about 5 minutes. Reduce the heat and simmer, covered, stirring as needed, until the vegetables are cooked through and the flavors are blended, about 5 minutes. Serve the pasta, topped with the sausage mixture; sprinkle with the pine nuts.

PER SERVING: 402 Calories, 14 g Total Fat, 4 g Saturated Fat, 22 mg Cholesterol, 272 mg Sodium, 55 g Total Carbohydrate, 10 g Dietary Fiber, 17 g Protein, 77 mg Calcium.

SERVING PROVIDES: 2 Breads, 2 Fruit/Vegetables, 1 Protein/Milk, 1 Fat.

POINTS PER SERVING: 7.

uscan Pasta

MAKES 4 SERVINGS

Renee J. Hense
Chicago, Illinois

Renee has given up cooking rich, high-fat dinners in favor of flavor-intense, low-fat dishes like this delicious pasta. "It's a favorite for us because it is easy to prepare and follows the Weight Watchers guidelines, yet feels like a special dish," she writes.

2 teaspoons olive oil

1 onion, chopped

2 garlic cloves, minced

One 19-ounce can red kidney beans, rinsed and drained

One 14¹/₂-ounce can Italian-style stewed tomatoes

¹/₄ pound Canadian-style bacon, cut into strips

¹/₄ cup dry red wine

1 teaspoon dried basil

¹/₂ teaspoon dried oregano

¹/₂ teaspoon freshly ground black pepper

4 cups hot cooked farfalle

(See photo.)

1. In a large nonstick skillet, heat the oil. Add the onion and garlic; cook, stirring as needed, until softened, about 5 minutes.

2. Add the beans, tomatoes, bacon, wine, basil, oregano and pepper; bring to a boil. Reduce the heat and simmer, uncovered, until slightly thickened, about 15 minutes.

3. Place the pasta in a large serving bowl. Top with the sauce; toss to coat.

PER SERVING: 404 Calories, 6 g Total Fat, 1 g Saturated Fat, 14 mg Cholesterol, 1,020 mg Sodium, 65 g Total Carbohydrate, 10 g Dietary Fiber, 21 g Protein, 78 mg Calcium.

SERVING PROVIDES: 2 Breads, 1 Fruit/Vegetable, 3 Protein/Milks, 1 Fat.

POINTS PER SERVING: 7.

CHAPTER

9

Baked Goods and Desserts

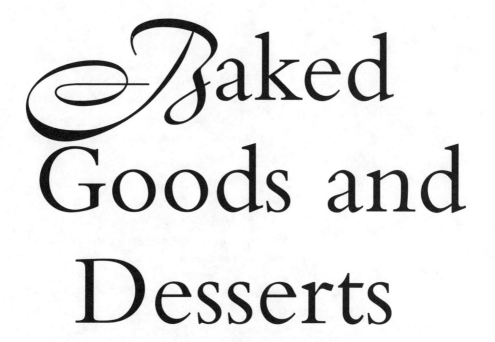

Apple Cake

MAKES 18 SERVINGS

Deborah Tisch
Humble, Texas

Deborah likes to serve this fragrant apple cake hot from the oven, topped with a scoop of vanilla nonfat frozen yogurt. What could be more warming on a blustery autumn day?

3¹/₃ cups all-purpose flour

1 teaspoon baking soda

1 teaspoon cinnamon

Dash salt

1 cup sugar

4 egg whites

4 apples, cored and diced

1¹/₂ cups unsweetened
applesauce

2 teaspoons vanilla extract

1. Preheat the oven to 350° F. Spray a 10" tube pan with nonstick cooking spray.

2. In a medium bowl, combine the flour, baking soda, cinnamon and salt.

3. In a large bowl, with an electric mixer at high speed, beat the sugar and egg whites until soft peaks form. With the mixer at low speed, blend in the apples, applesauce and vanilla. Add the flour mixture; stir until just combined (do not overmix).

4. Scrape the batter into the pan; spread it smooth. Bake until golden and a toothpick inserted in the center comes out clean, about 55 minutes. Cool in the pan on a rack 10 minutes. Remove from the pan and cool on the rack 20 minutes longer; serve warm.

PER SERVING: 156 Calories, 0 g Total Fat, 0 g Saturated Fat, 0 mg Cholesterol, 91 mg Sodium, 35 g Total Carbohydrate, 1 g Dietary Fiber, 3 g Protein, 8 mg Calcium.

SERVING PROVIDES: 1 Bread, 50 Bonus Calories.

POINTS PER SERVING: 3.

$\mathcal{C}$arrot Cake

MAKES 16 SERVINGS

Meryl Lewis
Berkley, Massachusetts

Since joining Weight Watchers in 1993, Meryl has lost 124 pounds.
Recipes such as this carrot cake helped, especially since she could share it
at get-togethers while she remained on the program.

1³/₄ cups all-purpose flour

¹/₂ cup whole-wheat flour

2 teaspoons baking soda

1 teaspoon cinnamon

1 teaspoon ground allspice

¹/₄ teaspoon grated nutmeg

¹/₈ teaspoon salt

¹/₂ cup firmly packed light
brown sugar

2 egg whites

6 carrots, shredded

Two 8-ounce cans crushed
unsweetened pineapple,
drained

²/₃ cup low-fat (1%)
buttermilk

¹/₂ cup raisins

3 tablespoons canola oil

2 teaspoons vanilla extract

1 teaspoon almond extract

1. Preheat the oven to 350° F. Spray a 13 × 9" baking pan with nonstick cooking spray.

2. In a medium bowl, combine the flours, baking soda, cinnamon, allspice, nutmeg and salt.

3. In a large bowl, with an electric mixer at high speed, beat the sugar and egg whites until thick and frothy. With the mixer at low speed, stir in the carrots, pineapple, buttermilk, raisins, oil and the extracts. Gradually add the flour mixture and stir until all the flour is just moistened.

4. Scrape the batter into the pan. Bake until golden and a toothpick inserted in the center comes out clean, about 35 minutes. Cool completely in the pan on a rack.

PER SERVING: 159 Calories, 3 g Total Fat, 0 g Saturated Fat, 1 mg Cholesterol, 214 mg Sodium, 31 g Total Carbohydrate, 2 g Dietary Fiber, 3 g Protein, 41 mg Calcium.

SERVING PROVIDES: 1 Bread, 1 Fruit/Vegetable, 1 Fat.

POINTS PER SERVING: 3.

Fat-Free Chocolate Cake

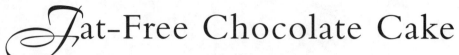

MAKES 24 SERVINGS

Michele E. Mosher
Quaker Hill, Connecticut

*Michele has come up with what every chocolate-lover dreams about: a dark
and delicious dessert that leaves you free of self-recrimination.*

3¹/₃ cups all-purpose flour

¹/₂ cup unsweetened cocoa powder, sifted

1¹/₂ teaspoons baking soda

¹/₂ teaspoon salt

1¹/₂ cups granulated sugar

¹/₂ cup plain nonfat yogurt

2 egg whites

1 tablespoon vanilla extract

1 tablespoon white vinegar

2 tablespoons confectioners' sugar

1. Preheat the oven to 350° F. Spray a 13 × 9" baking pan with nonstick cooking spray.

2. In a medium bowl, combine the flour, cocoa, baking soda and salt.

3. In a large bowl, with an electric mixer at medium speed, beat the granulated sugar, yogurt, egg whites, vanilla and vinegar until fluffy, about 2 minutes. With the mixer at low speed, gradually add the flour mixture; stir until just combined (do not overmix). Add 2 cups water and stir until just smooth.

4. Pour the batter into the pan. Bake until a toothpick inserted in the center comes out clean, about 40 minutes. Cool completely in the pan on a rack. Dust with the confectioners' sugar.

PER SERVING: 124 Calories, 0 g Total Fat, 0 g Saturated Fat, 0 mg Cholesterol, 133 mg Sodium, 28 g Total Carbohydrate, 1 g Dietary Fiber, 3 g Protein, 15 mg Calcium.

SERVING PROVIDES: 1 Bread, 60 Bonus Calories.

POINTS PER SERVING: 2.

*G*ingerbread Cake

MAKES 24 SERVINGS

Kim Cullison
Bel Air, Maryland

Kim loved her grandmother's gingerbread cake but had a problem with all the fat, cholesterol and calories that accompanied every bite. Her solution? This streamlined version, one that banishes the fat but keeps the old-fashioned goodness.

2¹/₄ cups all-purpose flour

2 teaspoons baking soda

1 teaspoon cinnamon

¹/₂ teaspoon ground ginger

¹/₂ teaspoon ground allspice

¹/₄ teaspoon salt

1 cup unsweetened applesauce

1 cup light molasses

²/₃ cup fat-free egg substitute

¹/₂ cup sugar

¹/₂ cup pitted prunes, finely chopped

1 cup boiling water

1. Preheat the oven to 350° F. Spray a 13 × 9" baking pan with nonstick cooking spray.

2. In a medium bowl, combine the flour, baking soda, cinnamon, ginger, allspice and salt.

3. In a large bowl, with an electric mixer at medium speed, beat the applesauce, molasses, egg substitute, sugar and prunes until frothy, about 2 minutes. With the mixer at low speed, gradually add the flour mixture; stir until just combined (do not overmix). Add the water and stir until just smooth.

4. Pour the batter into the pan. Bake until a toothpick inserted in the center comes out clean, about 40 minutes. Cool completely in the pan on a rack.

PER SERVING: 112 Calories, 0 g Total Fat, 0 g Saturated Fat, 0 mg Cholesterol, 144 mg Sodium, 26 g Total Carbohydrate, 1 g Dietary Fiber, 2 g Protein, 36 mg Calcium.

SERVING PROVIDES: 1 Bread, 50 Bonus Calories.

POINTS PER SERVING: 2.

Pineapple Right-Side-Up Cake

MAKES 12 SERVINGS

Kim Cullison
Bel Air, Maryland

Amazing, isn't it? Kim took a longtime loaded-with-fat family favorite and, with a few clever substitutions, transformed it into something light and lovely. "The best part," she writes, "is that no one can tell the difference from the original recipe."

½ cup unsweetened applesauce

One 8-ounce can unsweetened crushed pineapple, drained (reserve the juice)

⅓ cup skim milk

⅓ cup fat-free egg substitute

½ teaspoon vanilla extract

1¾ cups all-purpose flour

⅓ cup granulated sugar

2 teaspoons double-acting baking powder

¼ cup firmly packed light brown sugar

1. Preheat the oven to 350° F. Spray a 9" square baking pan with nonstick cooking spray.

2. In a medium bowl, with a wooden spoon, stir together the applesauce, pineapple juice, milk, egg substitute and vanilla.

3. In a large bowl, combine the flour, granulated sugar and baking powder; make a well in the center. Add the applesauce mixture; stir until just combined (do not overmix).

4. Scrape the batter into the pan. Spoon the crushed pineapple over the batter and sprinkle with the brown sugar. Bake until golden and a toothpick inserted in the center comes out clean, about 30 minutes. Cool in the pan on a rack 10 minutes; serve warm.

PER SERVING: 124 Calories, 0 g Total Fat, 0 g Saturated Fat, 0 mg Cholesterol, 98 mg Sodium, 28 g Total Carbohydrate, 1 g Dietary Fiber, 3 g Protein, 65 mg Calcium.

SERVING PROVIDES: 1 Bread, 50 Bonus Calories.

POINTS PER SERVING: 2.

*F*ruit-Spread Coffee Cake

MAKES 18 SERVINGS

Marcia Morris
Gosport, Indiana

After losing 136 pounds on Weight Watchers, Marcia used her newfound knowledge to become a family nutrition adviser at a local university. She likes to serve this coffee cake on holiday mornings or when company comes to visit.

3⅓ cups reduced-fat buttermilk baking mix

½ cup granulated sugar

3 tablespoons cold unsalted stick margarine, diced

⅔ cup fat-free egg substitute

½ cup skim milk

1 teaspoon vanilla extract

½ teaspoon almond extract

1 cup spreadable fruit (any flavor)

½ cup confectioners' sugar

1. Preheat the oven to 350° F. Spray a 15 × 10" jelly-roll pan with nonstick cooking spray.

2. In a large bowl, combine the baking mix and granulated sugar. With a pastry blender or 2 knives, cut in the margarine until the mixture resembles coarse crumbs. Add the egg substitute, milk, and the extracts; with a wooden spoon, stir until just combined (do not overmix).

3. Spread two-thirds of the batter into the pan, smoothing the top; spoon the spreadable fruit evenly over the batter. Drop the remaining batter by tablespoonfuls evenly over the fruit. Bake until light brown and a toothpick inserted in the center comes out clean, about 25 minutes. Cool in the pan on a rack 10 minutes.

4. Meanwhile, whisk the confectioners' sugar with 1 tablespoon water until smooth; drizzle evenly over the top of the cake while it is still warm.

PER SERVING: 175 Calories, 3 g Total Fat, 1 g Saturated Fat, 0 mg Cholesterol, 263 mg Sodium, 33 g Total Carbohydrate, 0 g Dietary Fiber, 3 g Protein, 34 mg Calcium.

SERVING PROVIDES: 1 Bread, 1 Fruit/Vegetable, 1 Fat, 50 Bonus Calories.

POINTS PER SERVING: 4.

Easy Yogurt Cheesecake

MAKES 8 SERVINGS

Sandra O'Shaughnessy
Centerville, Massachusetts

Remember cheesecake? Be wistful no more. Sandra's version is not only rich, satisfying, fat-free and easy, but it actually makes its own crust!

2 cups yogurt cheese★

²/₃ cup fat-free egg substitute

¹/₂ cup + 2 tablespoons sugar

2 tablespoons all-purpose flour

2 teaspoons vanilla extract

³/₄ cup nonfat sour cream

1 tablespoon raspberry syrup

1. Preheat the oven to 325° F. Spray a 9" pie plate with nonstick cooking spray.

2. In a large bowl, whisk the yogurt cheese, egg substitute, ¹/₂ cup of the sugar, the flour and vanilla until smooth. Pour the mixture into the pie plate and bake until firm and a knife inserted in the center comes out clean, about 50 minutes.

3. Meanwhile, in a small bowl, combine the sour cream and the remaining 2 tablespoons of the sugar. Pour over the cheesecake; drizzle with the syrup and bake until the topping is cooked through, about 15 minutes longer. Cool completely on a rack. Refrigerate, covered, until chilled, about 2 hours.

PER SERVING: 143 Calories, 0 g Total Fat, 0 g Saturated Fat, 0 mg Cholesterol, 89 mg Sodium, 25 g Total Carbohydrate, 0 g Dietary Fiber, 8 g Protein, 175 mg Calcium.

SERVING PROVIDES: 1 Protein/Milk, 80 Bonus Calories.

POINTS PER SERVING: 3.

★To prepare the yogurt cheese, spoon 4 cups plain nonfat yogurt into 2 coffee filters or a cheesecloth-lined strainer; place over a bowl. Refrigerate, covered, at least 5 hours or overnight. Discard the liquid in the bowl. Makes 2 cups yogurt cheese.

Chocolate-Amaretto Cheesecake

MAKES 12 SERVINGS

De'Ann Tollefsrud
Phoenix, Arizona

This winning cheesecake fits into the new lifestyle of healthy eating De'Ann has adopted, but it does not make her feel deprived at all. Serve it with your favorite fresh berries. Not one of our tasters could believe this rich dessert wasn't a decadent, diet-busting indulgence.

Six 2¹/₂" chocolate graham cracker squares, made into crumbs

2¹/₃ cups part-skim ricotta cheese

4 ounces nonfat cream cheese

¹/₂ cup sugar

¹/₄ cup unsweetened cocoa powder

1 egg

3 tablespoons all-purpose flour

2 tablespoons Amaretto liqueur

1 teaspoon vanilla extract

2 tablespoons semisweet chocolate chips

(See photo.)

1. Preheat the oven to 300° F. Spray an 8" springform pan with nonstick cooking spray. Sprinkle the cracker crumbs evenly over the bottom of the pan.

2. In a blender or food processor, puree the ricotta and cream cheeses, the sugar, cocoa, egg, flour, liqueur and vanilla; stir in the chocolate chips.

3. Pour the cheese mixture over the crumbs. Bake until a knife inserted in the center comes out clean, about 1¹/₂ hours. Cool completely on a rack. Refrigerate, covered, until chilled, at least 3 hours.

PER SERVING: 99 Calories, 2 g Total Fat, 1 g Saturated Fat, 21 mg Cholesterol, 82 mg Sodium, 17 g Total Carbohydrate, 1 g Dietary Fiber, 3 g Protein, 50 mg Calcium.

SERVING PROVIDES: 1 Protein/Milk, 70 Bonus Calories.

POINTS PER SERVING: 2.

Chipper Banana Muffins

MAKES 18 SERVINGS

Marsha M. Williams
Boise, Idaho

*Marsha likes to bake a batch of muffins on the weekend
and freeze them for hectic weekday mornings.*

2¼ cups all-purpose flour

1½ teaspoons double-
acting baking powder

1½ teaspoons baking soda

½ cup sugar

½ cup unsweetened
applesauce

2 eggs

⅓ cup canola oil

2 very ripe bananas,
mashed

½ cup skim buttermilk

¼ cup semisweet chocolate
chips

1. Preheat the oven to 350° F. Line eighteen 2¾" muffin cups with paper liners.

2. In a medium bowl, combine the flour, baking powder and baking soda.

3. In a large bowl, with an electric mixer at medium speed, beat the sugar, applesauce, eggs and oil until frothy. With the mixer at low speed, alternately add the bananas and buttermilk with the flour mixture; stir until just combined (do not overmix). Fold in the chocolate chips.

4. Spoon the batter into the cups, filling each about two-thirds full. Bake until golden and a toothpick inserted in the center comes out clean, 20–25 minutes. Remove from the cups and cool completely on a rack.

PER SERVING: 150 Calories, 5 g Total Fat, 1 g Saturated Fat, 24 mg Cholesterol, 161 mg Sodium, 23 g Total Carbohydrate, 1 g Dietary Fiber, 3 g Protein, 38 mg Calcium.

SERVING PROVIDES: 1 Bread, 1 Fat, 50 Bonus Calories.

POINTS PER SERVING: 3.

Cranberry-Blueberry Muffins

MAKES 18 SERVINGS

Annette Snoek
Grafton, Ontario, Canada

Annette found herself stopping far too often at the local coffee shop for their high-fat muffins, so she developed this recipe for low-fat Cranberry-Blueberry Muffins. She keeps them on hand in the freezer. Our tasters especially liked the flavor contrast of the three fruits.

2½ cups whole-wheat flour

⅔ cup sugar

2 teaspoons double-acting baking powder

1 teaspoon baking soda

¼ teaspoon salt

⅓ cup cold reduced-calorie margarine, diced

¾ cup plain nonfat yogurt

⅓ cup thawed frozen orange juice concentrate

2 eggs

1½ cups fresh or frozen blueberries

1 cup fresh or frozen cranberries

24 dried apricot halves, chopped

(See photo.)

1. Preheat the oven to 400° F. Spray eighteen 2¾" non-stick muffin cups with nonstick cooking spray, or line with paper liners.

2. In a large bowl, combine the flour, sugar, baking powder, baking soda and salt. Using a pastry blender or 2 knives, cut in the margarine until the mixture resembles coarse crumbs.

3. In a medium bowl, combine the yogurt, orange juice concentrate and eggs. Stir into the flour mixture until just combined (do not overmix). Gently stir in the blueberries, cranberries and apricots.

4. Spoon the batter into the cups, filling each about two-thirds full. Bake until golden and a toothpick inserted in the center comes out clean, 15–20 minutes. Cool on a rack 10 minutes; remove from the cups and cool completely on the rack.

PER SERVING: 144 Calories, 3 g Total Fat, 0 g Saturated Fat, 24 mg Cholesterol, 211 mg Sodium, 28 g Total Carbohydrate, 3 g Dietary Fiber, 4 g Protein, 63 mg Calcium.

SERVING PROVIDES: 1 Bread, 1 Fruit/Vegetable, 1 Fat.

POINTS PER SERVING: 3.

ate-Bran Muffins

MAKES 18 SERVINGS

Carolyn Webb
Sault Ste. Marie, Ontario, Canada

A treat rather than a transgression, these high-fiber, low-fat muffins help keep
Carolyn satisfied and on the program at breakfast time. And, yes, they freeze well, too.

1½ cups skim buttermilk

1⅓ cups whole bran cereal

1¾ cups whole-wheat flour

2 teaspoons cinnamon

1 teaspoon baking soda

1 teaspoon double-acting baking powder

½ teaspoon salt

½ cup firmly packed light brown sugar

12 pitted prunes, finely chopped

1 egg

3 tablespoons vegetable oil

24 pitted dates, chopped

2 apples, grated

1. Preheat the oven to 400° F. Spray eighteen 2¾" muffin cups with nonstick cooking spray.

2. In a large bowl, combine the buttermilk and cereal; let stand 5 minutes.

3. Meanwhile in a medium bowl, combine the flour, cinnamon, baking soda, baking powder and salt.

4. Add the sugar, prunes, egg and oil to the cereal mixture; mix well with a wooden spoon. Stir in the dates, apples and the flour mixture until just combined (do not overmix).

5. Spoon the batter evenly into the cups, filling each about two-thirds full. Bake until golden and a toothpick inserted in the center comes out clean, 20–25 minutes. Cool on a rack 10 minutes; remove from the cups and cool completely on the rack.

PER SERVING: 165 Calories, 3 g Total Fat, 0 g Saturated Fat, 12 mg Cholesterol, 231 mg Sodium, 34 g Total Carbohydrate, 4 g Dietary Fiber, 4 g Protein, 77 mg Calcium.

SERVING PROVIDES: 1 Bread, 1 Fruit/Vegetable, 1 Fat.

POINTS PER SERVING: 3.

*C*hocolate Chocolate-Chip "Cakies"

MAKES 24 SERVINGS

Barbara K. McConnell
Richmond, Michigan

These chocolaty drop cookies have an old-fashioned, cakelike texture and rich flavor, but their nutritional profile is positively modern.

2 cups all-purpose flour

¹/₄ cup unsweetened cocoa powder, sifted

1 teaspoon baking soda

¹/₄ teaspoon salt

¹/₂ cup firmly packed light brown sugar

¹/₄ cup unsalted stick margarine

¹/₃ cup fat-free egg substitute

³/₄ cup plain low-fat yogurt

1 teaspoon vanilla extract

1 cup semisweet chocolate chips

(See photo.)

1. Arrange the oven racks to divide the oven into thirds; preheat the oven to 375° F.

2. In a medium bowl, combine the flour, cocoa, baking soda and salt.

3. In a large bowl, with an electric mixer at high speed, beat the sugar, margarine and egg substitute until light and fluffy. With the mixer at low speed, gradually add the flour mixture, the yogurt, vanilla and chocolate chips; stir until just combined (do not overmix).

4. Drop the dough by tablespoons onto 2 ungreased baking sheets, making 24 cookies. Bake until firm, about 10 minutes. Cool completely on a rack; store in an airtight container for 3–4 days.

PER SERVING: 97 Calories, 3 g Total Fat, 1 g Saturated Fat, 0 mg Cholesterol, 88 mg Sodium, 16 g Total Carbohydrate, 1 g Dietary Fiber, 2 g Protein, 22 mg Calcium.

SERVING PROVIDES: 1 Bread, 1 Fat, 60 Bonus Calories.

POINTS PER SERVING: 1.

Oatmeal-Raisin Cookies

MAKES 24 SERVINGS

Elizabeth Long
Brooklyn Park, Minnesota

Elizabeth, a Weight Watchers staffer for the past nine years, has put a light, new spin on her great-grandmother's oatmeal cookie recipe, ever the crowd pleaser.

1³/₄ cups quick-cooking oatmeal

1 cup all-purpose flour

2 tablespoons nonfat dry milk

1 teaspoon double-acting baking powder

1 teaspoon cinnamon

¹/₄ teaspoon salt

¹/₂ cup firmly packed light brown sugar

¹/₄ cup unsalted stick margarine

1 egg white

¹/₂ cup skim milk

³/₄ cup raisins

1 teaspoon vanilla extract

(See photo.)

1. Arrange the oven racks to divide the oven into thirds; preheat the oven to 375° F. Spray 2 nonstick baking sheets with nonstick cooking spray.

2. In a large bowl, combine the oatmeal, flour, dry milk, baking powder, cinnamon and salt.

3. In another large bowl, with an electric mixer at high speed, beat the sugar, margarine and egg white until light and fluffy. With the mixer at low speed, alternately add the skim milk and the flour mixture with the raisins and vanilla; stir until just combined (do not overmix).

4. Drop the dough by tablespoons onto the baking sheets, making 24 cookies. Bake until golden, about 15 minutes. Cool completely on a rack; store in an airtight container for 3–4 days.

PER SERVING: 95 Calories, 2 g Total Fat, 0 g Saturated Fat, 0 mg Cholesterol, 52 mg Sodium, 17 g Total Carbohydrate, 1 g Dietary Fiber, 2 g Protein, 34 mg Calcium.

SERVING PROVIDES: 1 Bread, 1 Fat.

POINTS PER SERVING: 2.

lmond Biscotti

MAKES 24 SERVINGS

Jan Kiser
Napa, California

*Jan keeps these crunchy biscotti on hand to serve to friends who drop by.
What could go better with good coffee and good conversation?*

2¼ cups all-purpose flour

2 teaspoons double-acting baking powder

½ cup sugar

5 tablespoons unsalted stick margarine

2 eggs

1½ teaspoons grated lemon zest

1 teaspoon vanilla extract

1 cup slivered almonds, finely chopped

(See photo.)

1. Preheat the oven to 350° F. In a medium bowl, combine the flour and baking powder.

2. In a large bowl, with an electric mixer at high speed, beat the sugar and margarine until light and fluffy. Beat in the eggs, lemon zest and vanilla. With the mixer at low speed, gradually add the flour mixture and the almonds; stir until just combined (do not overmix).

3. Divide the dough into halves. With moistened hands, form each half into a 12 × 1½" log. Place the logs on a nonstick baking sheet. With a moistened rolling pin, flatten each log to ½" thickness. Bake until firm, about 18 minutes.

4. Carefully transfer the logs to a cutting board; dipping a serrated knife into water before each cut, cut each log into 12 slices on the diagonal. Lay the slices, cut-side down, on the baking sheet and bake until dry and lightly browned, about 12 minutes. Cool completely on a rack; store in an airtight container for up to 1 week, or wrap in heavy-duty foil and freeze for up to 3 months.

PER SERVING: 120 Calories, 6 g Total Fat, 1 g Saturated Fat, 18 mg Cholesterol, 47 mg Sodium, 14 g Total Carbohydrate, 1 g Dietary Fiber, 3 g Protein, 42 mg Calcium.

SERVING PROVIDES: 1 Bread, 1 Fat.

POINTS PER SERVING: 3.

$\mathscr{A}$pricot-Nectarine Delight

MAKES 8 SERVINGS

Nancy Haines
Beacon, New York

*Since she's been a Weight Watchers member, Nancy has lost 217½ pounds. Although she's a
lifetime member, she still attends weekly meetings for the support. Her family enjoys
the healthful recipes she makes—in fact, they prefer the new, low-fat versions.
This satisfying cake bursts with fruit and great flavor.*

TOPPING

¼ cup sugar

3 tablespoons all-purpose flour

2 teaspoons cold unsalted stick margarine, diced

CAKE

1⅓ cups all-purpose flour

2 teaspoons double-acting baking powder

½ teaspoon cinnamon

¼ teaspoon grated nutmeg

⅛ teaspoon salt

½ cup skim milk

½ cup unsweetened applesauce

⅓ cup fat-free egg substitute

¼ cup + 2 tablespoons sugar

2 teaspoons vanilla extract

3 nectarines, peeled and thinly sliced

2 tablespoons apricot spreadable fruit

1. Preheat the oven to 375° F. Spray an 8" square baking pan with nonstick cooking spray.

2. To prepare the topping, in a small bowl, combine the sugar and flour. Using a pastry blender or 2 knives, cut in the margarine until the mixture resembles coarse crumbs.

3. To prepare the cake, in a medium bowl, combine the flour, baking powder, cinnamon, nutmeg and salt.

4. In a large bowl, whisk together the milk, applesauce, egg substitute, sugar and vanilla. Gradually whisk in the flour mixture until all of the flour is just moistened.

5. Pour half of the batter into the pan; top with the nectarines and spreadable fruit. Pour the remaining batter on top; spread it smooth. Sprinkle with the topping. Bake until golden and a toothpick inserted in the center comes out clean, 30–35 minutes. Cool on a rack 10 minutes; serve warm.

PER SERVING: 207 Calories, 2 g Total Fat, 0 g Saturated Fat, 0 mg Cholesterol, 182 mg Sodium, 44 g Total Carbohydrate, 1 g Dietary Fiber, 4 g Protein, 98 mg Calcium.

SERVING PROVIDES: 1 Bread, 1 Fruit/Vegetable, 70 Bonus Calories.

POINTS PER SERVING: 4.

Strawberry-Apple Bake

MAKES 6 SERVINGS

Nadine A. Walther
Lebanon, New Jersey

As the adoptive mother of 10 children, Nadine tries to keep her food budget down while coming up with "healthy alternatives to sugary desserts." This apple bake, a perfect fit for Nadine's Weight Watchers program, does triple-duty as breakfast, snack or dessert.

3 Empire or other firm apples, peeled, cored and thinly sliced

2 cups fresh or frozen unsweetened whole strawberries

4 tablespoons sugar

1 teaspoon cinnamon

1³/₄ cups all-purpose flour

1 tablespoon double-acting baking powder

¹/₂ cup skim milk

¹/₂ cup unsweetened applesauce

2 egg whites

1. Preheat the oven to 400° F. Spray a 10 × 6" baking dish with nonstick cooking spray.

2. Arrange the apples and strawberries in the dish; sprinkle evenly with 2 tablespoons of the sugar and the cinnamon.

3. In a medium bowl, combine the flour, baking powder and the remaining 2 tablespoons of the sugar. Add the milk, applesauce and egg whites; stir until the flour is just moistened.

4. Spread the batter evenly over the apple mixture. Bake until the top is golden and the fruit is bubbling, 35–40 minutes. Cool on a rack 20 minutes; serve warm.

PER SERVING: 232 Calories, 1 g Total Fat, 0 g Saturated Fat, 0 mg Cholesterol, 274 mg Sodium, 51 g Total Carbohydrate, 4 g Dietary Fiber, 6 g Protein, 181 mg Calcium.

SERVING PROVIDES: 2 Breads, 1 Fruit/Vegetable, 40 Bonus Calories.

POINTS PER SERVING: 4.

*H*oliday
Apple-Cranberry Pie

MAKES 8 SERVINGS

Linda Shafritz
Los Angeles, California

Last Thanksgiving, Linda served this delicious festive pie for dessert.
It was so well received by her family and friends that she sent it to us. We give thanks.

1½ cups low-fat granola

1 egg white

1 teaspoon fresh lemon juice

6 Granny Smith apples, peeled, cored and thinly sliced

¼ cup dried cranberries

2 tablespoons sugar

2 teaspoons cinnamon

1. Preheat the oven to 325° F. Spray a 9" pie plate with nonstick cooking spray.

2. Place the granola in a food processor or blender; pulse several times, until finely chopped. Add the egg white, lemon juice and 1 tablespoon water; pulse several times, until the mixture holds together. With moistened fingers, press the crumb mixture onto the bottom and up the sides of the pie plate.

3. In a medium bowl, combine the apples, cranberries, sugar and cinnamon. Spread evenly over the crust and sprinkle with 1 tablespoon water. Cover with foil and bake until the apples are tender, 45–50 minutes. Cool on a rack 10 minutes; serve warm.

PER SERVING: 128 Calories, 1 g Total Fat, 0 g Saturated Fat, 0 mg Cholesterol, 45 mg Sodium, 29 g Total Carbohydrate, 2 g Dietary Fiber, 2 g Protein, 16 mg Calcium.

SERVING PROVIDES: 1 Bread, 2 Fruit/Vegetables, 60 Bonus Calories.

POINTS PER SERVING: 2.

Beef in a Leaf

Oven Beef Stew

Apple Dumplings

Almond Biscotti, Oatmeal-Raisin Cookies and Chocolate Chocolate-Chip "Cakies"

Brownie Pie

MAKES 8 SERVINGS

Diane Honer
Ivoryton, Connecticut

"This pie is so good that my nine-year-old requested it this year for his birthday cake,"
writes Diane. We loved it too, especially with a few sliced strawberries.

3 egg whites

2 tablespoons firmly packed light brown sugar

Eighteen 2¹/₂" chocolate graham cracker squares, made into crumbs

¹/₄ cup walnuts, finely chopped

¹/₂ teaspoon vanilla extract

1 pint vanilla nonfat frozen yogurt, slightly softened

(See photo.)

1. Preheat the oven to 325° F. Spray a 9" pie plate with nonstick cooking spray.

2. In a large bowl, with an electric mixer at medium-high speed, beat the egg whites until soft peaks form, 3–4 minutes. With the mixer at medium-high speed, gradually add the sugar and beat until stiff peaks form, 2–3 minutes.

3. Using a rubber scraper, gently fold in the cracker crumbs, nuts and vanilla until just blended. Scrape the mixture into the pie plate. Bake until firm and a toothpick inserted in the center comes out clean, about 25 minutes. Cool completely on a rack.

4. Spread the frozen yogurt over the pie; freeze, covered, until the yogurt is very firm, 2–3 hours.

PER SERVING: 113 Calories, 4 g Total Fat, 0 g Saturated Fat, 0 mg Cholesterol, 124 mg Sodium, 17 g Total Carbohydrate, 1 g Dietary Fiber, 3 g Protein, 7 mg Calcium.

SERVING PROVIDES: 1 Bread.

POINTS PER SERVING: 2.

 pple Dumplings

MAKES 6 SERVINGS

Susan Arick
Newark, Ohio

For an extra special treat, serve these dumplings warm with a little frozen nonfat yogurt.
With or without, they will remind you of Grandmother's kitchen.

2 tablespoons firmly packed
light brown sugar

1½ teaspoons cinnamon

1 teaspoon cornstarch

1 teaspoon vanilla extract

6 McIntosh apples, peeled
and cored

6 square egg roll wrappers

(See photo.)

1. Preheat the oven to 375° F. Spray six 2³/₄" muffin cups with nonstick cooking spray.

2. In a large bowl, combine the sugar, cinnamon, cornstarch, vanilla and 1 tablespoon water. Add the apples; toss to coat.

3. Place one apple in the center of each egg roll wrapper. Bring the corners up to the top of the apple, pressing and folding to seal the edges. Stand each dumpling in a muffin cup and lightly spray the tops with nonstick cooking spray. Bake until golden, about 20 minutes. Cool on a rack 15 minutes; serve warm.

PER SERVING: 165 Calories, 1 g Total Fat, 0 g Saturated Fat, 3 mg Cholesterol, 164 mg Sodium, 36 g Total Carbohydrate, 2 g Dietary Fiber, 3 g Protein, 28 mg Calcium.

SERVING PROVIDES: 1 Bread, 1 Fruit/Vegetable.

POINTS PER SERVING: 3.

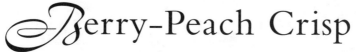

Berry-Peach Crisp

MAKES 8 SERVINGS

Alice Molter
Cleveland Heights, Ohio

Alice, a former Weight Watchers leader, used to love to transform members' favorite dishes into on-the-program recipes. While not every recipe could be converted, many, like this colorful dessert, worked beautifully.

3 cups fresh blueberries

4 peaches, peeled and sliced

3 tablespoons granulated sugar

1 tablespoon cornstarch

2 tablespoons fresh lemon juice

1/2 cup quick-cooking oatmeal

1/3 cup all-purpose flour

2 tablespoons firmly packed brown sugar

1 teaspoon cinnamon

1/2 teaspoon grated nutmeg

3 tablespoons cold unsalted stick margarine, diced

1. Preheat the oven to 375° F. Spray an 8" square baking pan with nonstick cooking spray.

2. In a medium bowl, combine the blueberries, peaches, granulated sugar, cornstarch and lemon juice; transfer to the pan and spread smooth.

3. In a small bowl, combine the oatmeal, flour, brown sugar, cinnamon and nutmeg. Using a pastry blender or 2 knives, cut in the margarine until the mixture resembles coarse crumbs. Sprinkle evenly over the fruit mixture. Bake until the top is golden and the fruit is hot and bubbling, about 40 minutes. Cool on a rack 15 minutes; serve warm.

PER SERVING: 175 Calories, 5 g Total Fat, 1 g Saturated Fat, 0 mg Cholesterol, 50 mg Sodium, 33 g Total Carbohydrate, 3 g Dietary Fiber, 2 g Protein, 19 mg Calcium.

SERVING PROVIDES: 1 Bread, 1 Fruit/Vegetable, 1 Fat.

POINTS PER SERVING: 3.

Quick Berry Soufflé

MAKES 2 SERVINGS

Janice Nieder
San Francisco, California

*After losing 20 pounds a few years ago, Janice became a professional food consultant
and fitness trainer. Now, she sends overweight clients to Weight Watchers because,
she says, "I know they're in good hands." This delightful dessert recipe,
a favorite among Janice's clients, is bursting with ripe, sweet raspberries.*

3 egg whites

2 teaspoons sugar

1/2 teaspoon vanilla extract

3/4 cup raspberries

3 tablespoons thawed
frozen orange juice
concentrate

1/4 teaspoon cinnamon

1. Place the broiler rack 6" from the heat; preheat the broiler.

2. In a large bowl, with an electric mixer at medium-high speed, beat the egg whites until soft peaks form, 3–4 minutes. With the mixer at medium-high speed, gradually add the sugar and vanilla; beat until stiff peaks form, 2–3 minutes.

3. In a large nonstick ovenproof skillet, combine the berries and orange juice concentrate. Cook until heated through, about 2 minutes. Spread the egg white mixture evenly over the raspberries; sprinkle evenly with the cinnamon.

4. Broil until the egg white mixture is set and the top is golden, 3–4 minutes. Run a rubber scraper around the inside edge of the pan and invert the soufflé onto a large plate. Serve at once.

PER SERVING: 111 Calories, 0 g Total Fat, 0 g Saturated Fat, 0 mg Cholesterol, 83 mg Sodium, 21 g Total Carbohydrate, 2 g Dietary Fiber, 6 g Protein, 25 mg Calcium.

SERVING PROVIDES: 1 Fruit/Vegetable.

POINTS PER SERVING: 2.

 Bread Pudding

MAKES 8 SERVINGS

Carolyn Ladd
Ellington, Connecticut

Carolyn has a long commute to work each morning; since she eats breakfast so early,
she needs something hearty that will satisfy her until midday. This versatile
bread pudding, which she heats up in the microwave, does the trick.
We think it also makes a wonderful dessert.

8 slices reduced-calorie whole-wheat bread, cut into 1" pieces

$^1/_2$ cup raisins

4 cups skim milk

$1^1/_3$ cups fat-free egg substitute

3 tablespoons sugar

1 tablespoon vanilla extract

$^1/_2$ teaspoon cinnamon

I. Preheat the oven to 350° F. Spray a 2-quart casserole with nonstick cooking spray.

2. Place the bread in the casserole; sprinkle with the raisins.

3. In a medium bowl, combine the milk, egg substitute, sugar, vanilla and cinnamon; pour evenly over the bread mixture.

4. Bake until a knife inserted in the center comes out clean, about 55 minutes. Cool in the pan on a rack 10 minutes; serve warm.

PER SERVING: 161 Calories, 1 g Total Fat, 0 g Saturated Fat, 2 mg Cholesterol, 249 mg Sodium, 29 g Total Carbohydrate, 3 g Dietary Fiber, 11 g Protein, 189 mg Calcium.

SERVING PROVIDES: 1 Bread, 1 Fruit/Vegetable, 1 Protein/Milk.

POINTS PER SERVING: 3.

Strawberry Crêpes

MAKES 2 SERVINGS

Karen Adcock
Centerville, Ohio

*When Karen and her husband, Frank, go camping in their recreational vehicle,
they make these delicious fruit-and-cheese crêpes for breakfast. Sometimes,
it's perfectly fine to start the day with your favorite dessert.*

2 cups strawberries, sliced

2 teaspoons sugar

1/3 cup nonfat cottage cheese

2 tablespoons plain nonfat yogurt

1/8 teaspoon cinnamon

1/2 cup + 1 tablespoon reduced-fat buttermilk baking mix

1/2 cup skim milk

1. In a medium nonstick saucepan, cook the strawberries and 1 teaspoon of the sugar, stirring as needed, until the strawberries are softened and give off liquid, about 5 minutes. Remove from the heat and cool slightly.

2. In a blender or food processor, puree the cottage cheese, yogurt, cinnamon and the remaining 1 teaspoon of the sugar. Transfer to a small bowl.

3. To make the crêpes, in a medium bowl, combine the baking mix and milk; stir until smooth. Spray a small nonstick skillet with nonstick cooking spray; heat until a drop of water sizzles. Pour a generous 2 tablespoons batter into the skillet, tilting to cover the bottom of the pan. Cook until the underside is set, about 1 minute. Turn and cook the other side until lightly browned, about 1 minute. Slide the crêpe onto wax paper. Repeat with the remaining batter, making 4 crêpes.

4. Divide the strawberries and the cheese mixture among the 4 crêpes; roll up and serve.

PER SERVING: 269 Calories, 5 g Total Fat, 1 g Saturated Fat, 7 mg Cholesterol, 616 mg Sodium, 44 g Total Carbohydrate, 4 g Dietary Fiber, 14 g Protein, 190 mg Calcium.

SERVING PROVIDES: 2 Breads, 1 Fruit/Vegetable, 1 Protein/Milk, 40 Bonus Calories.

POINTS PER SERVING: 5.

Microwave-Baked Apple

MAKES 1 SERVING

Carolyn Webb
Sault Ste. Marie, Ontario, Canada

*Carolyn loves desserts. She especially enjoys this baked apple—so much so that she
eats it for breakfast occasionally. She says starting the day off with a
Weight Watchers–style recipe helps keep her on track all day.*

1 large Granny Smith
apple, cored

³/₄ cup wheat and barley
nugget-type cereal

2 tablespoons apple juice

¹/₄ teaspoon cinnamon

¹/₈ teaspoon ground allspice

¹/₈ teaspoon ground
cardamom

¹/₄ cup aspartame-sweetened
caramel-apple nonfat
yogurt

1. Spray a 2-cup microwavable dish with nonstick cooking spray. Place the apple in the dish.

2. In a small bowl, combine the cereal, apple juice, cinnamon, allspice, cardamom and 1 tablespoon water. Spoon the mixture into the apple cavity and around the apple. Microwave, covered, on High until the apple is tender, 4 minutes. Cool on a rack 10 minutes.

3. Transfer the apple and cereal mixture to a plate; top with the yogurt.

PER SERVING: 473 Calories, 3 g Total Fat, 0 g Saturated Fat, 0 mg Cholesterol, 561 mg Sodium, 111 g Total Carbohydrate, 12 g Dietary Fiber, 12 g Protein, 144 mg Calcium.

SERVING PROVIDES: 1 Bread, 2 Fruit/Vegetables.

POINTS PER SERVING: 7.

*M*icrowave
Apple and Pear Crisp

MAKES 4 SERVINGS

Mary Schilling
Cincinnati, Ohio

*Mary is a college professor and a Weight Watchers leader. She uses this dessert—
a modification of her mom's recipe—as a snack between afternoon classes.*

2 Empire or other firm apples, peeled, cored and thinly sliced

2 pears, cored and thinly sliced

1/2 cup quick-cooking oatmeal

1/4 cup firmly packed light brown sugar

3 tablespoons all-purpose flour

1 teaspoon cinnamon

1/4 teaspoon grated nutmeg

4 teaspoons cold reduced-calorie margarine, diced

1. Spray a 9" square microwavable baking pan with nonstick cooking spray.

2. Place the apples and pears in the pan; with a vented cover, microwave on High, stirring once, until the fruit is tender-crisp, 6 minutes.

3. Meanwhile, in a small bowl, combine the oatmeal, sugar, flour, cinnamon and nutmeg. Using a pastry blender or 2 knives, cut in the margarine until the mixture resembles coarse crumbs. Sprinkle evenly over the fruit mixture.

4. Microwave on High, uncovered, until the fruit is tender and the topping is cooked, about 6 minutes.

PER SERVING: 206 Calories, 3 g Total Fat, 0 g Saturated Fat, 0 mg Cholesterol, 51 mg Sodium, 44 g Total Carbohydrate, 4 g Dietary Fiber, 3 g Protein, 36 mg Calcium.

SERVING PROVIDES: 1 Bread, 1 Fruit/Vegetable, 1 Fat, 50 Bonus Calories.

POINTS PER SERVING: 4.

Creamy Brown Rice Pudding

MAKES 8 SERVINGS

Karen Boden
Edberg, Alberta, Canada

Although Karen likes to eat this comforting rice pudding for breakfast, she's also proud to serve it for dessert, garnished with a sprinkling of raisins.

4 cups skim milk

3 cups cooked brown rice

2 eggs

2 tablespoons cornstarch

1/4 cup firmly packed light brown sugar

1 teaspoon cinnamon

2 teaspoons vanilla extract

1. In a large nonstick saucepan, bring the milk and rice to a boil, stirring as needed. Reduce the heat and simmer, uncovered, stirring as needed, until thickened, about 5 minutes.

2. In a small bowl, lightly beat the eggs. Add the cornstarch and 1/3 cup water; stir until smooth. Add to the rice mixture and cook, stirring constantly, until the mixture thickens, 2–3 minutes. Remove from the heat and stir in the sugar, cinnamon and vanilla; cool slightly. Serve warm or refrigerate, covered, until chilled, at least 3 hours.

PER SERVING: 181 Calories, 2 g Total Fat, 1 g Saturated Fat, 56 mg Cholesterol, 86 mg Sodium, 32 g Total Carbohydrate, 1 g Dietary Fiber, 8 g Protein, 173 mg Calcium.

SERVING PROVIDES: 1 Bread, 1 Protein/Milk.

POINTS PER SERVING: 4.

Ginger Rice Pudding

MAKES 2 SERVINGS

Carolyn Webb
Sault Ste. Marie, Ontario, Canada

*So creamy, so satisfying, so healthful. Carolyn likes to have one serving for dessert
and the other for breakfast the next day. Sure beats dry cereal from a box.*

¹/₄ cup raisins

1 teaspoon grated peeled
  gingerroot

¹/₄ teaspoon cinnamon

¹/₈ teaspoon salt

¹/₈ teaspoon allspice

1 cup quick-cooking
  brown rice

1 cup aspartame-sweetened
  lemon nonfat yogurt

In a medium saucepan, combine the raisins, ginger, cinnamon, salt and allspice with 1 cup water; bring to a boil. Stir in the rice and return to a boil. Reduce the heat and simmer, covered, 5 minutes. Remove from the heat; stir once, then cover and let stand until all of the liquid is absorbed, about 5 minutes. Stir in the yogurt. Serve warm or refrigerate, covered, until chilled, at least 2 hours.

PER SERVING: 286 Calories, 2 g Total Fat, 0 g Saturated Fat, 0 mg Cholesterol, 233 mg Sodium, 66 g Total Carbohydrate, 3 g Dietary Fiber, 9 g Protein, 189 mg Calcium.

SERVING PROVIDES: 2 Breads, 1 Fruit/Vegetable.

POINTS PER SERVING: 5.

No-Bake Lemon Cheesecake

MAKES 8 SERVINGS

Leone Ottenbreit
Yorkton, Saskatchewan, Canada

*Leone, the mother of three young children, lets her refrigerator do most of
the work in making this light, lemony cheesecake. How very clever!*

1 envelope (four $^1/_2$-cup servings) sugar-free lemon-flavored gelatin mix

1 cup boiling water

3 tablespoons fresh lemon juice

One 7$^1/_2$-ounce package pot cheese (no salt added)

$^1/_2$ cup sugar

1 teaspoon vanilla extract

One 12-ounce can evaporated skimmed milk

3 tablespoons graham cracker crumbs

1. In a medium bowl, combine the gelatin mix and water; stir until the gelatin is completely dissolved, about 2 minutes; stir in the lemon juice and cool slightly.

2. In a blender or food processor, puree the pot cheese, sugar and vanilla. Add the gelatin mixture and the milk; puree until blended. Pour the mixture into a 12 × 8" glass baking dish. Refrigerate, covered, until set, at least 4 hours. Sprinkle with the cracker crumbs.

PER SERVING: 144 Calories, 3 g Total Fat, 2 g Saturated Fat, 12 mg Cholesterol, 191 mg Sodium, 22 g Total Carbohydrate, 0 g Dietary Fiber, 8 g Protein, 169 mg Calcium.

SERVING PROVIDES: 1 Protein/Milk, 50 Bonus Calories.

POINTS PER SERVING: 3.

$\mathcal{U}$pside-Down No-Bake Cheesecake

MAKES 8 SERVINGS

Emily F. Fritts
North Haven, Connecticut

A dedicated gardener, Emily makes good use of the fresh fruits and vegetables she grows. "A handful of freshly picked, ripe red raspberries on top of this cheesecake makes an elegant dessert," she says.

1 tablespoon fresh lemon juice

1 envelope unflavored gelatin

$1/2$ cup evaporated skimmed milk

$1/4$ cup sugar

2 cups nonfat cottage cheese

1 cup aspartame-sweetened vanilla nonfat yogurt

2 tablespoons nonfat sour cream

1 teaspoon vanilla extract

$1/8$ teaspoon almond extract

Twelve $2^1/2$" graham cracker squares, made into crumbs

$1^1/2$ cups fresh raspberries (or $1^1/2$ cups sliced fresh strawberries)

1. In a small bowl, combine the lemon juice and 2 tablespoons cold water; sprinkle with the gelatin and let soften 5 minutes.

2. Meanwhile, in a small saucepan over medium heat, heat the milk and sugar until the sugar is dissolved and the milk is just heated through, 2–3 minutes. Remove from the heat and stir in the gelatin mixture, stirring until the gelatin is thoroughly dissolved.

3. In a blender or food processor, puree the cottage cheese, yogurt, sour cream, extracts and the gelatin mixture. Pour into a 10 × 6" glass baking dish; sprinkle evenly with the cracker crumbs. Refrigerate, covered, until firm, at least 3 hours. Top with the raspberries.

PER SERVING: 158 Calories, 1 g Total Fat, 0 g Saturated Fat, 6 mg Cholesterol, 303 mg Sodium, 25 g Total Carbohydrate, 1 g Dietary Fiber, 11 g Protein, 127 mg Calcium.

SERVING PROVIDES: 1 Bread, 1 Protein/Milk.

POINTS PER SERVING: 3.

Chocolate-Drizzled Oranges in Strawberry Cream

MAKES 2 SERVINGS

Marsha Thomas
Reno, Nevada

Marsha, a Weight Watchers leader who calls herself "The Recipe Lady,"
came up with this one for Valentine's Day. "I wanted something that had the
flavor of chocolate, looked sensual and yet kept me on my program," she writes.
Whoever said that romance and practicality don't mix?

1 cup strawberries

1 tablespoon sugar

1 tablespoon orange liqueur

1 tablespoon frozen light whipped topping (10 calories per tablespoon)

2 teaspoons cornstarch

2 navel oranges, peeled and sliced ¼" thick

1 teaspoon light chocolate syrup

Mint sprigs

1. In a blender or food processor, puree the strawberries, sugar, liqueur and whipped topping.

2. In a small saucepan, combine the cornstarch with 3 tablespoons cold water; stir in the strawberry mixture. Cook over medium heat, stirring constantly, until the mixture boils and thickens, 2–3 minutes. Remove from the heat and cool slightly. Refrigerate, covered, until chilled, 1–2 hours.

3. Pour the strawberry cream onto 2 dessert plates. Arrange the orange slices on top. Drizzle with the chocolate syrup and serve, garnished with the mint.

PER SERVING: 140 Calories, 1 g Total Fat, 0 g Saturated Fat, 0 mg Cholesterol, 5 mg Sodium, 31 g Total Carbohydrate, 5 g Dietary Fiber, 2 g Protein, 57 mg Calcium.

SERVING PROVIDES: 2 Fruit/Vegetables, 70 Bonus Calories.

POINTS PER SERVING: 2.

Fruit and Cream Freezes

MAKES 12 SERVINGS

Garnett L. Stickler
Kenova, West Virginia

Garnett got the recipe for this refreshing treat from her mother-in-law.
Eating one, she writes, is "like eating a banana split."

¹/₄ cup walnuts

2 very ripe bananas

2 cups nonfat sour cream

One 8-ounce can unsweet-
ened crushed pineapple
(reserve the juice)

¹/₃ cup mini marshmallows

¹/₄ cup sugar

1 teaspoon vanilla extract

6 maraschino cherries,
halved

1. Line twelve 2³/₄" muffin cups with foil liners.

2. Place the walnuts in a blender or food processor and pulse several times, until coarsely chopped. Add the bananas and pulse until just blended. Add the sour cream, pineapple and its juice, the marshmallows, sugar and vanilla; pulse until just blended.

3. Spoon ¹/₄ cup of the mixture into each lined cup. Freeze until firm, at least 2 hours. Soften in the refrigerator 15–20 minutes and serve, garnished with the cherry halves.

PER SERVING: 94 Calories, 2 g Total Fat, 0 g Saturated Fat, 0 mg Cholesterol, 28 mg Sodium, 16 g Total Carbohydrate, 1 g Dietary Fiber, 3 g Protein, 57 mg Calcium.

SERVING PROVIDES: 1 Fruit/Vegetable, 50 Bonus Calories.

POINTS PER SERVING: 2.

$\mathcal{L}$uscious Lemon Pie

MAKES 8 SERVINGS

Laurie Rolan
Bloomfield, Ohio

Although Laurie lost 120 pounds with Weight Watchers, she still hasn't lost her sweet tooth. This summery, cool dessert keeps her both happy and at her goal weight.

Twelve 2½" graham cracker squares

4 teaspoons cold reduced-calorie margarine

1 envelope (four ½-cup servings) sugar-free lemon-flavored gelatin mix

½ cup boiling water

1 envelope (four ½-cup servings) reduced-calorie instant vanilla pudding mix

2 cups aspartame-sweetened lemon nonfat yogurt

1 cup skim milk

1 cup plain nonfat yogurt

1. Preheat the oven to 350° F. Spray a 9" pie plate with nonstick cooking spray. In a food processor or blender, process the crackers until finely crumbled. Add the margarine; process until evenly moistened. Press the crumb mixture evenly onto the bottom and part way up the sides of the pie plate. Bake until browned, 6–8 minutes. Cool completely on a rack.

2. In a small bowl, combine the gelatin mix and water; stir until the gelatin is completely dissolved, about 2 minutes. Set aside to cool slightly.

3. In a large bowl, with an electric mixer at medium speed, beat together the pudding mix, 1 cup of the lemon yogurt, the milk and plain yogurt. Add the gelatin mixture and stir until thoroughly combined.

4. Pour into the cooled pie crust; refrigerate, covered, until firm, at least 8 hours. Cut into 8 wedges; top each wedge with 2 tablespoons of the remaining lemon yogurt.

PER SERVING: 122 Calories, 2 g Total Fat, 0 g Saturated Fat, 1 mg Cholesterol, 345 mg Sodium, 19 g Total Carbohydrate, 0 g Dietary Fiber, 6 g Protein, 184 mg Calcium.

SERVING PROVIDES: 1 Bread.

POINTS PER SERVING: 3.

Strawberry–Tapioca Parfait

MAKES 6 SERVINGS

Marion Timmons
Lower Sackville, Nova Scotia, Canada

*This is one of Marion's favorite desserts. To keep things interesting,
she likes to vary it from time to time, using other fruits (blueberries would work well)
or unsweetened applesauce sprinkled with a dash of nutmeg.*

3 cups skim milk

4 tablespoons sugar

3 tablespoons quick-cooking tapioca

1 egg white, lightly beaten

1 teaspoon vanilla extract

3 cups strawberries, hulled and sliced

Mint sprigs

1. In a large nonstick saucepan, combine the milk, 2 tablespoons of the sugar, the tapioca and egg white. Cook over medium heat, stirring constantly, until the mixture boils and thickens, 5–6 minutes. Remove from the heat and stir in the vanilla. Refrigerate, covered, until chilled, at least 2 hours.

2. In a small bowl, combine the strawberries and the remaining 2 tablespoons of the sugar; refrigerate, covered, until chilled, 1–2 hours.

3. In 6 parfait glasses, alternately layer the tapioca mixture and the strawberries, making 2 layers of each. Serve at once, garnished with the mint.

PER SERVING: 121 Calories, 1 g Total Fat, 0 g Saturated Fat, 2 mg Cholesterol, 96 mg Sodium, 24 g Total Carbohydrate, 2 g Dietary Fiber, 5 g Protein, 162 mg Calcium.

SERVING PROVIDES: 1 Fruit/Vegetable, 60 Bonus Calories.

POINTS PER SERVING: 2.

Strawberry-Yogurt Pie

MAKES 6 SERVINGS

Dawn Reed
Meriden, Kansas

"My mom used to make this in the summertime as a cool, refreshing treat," writes Dawn.
"It's a great dessert or end-of-the-day reward, and kids as well as adults enjoy it."

1 cup + 2 tablespoons graham cracker crumbs

2 tablespoons unsalted stick margarine, melted

3 cups aspartame-sweetened strawberry nonfat yogurt

1/2 cup frozen light whipped topping

3 cups strawberries, coarsely chopped

1. Preheat the oven to 350° F. Spray a 9" pie plate with nonstick cooking spray.

2. In a medium bowl, combine the cracker crumbs and margarine until evenly moistened. Press the crumb mixture evenly onto the bottom and up the sides of the pie plate. Bake until lightly browned, about 8 minutes. Cool on a rack 15 minutes.

3. Meanwhile, in a large bowl, whisk the yogurt and whipped topping until smooth; fold in the strawberries. Pour into the crust and freeze until firm, about 3 hours.

PER SERVING: 211 Calories, 6 g Total Fat, 1 g Saturated Fat, 0 mg Cholesterol, 206 mg Sodium, 32 g Total Carbohydrate, 3 g Dietary Fiber, 6 g Protein, 186 mg Calcium.

SERVING PROVIDES: 1 Bread, 1 Fruit/Vegetable, 1 Fat.

POINTS PER SERVING: 4.

Strawberry Sorbet

MAKES 8 SERVINGS

Donna Hill
New York, New York

With lovely strawberries available most of the year, it's hard to resist making Donna's summery sorbet, no matter what the calendar reads. The bonus is that you don't need an ice cream maker, and any leftovers may be stored in the freezer for up to a month!

6 cups strawberries, hulled and washed

¹/₂ cup superfine sugar

¹/₄ cup fresh lemon juice

2 tablespoons strawberry liqueur

Mint sprigs

1. In a food processor or blender, puree the strawberries, sugar, lemon juice and liqueur. Pour the mixture into a 12 × 8" glass baking dish; freeze, covered, until the mixture is frozen 1" around the edges, about 2 hours. With a whisk, beat the mixture to break up the large frozen crystals, 1–2 minutes. Return to the freezer and freeze, covered, until firm, at least 3 hours.

2. Soften in the refrigerator 20 minutes and serve, garnished with the mint sprigs.

PER SERVING: 95 Calories, 0 g Total Fat, 0 g Saturated Fat, 0 mg Cholesterol, 1 mg Sodium, 22 g Total Carbohydrate, 3 g Dietary Fiber, 1 g Protein, 17 mg Calcium.

SERVING PROVIDES: 1 Fruit/Vegetable, 60 Bonus Calories.

POINTS PER SERVING: 1.

Tropical Trifle

MAKES 16 SERVINGS

Stella A. Spikell
Boardman, Ohio

The guests at Stella's parties know they can invariably look forward to something sweet for dessert. If they're really lucky, they might be served this festive, luscious trifle.

¹/₄ cup sliced unblanched almonds

1 tablespoon shredded unsweetened coconut

1 envelope (four ¹/₂-cup servings) reduced-calorie vanilla pudding mix

2 cups skim milk

1 tablespoon grated orange zest

2 cups frozen light whipped topping

10 ounces angel food cake, cut into 2" cubes

1 cup orange juice

One 20-ounce can unsweetened pineapple tidbits, drained

One 11-ounce can mandarin orange sections, drained

1. In a large nonstick skillet, toast the almonds, stirring constantly, 2 minutes. Add the coconut and toast, stirring constantly, until both are lightly browned, about 2 minutes longer. Transfer to a heatproof plate.

2. Prepare the pudding with the milk according to package directions; stir in the orange zest and 1 cup of the whipped topping.

3. Place one-third of the cake cubes in a 2- to 3-quart glass bowl; drizzle with one-third of the orange juice. Spread one-third of the pudding mixture over the cake and top with one-third each of the pineapple and orange. Repeat the layering twice more.

4. Spread the remaining 1 cup whipped topping over the top. Refrigerate, covered, at least 2 hours. Just before serving, sprinkle with the toasted almond and coconut mixture.

PER SERVING: 129 Calories, 2 g Total Fat, 1 g Saturated Fat, 1 mg Cholesterol, 231 mg Sodium, 25 g Total Carbohydrate, 1 g Dietary Fiber, 3 g Protein, 76 mg Calcium.

SERVING PROVIDES: 1 Fruit/Vegetable, 80 Bonus Calories.

POINTS PER SERVING: 3.

Tropical Tarts

MAKES 6 SERVINGS

Rebecca Raiewski
Petaluma, California

"This recipe is the result of my sweet tooth and my love for creamy, rich-tasting desserts,"
writes Rebecca. In the summer, she varies it by using strawberry yogurt and fresh strawberries.

2 peaches or nectarines, diced

1 cup apricot-mango nonfat yogurt

1/4 cup frozen light whipped topping

6 single-serve graham cracker crusts

Mint sprigs

In a medium bowl, combine the peaches and yogurt; gently fold in the whipped topping. Spoon about 1/3 cup of the peach mixture into each crust. Refrigerate, covered, until chilled, at least 2 hours. Serve, garnished with the mint.

PER SERVING: 150 Calories, 7 g Total Fat, 2 g Saturated Fat, 0 mg Cholesterol, 134 mg Sodium, 18 g Total Carbohydrate, 1 g Dietary Fiber, 3 g Protein, 63 mg Calcium.

SERVING PROVIDES: 1 Bread, 1 Fat.

POINTS PER SERVING: 3.

Index

Metric Conversions

If you are converting the recipes in this book to metric measurements, use the following chart as a guide.

VOLUME		WEIGHT		LENGTH		OVEN TEMPERATURES	
¼ teaspoon	1 milliliter	1 ounce	30 grams	1 inch	25 millimeters	250°F	120°C
½ teaspoon	2 milliliters	¼ pound	120 grams	1 inch	2.5 centimeters	275°F	140°C
1 teaspoon	5 milliliters	½ pound	240 grams			300°F	150°C
1 tablespoon	15 milliliters	¾ pound	360 grams			325°F	160°C
2 tablespoons	30 milliliters	1 pound	480 grams			350°F	180°C
3 tablespoons	45 milliliters					375°F	190°C
¼ cup	50 milliliters					400°F	200°C
⅓ cup	75 milliliters					425°F	220°C
½ cup	125 milliliters					450°F	230°C
⅔ cup	150 milliliters					475°F	250°C
¾ cup	175 milliliters					500°F	260°C
1 cup	250 milliliters					525°F	270°C
1 quart	1 liter						

Dry and Liquid Measurement Equivalents

TEASPOONS	TABLESPOONS	CUPS	FLUID OUNCES
3 teaspoons	1 tablespoon		½ fluid ounce
6 teaspoons	2 tablespoons	⅛ cup	1 fluid ounce
8 teaspoons	2 tablespoons plus 2 teaspoons	⅙ cup	
12 teaspoons	4 tablespoons	¼ cup	2 fluid ounces
15 teaspoons	5 tablespoons	⅓ cup minus 1 teaspoon	
16 teaspoons	5 tablespoons plus 1 teaspoon	⅓ cup	
18 teaspoons	6 tablespoons	⅓ cup plus two teaspoons	3 fluid ounces
24 teaspoons	8 tablespoons	½ cup	4 fluid ounces
30 teaspoons	10 tablespoons	½ cup plus 2 tablespoons	5 fluid ounces
32 teaspoons	10 tablespoons plus 2 teaspoons	⅔ cup	
36 teaspoons	12 tablespoons	¾ cup	6 fluid ounces
42 teaspoons	14 tablespoons	1 cup plus 2 tablespoons	7 fluid ounces
45 teaspoons	15 tablespoons	1 cup minus 1 tablespoon	
48 teaspoons	16 tablespoons	1 cup	8 fluid ounces

Note: Measurement of less than ⅛ teaspoon is considered a dash or a pinch.